E X C H A N G E - V A L U E S

The
Final XIV
Interviews

+

one

Curated by
TOM BECKETT

Otoliths

EXCHANGE VALUES: The Final XIV Interviews + one

Copyright © 2007, 2008
by the individual contributors.

Back cover pwoemrds
by Karri Kokko, typeset by Geof Huth

Cover design by harry k stammer

Typsetting & Layout by
Soares, Caeiro et Pessoa Import/Export Co.

ISBN 978-0-9805096-1-8

Printed in the USA

Otoliths
8 Kennedy St
Rockhampton
QLD 4700
AUSTRALIA

http://the-otolith.blogspot.com
http://stores.lulu.com/l_m_young

The Interviews

The E-X-C-H-A-N-G-E-V-A-L-U-E-S project debuted in January 2005 with my interview of Crag Hill. The work at the website ended in January 2008 with Sheila E. Murphy's interview of Tom Mandel. Thirty-eight more interviews occurred in between those bookend pieces.

This third and final volume of exchanges includes the last 14 interviews which appeared at the website. Also included: a "bonus" interview of myself by Nicholas Manning which is published here for the first time. As in the previous two collections, each interview is supplemented with bio notes and by a generous selection from the interviewee's work.

Each poet-subject in conversation here constitutes a matrix of practices which, given due consideration, models approaches to experience through innovative art.

What you hold in your hand is not so much a book as a tool kit. Please use it.

It has been an honor and a privilege to work with everyone involved.

Tom Beckett
Kent, Ohio
April 12, 2008

http://willtoexchange.blogspot.com

Ernesto Priego
interviewed by Tom Beckett

Ernesto Priego was born in Mexico City. He studied English Literature at the National Autonomous University of Mexico (UNAM). He has also later taught literary criticism and American and British fiction from the 20th century there. He has a Master's degree from the University of East Anglia, Norwich, and is now a PhD student at University College London. His main blog is Never Neutral, hosted at wordpress.com. He lives in North London.

Tom Beckett: Where did/does poetry begin for you?

Ernesto Priego: It began with García Lorca. My parents gave me this little book of his poems for children, an illustrated one. I must have been 6 or 7. I knew that book by heart. I can still remember some of those: *"el lagarto está llorando/la lagarta está llorando..."* It was a very scary book, in a way, and now that I think of it I realize how influential it was to me. Not only the fact that for me the illustrations and the words were inseparable, and perhaps thus my fascination with illustrated books and comics, but also this sense of melancholy and inebriated sorrow that can be felt all over Lorca.

I started writing poetry and became interested in being a poet (whatever that means) after meeting Mexican poet and Latin American literature professor Eduardo Casar. His approach to poetry is so down-to-earth, and at the same time so carnavalesque, that it was impossible not to be fascinated by the possibility of experiencing life in a poetic way, which would mean, for me, when I was 15 at least, not growing up and thus becoming boring and pathetic. When I was a teenager Casar made me rediscover poetry's revolutionary power to disturb with beauty and a sense of humor the most solidified cysts of a conformed society. It may be the only case in my life in which meeting the person preceded reading the poetry. I met him at a poetry reading he gave at my high school in Coyoacán. Then I read his Caserías book and a whole world revealed to me. *"Basta la lluvia y se me nota todo"* was a line that made me realize how words could say more about us than we ever imagined.

In a non-chronological sense, poetry begins, for me, in dawn and dusk. Poetry is a space of indeterminacy: the threshold. It may sound like a commonplace, but I find poetry wherever I go, and I am constantly sniggling or even laughing on my own when I walk around a city. My idea of poetry is very referential and self-referential, trivial one could say, in that sense. I am always establishing connections, quoting, building bridges. Sometimes I become quite cryptic for other people because I have this whole textual universe which is almost private (though shared with some people I know and I don't know) and therefore I'm concerned about not getting whatever message I want to convey across. And when I see that this private, intimate network of words makes sense to other people, people who don't know me personally, like Jean Vengua, Eileen Tabios, Amy Bernier, John Bloomberg-Rissman or Mark Young I realize how much I underestimate the power of simple words. I am always surprised and what can happen when you send a word away, when you let it go. In that sense I was profoundly influenced by Cristina Peri-Rossi and Alejandra Pizarnik. I truly, sincerely believe that poetry must be a very humble act, just to

8

discover that what it can do, sometimes, can be the least humble thing.

TB: You're bilingual—fluent in Spanish and English. You think and write in both languages. Talk about that a little—how it affects your practice.

EP: It's essential. My relationship with English is a special and strange one, because I always feel a bit uncomfortable in it and still sometimes it's the language I feel expresses better some things. Since I was a kid my favorite authors were either USAmericans or British, and even though I read them in translations to Spanish I could always sense that what I was reading was merely an approximation to what the original was. There's also the fact that many of the translations I read came from Spain and therefore felt always pretty alien to me: that Spanish wasn't the Spanish I knew. So the experience of translation has also be a key one: the idea that no language is completely whole or self-sufficient and that only a Babelian mash-up of languages could probably come somewhere near to expressing the whole. Back when I was a teenager, by listening to pop music in English (mainly punk, hardcore, goth and some metal) and reading comic books and novels and poetry I started having this understanding of language and experience of it as a fragmentary one. It is through the experience of bilingualism that I have come to define for myself an understanding of what poetry could be: meanings are never final and univocal.

I get aesthetic pleasure from dictionaries: I collect them. They are an essential tool, not only when I'm writing poetry, but as a way of making a living, because I am a translator as well. Translation and writing poetry have always been related fields for me, not only because of my experience as a reader, learning a language by trying to understand poetry or song lyrics (most of my knowledge of French came first from Baudelaire and Rimbaud, for example) but also because of my need to say things that cannot be properly expressed in only one language. When I read Deleuze and Guattari's book on Kafka and minor literature I could perfectly relate to this idea of writing in a language that wasn't yours. And then I discovered Walter Benjamin and then Jacques Derrida and everything started making sense. But critical theory and deconstruction in particular became meaningful for me only because I already had this primitive, primal notion that meanings were perpetually deferred.

As a Mexican writer, it's very strange that I should decide to write poetry in English. But as a Mexican English Literature student, it was only logical, for me, to try my hand at it. But in Mexico it was some kind of unspoken rule, a cultural taboo, also because of our contradictory and conflictive relation to the US, that a Mexican Spanish native speaker should want to write in the language of the Northern neighbor, the language of Uncle Sam. In Mexican culture, the figure of the translator is the figure of the traitor. La Malinche is depicted by Mexican muralist painter David Alfaro Siqueiros Siqueiros as a prostitute who, bilingual, licks Hernán Cortés's ear. So right there, deep in the Mexican psyche lies the idea that to speak the oppressor's tongue is to sell yourself and therefore to sell your country. Again, this is quite contradictory in contemporary Mexican culture, because, for instance, Diego Rivera was very happy to paint his murals in the US and, in general, Mexicans have a fascination with English and make every possible effort to learn it. In recent times, our most talented filmmakers and actors have filmed in English, but there are not that many of us writer types writing originally in English. (Mexicans writers are translated into English, of course, but not the other way around). So, I must say, for me it's also a conscious decision, a political act of sorts if you will, to know that writing in English as a Mexican writer puts me in a strange situation which is also a non-place. Because my English is "awkward" because it's my second language and I'm not as fluent in it as I wish I were, and because in Mexico people will not take seriously any work of mine not written in Spanish. My hay(na)ku collection, *Not Even Dogs*, will not be reviewed in Mexico because it's in English and therefore it cannot be read nor sold nor distributed. There's no interest in Mexico for a book like mine, written in a language which is not mine. Then again, I would say that Spanish is not my language either.

TB: *Not Even Dogs* has, I believe, the distinction of being the first individually authored booklength collection of hay(na)ku. What is it about that form that appeals to you?

EP: I feel very honored that Eileen Tabios decided mine should be the first single-author hay(na)ku collection. I never expected that to happen. What interests me about the 1-2-3 form is that whenever I think of it different ideas come to my head. I have attempted to reply to this question of "why hay(na)ku?" before and I always come up with a different answer. By the time I first came across Eileen's concept of the hay(na)ku I had been playing around with those "magnetic poetry" sets at my friend's kitchens and would take photos of the resulting poems. I realized some of them imitated the three-line structure of the "American haiku" as imagined by Jack Kerouac, and when I read Eileen I even thought we were on very similar playgrounds there. Then I realized her concept was much more formally rigid than I thought at first, but this gave me an excuse to be bold and just attempt as many combinations as possible. There is something about the rhythm of the hay(na)ku that was strikingly familiar to pop music lyrics and to the Northern Mexican lyrical

tradition of corridos. I saw in the hay(na)ku structure a very seductive
tendency towards the stanza rather than a self-contained unit. I guess I always
thought of some lyrics by bands I like in terms of 1-2-3s:

Estaba
pensando sobre-
viviendo con mi

sister
en New
Jersey: ella me

dijo
que es
una vida buena

allá,
bien rica,
bien chévere! (Ey-oy!)

(From The Pixies, "Vamos")

Also, a case like this:

vuelve
ahí cabaretera
vuelve a ser

lo
que antes
eras en aquél

pobre
rincón ahí
quemaron tus alas

mariposa
equivocada las
luces de Nueva-York

(From La Sonora Santanera, "Luces de New York")

So I thought that the hay(na)ku, instead of promoting a way of reading that would isolate individual words in a negative sense, would be all about fluidity and run-ons. The stanzaic form, though, does promote a reading that places attention on the graphic situation of each word and on the blank spaces after each end of line. This gap between lines, the line-break proper, is something I see as the space between panels in comic books, what Scott McCloud calls "the gutter". For him the whole mechanism of graphic narrative is activated by this blank space between panels. For me, the hay(na)ku is activated by this blank space between lines and between stanzas. I have never been into metrical patterns, even though I had to study that in the university. But I always thought that poetry was somewhere else, not in technical or metrical precision. So here was this form that was cunningly simple. 1, 2, 3. Like punk rock:

Beat
on the
brat -beat on

the
brat with
a baseball bat

(From The Ramones, "Blitzkrieg Bop")

I am only thinking of this as I try to reply to your question. But the more I think of it the more I realize that my visual memory of pop music lyrics had a tendency to be in a hay(na)ku-like stanzaic form even if they hadn't been originally conceived as that, of course. The hay(na)ku appealed to my imagination and my sentimental education. I was thinking of Sonic Youth's Kim Gordon whispering,

I
swear I
never mean it

I
swear it
wasn't meant to

be

(From "Shadow of a Doubt")

and then, I don't know, I just started trying my hand at it. I would start talking in hay(na)ku form, even if nobody noticed. When I first read my hay(na)ku in my book's launch in Xalapa, México, last year, a member of the audience asked me to read more emphatically as to underline the 1 2 3 stanzaic form, because he could not "see" it as I was reading it. I did not want to, because for me the whole thing was about being fluid, about running into the next stanza. Some of my hay(na)ku sequences, as they have become known, do require some more isolated reading, separating each stanza as a single unit, making pauses between them, but in general I would say that what I want to achieve is a two-fold combination of both an emphasis on the haiku-like 3-line snapshot and underscoring simultaneously that these instants are always part of a longer current of words and images and thoughts that flow into each other.

I guess that another reason why I have been so in love with the form is because of the differences between the English syntax and the Spanish one. I have always been fascinated by antepositions and all the possible relationships between adjectives, adverbs and nouns. Adjectival nouns are so marvelous in English. I don't think there is an equivalence in Spanish. So the possibility of leaving a word on its own is an invitation to consider its different functions, both as a part of speech and as an element within a syntactical structure.

TB: Who do you think of as your poetic forebears?

EP: That's a very interesting question. I don't know! I was just reading the issue of MiPoesias that Nick Carbo edited and I could relate so much to the poetics there. Sometimes I feel more connected to the poetry being written by Filipino-Americans and Asian-Americans than with the one written by Latinos or Chicanos. So I was wondering, just today, if there was something common, yet-unexplored, between the poetic experience and ancestry of Asian Americans and the place I think I come from. I would as well, say that there would be no way I'd be interested in poetry were it not for Allen Ginsberg and Jack Kerouac. The whole Beat generation was foundational for me and I guess that for a lot of people of my generation in Mexico. But I was also influenced by a sense of poetic writing from authors like Borges, Cortázar and Pizarnik. Of course that Mexican poetry was influential, especially Octavio Paz and Xavier Villaurrutia. Villaurrutia, whom I read because of Elías Nandino, another poet whose sense of sadness affected me deeply, has to be the the Mexican poet that most made me see what could be done with words. I always felt a bit alienated from Octavio Paz's work, due to political reasons, and it took me until my late 20s "to give him a second chance" and read his poetry trying to leave my prejudices behind.

I don't think I write with a sense of historical or literary genealogy in mind. In a way, for me to write is to be trapped within a very complex double-bind: I write to liberate myself from any sense of rootedness, while, at the same time, I know I write as a means to ground myself somewhere. I just don't have a "national" conception of poetry, and my forebears would have to be all these authors from different times and ages and countries and languages. To be honest, I feel closer to Charles Thompson (aka Black Francis or Frank Black; the Pixies's lead singer, not the ragtime musician) than to López Velarde. I think this is also in some sort of reaction to an attitude I perceive in some Mexican writers of my generation and even much younger ones, that their poetic tradition, to give it a name, is pretty much Mexican or Latin American. I know that my love for the English language annoys (or, in the best case, amuses) my fellow wordsmen at my home country. I just can't separate myself from the political context and I do feel a connection between revering the mainstream literary tradition in Mexico and alligning yourself to some sort of literary or cultural status quo. To be honest, I don't give a flying cucumber about that. So I try to keep myself as far away as possible from the literary mainstream, even though I have mingled with it quite closely you could say, but in terms of recognizing a tradition I can't lie and say that I like better Octavio Paz than T.S. Eliot or Carlos Fuentes than Nick Hornby. I guess this is also connected to this idea I have that a writer is not someone who calls himself a writer but someone who writes. I get the impression some people write because they want to be writers and the social recognition it brings, even if in a country like Mexico that is so paradoxical because even the most recognized and best-selling authors struggle to make a living from their work. Maybe this will sound like bollocks to some, but I honestly write for pleasure. That's why I blog. I guess the reason why most of my contemporaries in Mexico do not blog is because they see writing as a way of making a life and see no reason to do it for free. It's just an hypothesis, but I would sustain it. Others blog but leave their "more serious" work out of the blog, so they can publish it later somewhere else, most importantly on paper. What I like about my book is the fact that most of the poems there were previously posted on my blog and people had already read them even if in a slightly different form. I write in English, I think, because my true passion is pop culture and that implies a recognition that we live in an heterogeneous, cacophonic culture, and this has allowed me so much freedom to write whatever I want without thinking of pleasing specific literary mafias or cliques in Mexico. Now it may seem like I am straying too much away from the main question, as I usually seem to do (you should see me teach a class!), but I guess what I am trying to say is that an idea of who your forebears are is strictly related to who you want to be and what you want to do with your writing. So I acknowledge the importance that some writers had on my personal life, but that does not mean I would like to write like them or to be related to them in any way.

When I think about it, most poets who really influenced me were really rock and roll, if you know what I mean. Eduardo Casar is so rock and roll. When he writes,

Sucede que yo no me enamoro.
Simple, infinitivamente me tatúo.

he is playing with language and is giving a very long, emphatic finger to so much of the mainstream poetics and its politics. (I am quoting here by heart; so the actual poem may be slightly different). Paul Celan, Rainer Maria Rilke, Giuseppe Ungaretti, Constantine Cavafy, Xavier Villaurrutia, Cristina Peri-Rossi, Philip Larkin, W.B. Yeats, the English Romantics, all of them are grouped in my own personal pantheon as pure, absolute rock and roll. And even though I do enjoy some experimental and avant garde music, I will always prefer John Cale to John Cage. (And I do like Cage, mind you, just like I enjoy Pierre Henry, but if this flat were on fire I'd take The Velvet Underground over Cage's *Etudes Australes* without a thought). I come from a lyrical tradition, and this must be my strongest connection to what could be my own personal "national" tradition. Maybe this explains my conflict with the terms "experimental" and "post-avant", which I never know if they are meant to be chronological or formal. I understand the postmodern age I have experienced as one of intertextuality rather than one where language should be used as some sort of malleable substance that does have to stray away from the traditional sense of "meaning". So I come from both these sides, from both a need to experiment with languages and a need to keep saying things. Mexican culture is a lyrical culture, full of popular sayings, idiomatic expressions and carefree music about heartbreak and impossibility. Even the most experimental Mexican composers, who have had to deal with the ghosts of people like Manuel M. Ponce, Blas Galindo, Silvestre Revueltas and Carlos Chávez, seem to move within a lyrical context, even if its only "emotional", and not lyric-wise. I don't know if this makes any sense, because I am not a professional musicologist, but even one of the most prolific contemporary composers, Javier Álvarez, who by the way studied here in London and now teaches in Mexico, seems to be trapped within a need to deconstruct the burden of "Mexicanity" (I am thinking here of his piece "Temazcal"). Something similar, I think, happens with contemporary poetry in Mexico: there are some precious exceptions, but in general I think that the most recognized young poets writing in Spanish in Mexico are still trapped under the (political and formal) shadow of Octavio

Paz. To be honest, I am interested in this as a cultural phenomenon, but I think that there are more interesting things being done at the level of underground pop culture, both in music and in poetry. So my forebears are the poets and the writers and the musicians and the artists in general that I have enjoyed during these three decades of my life, but that does not mean in any way that that is actually reflected on what I do. Maybe it does. I don't know.

TB: Well, Ernesto, I believe that what/whom one loves matters in infinite numbers of ways which aren't always apparent to oneself. I'm a great believer in acknowledging those loves.

Do you think that poets have any unique social responsibilities?

EP: Yeah, you are right. I never quite believed Miles when he said he had no influences. It wasn't for him to say, after all. And sure, acknowledging one's loves is truly important. I keep dedicating poems to people or writing them after their work or their names or what they do. I do believe that poetry is a social activity and could never be detached from the rest of the world and other people. In that sense, your question is truly important. I'm not sure about "unique" social responsibilities, but I do believe that poets have social responsibilities they are not always willing to accept. By "social responsibility" I don't mean here some kind of very direct activism, or charity work, which here in the UK is perceived as the main form of being ethical or socially responsible, but an acknowledgment of the political role of poetry. Because poetry is not a "productive" activity in the same sense gardening or medicine is, and because it is still practiced and consumed by a comparatively small group in the context of the mainstream cultural activity, poets should be constantly aware of their role in the world. It comes to mind that language, especially "powerful" languages such as English, that dominate others and that have become the lingua franca of global business and mass communication, is also the material with which poetry is made. So poets should be more sensitive to the powers of languages, to what they can say and do. Not content-wise, not in the sense of Sartre's "engaged literature" or of the Latin American idea of "protesta", but in the sense of being open to difference through language. It is also in this sense that I understand Adorno's famous and so often misunderstood idea of "no poetry after Auschwitz". Because language was a key element in the implementation of Nazism and the destruction of European otherness. Because poetry could never be the same after such barbaric event. My idea of social responsibility in poetry is the one I read in Paul Celan, and more recently in the poetry of people like Barbara Jane Reyes and Michele Bautista, where language is reflecting, in my reading, the severe traumas of the contemporary world.

That's also one of the reasons why I dislike some poetry written according to very formal metric standards or using a language that is completely detached from most people's reality. It's not about being "populist" or about dumbing down poetry, but about realizing that language can alienate and be used as a means to alienate poetic language itself.

The problem with the avant garde is that it also saw people like Marinetti and Italian futurism, whose radical elitism shaped their idea of "hygiene" through war. Futurism became an aesthetics of war, and in this sense it represented, for me, the end of the promise of poetry as a revolutionary force. Because, after all, I do believe in the revolutionary power of poetry, but not in the propagandistic sense. By "the revolutionary power of poetry" I mean the ability to make language say more than what the status quo has allowed it to say. Poetry should celebrate imagination, not alienation. My interest in popular culture is also an interest in the carnivalesque, in the possibilities for disrupting the established order of things. As long as poets have the will and the initiative to seek different forms and forums for expression, as long as they do not passively accept the traditional channels and forms of mainstream and established literature, I think there is hope for poetry as a socially responsible practice.

I don't think that the poet is a "unique" character that should receive special considerations in society. But I believe, at the same time, that some societies have been completely detached from their poetic traditions and have learned to live without poetry. This is very sad. When I visit a house of a friend that has no poetry books, the next time I take a poetry book as a gift. It disturbs me, it saddens me deeply to see a house without poetry books, the same way that I still can't understand how some people can live their lives without listening to music. And then there's the fact that poetry books are very expensive and printed on very limited runs. And the official campaigns to promote poetry reading, not only in Mexico but even here in London, as in the case of the Underground Poetry campaign here in the tube, have not been that intelligent nor successful in attracting new readers. The truth is that the general public feels completely detached, if not alienated, from poetry or poetic experience. Walter Benjamin and his idea of modernity as the decay of the poetic experience comes to mind. I do believe that poetry can change lives, but that can only happen if poetry is read and poetry is written. So "social responsibility" in this sense would mean understanding the fundamental role of poetry as a life-changing experience and as an essential aspect of human development, of all human beings, not only cool urban hipsters or nerdy indie kids or tweed-wearing academics. And sometimes poetry feels so alienated form the rest of the world; so concerned with their own internal strifes, without realizing that nobody else but those within care about it. It reminds me of all the hours I spent in my 20s discussing what comics should be with Mexican cartoonists. We kept talking about it, spent weeks on message board discussions, burning precious time we should have employed in actually doing those comics. Comics share with poetry their reduced readership and their endangered species status. But, unlike comics, poetry is considered the highest literary activity. No one denies the cultural importance of poetry, while comics are still unfairly perceived as childish and immature. But this cultural recognition is merely nominal, because out of a few mainstream and well-established authors, poetry does not matter much in the cultural panorama. So poets have a responsibility to keep practicing poetry and to make it matter, to attract new readers, not only the same people who are already reading it.

TB: One last question: what is most encouraging/discouraging to you about the current poetry scene(s)?

EP: There are more encouraging things than discouraging ones. I have been very lucky in finding a receptive audience and fellow poets who have made me feel like what I do has some value. I would have never been so vocal about what I think of poetry outside of the unviersity's classrooms had it not been for blogging. I am indebted to many individuals who were very encouraging from the very beginning, like Bill Marsh, K. Silem Mohammad, Nick Piombino and of course Eileen Tabios. I think they might have been about the first ones to notice my work on my blog and to respond to it. I think the work that Ron Silliman does in terms of promoting poetry is awe-inspiring, even though some times I get depressed by reading the comments on his blog. Sometimes the Internet can emphasize a lot this navel-watching attitude of small groups or the "developed West" a lot, but at the same time it has, with blogging at its center, developed a very interesting community of people from different countries who support each other. I have recently been able to participate in a project by Bill Allegrezza, a poet whose blog I had followed for some time now but that only recently I established contact with. So "my scene" if it should be called like that, is basically my blog roll, a group of mutually-encouraging people interested in poetry and other things. I do find a bit discouraging to see that in spite of many important efforts poetry on the Internet still seems to replicate the political agendas of poetry off line. So there is not as much collaboration or exchange between poets of different nationalities, maybe because of the language barrier and what has been called "the technological divide", but I remain hopeful that this will change in the near future. When I was a teenager I published my own fanzines and was a DIY publications collector. Electronic self-publishing and blogging has been the next logical step. I wouldn't have been able to publish my poetry in English in Mexico, and it would have taken me a lot of time to get my stuff published in American or British journals using the traditional system of submitting by post. So as a blogger I have been self-publishing my stuff for more than 5 years now, and that has been a means of opening many doors. I still find the USA poetic scene(s) very intimidating, very localized and insular in many ways, but that may be because I don't know them first-hand and because all I know about them is what I read of them. I believe poetry should be all about exchange and dialogue, and I think that the Internet is and will keep playing a central role for contemporary poetry. As long as poets understand that the world is very diverse and complex and that the term "global" still has to find its true meaning implying a respectful recognition of otherness, including that of other languages and cultures, I think that poetry has a lot to offer in terms of encouragement. Maybe I'm too optimistic, but sometimes, when I write something and get a response I never expected, I can't help feeling that there is still some hope left in this world.

From *The Body Aches*

One day we will, no doubt,
be dust.
A slight cover
over every key
of the black dashboard
spelling our luck.

One day our names
will be read at the entrance of buildings
unrecognizable shadows
of a somewhat somewhere
a coincidence in time and space
once a trace, a signal, a landmark
indicating nothing, nowhere.

These words, one day, will
also cease as days go on
and be not even objects no one
recognizes in the lost & found.

You will remember my face, though:
A blurry memory as deep as your own wounds,
those dusty scars abandoned by the years,
a remembrance as forgotten as typewriters
and old journals on a wooden drawer.

The dust will become mud.

From *Not Even Dogs*

[For Tom Beckett]

This
begins with
a simple premise:

I don't know
who this
is.

Or,
should I
say, who I

is, in writing
it's the
body

written
superficially, here,
yet absent, nowhere,

found only precisely
here, non-place,
time,

river,
discourse, running,
flowing, flooding, naming,

bodies, names, roses,
The Nile,
things

blind
poets see
behind the whiteness

of the screen
in which
I

is
constructed yet
deleted & denied,

a sock puppet,
fabric of
words.

[After Tom Beckett]

He
was so
tired all the

time
they had
deleted sex from

their marital nights.
She was
so

frustrated
all the
time

they
preferred to
watch cut films

on cable tv
before bed
and

slowly
fall asleep
embracing each other.

In the morning
with breakfast
they

would
discuss it
over fresh OJ

and warm newspapers
holding their
hands.

This
eliminated the
all-too-common fight scenes

from their marriage.
Censorship saved
them.

Verbal Countries
For Jean Vengua

I don't write poesía en español
because I have stopped believing in origins.

I try, instead, to look for futures I obviously don't have.
Verb tenses not yet invented, dreams deferred for too long,
Infinitives as usual not completed and not yet began,
A glass of whiskey over a red bilingual dictionary.

Even if love were not what I wanted
I would still write en inglés
because that's the color of the ink within my skin
and the language and shape of these tattoos.

Look at me: you can tell it's not my tongue.
My language has abandoned me forever,
I am not who I am or who you think I am.
I write in something else to make you think you are not here.
In brief, we are always somewhere else, never here, always looking away.

And even if love were not what I wanted
I would still dream in these forever-foreign words,
por siempre extrañas, por siempre otras
words that embarrass me a little in their otherness.

I know I sound funny. I know this sounds weird.
It's a different accent. Picture me drunk, if you will,
or just a little bit dizzy. I stumble upon words like little stones en los frijoles.

Bite these words.
You may still remember me mañana, mas no hoy,
porque el hoy no llega aún.

I could not write these lines in my own language because there is no such thing
as anything to own.
We have been deprived from that privilege.
Despojados de la lengua propia, we dream in other verbal countries.

Este soy yo, in any language.

From "The Philosopher's Suite"

1.
Como
una flecha
clavada ha conservado

Antígona
su secreto
clavado en el corazón

2.
Yes
the belief
that any space

in
which nothing
is occurring to

stimulate
my senses
must be empty

3.
Beneath
the surface
of the sins,

the
unbroken nervure
of the flesh

4.
The
body is
not a site

on
which a
construction takes place;

it's
a destruction
creating the self

From *Gravity and Grace*

Grace and Gravity dream of amores porteños,
the bandonenón confesses

Sunday mornings when they don't have to work.
Grace and Gravity laugh sisterly, in secret suffering.

Their sailors, their immigrants, can't dance,
but drown themselves in longing and despair.

§

Gravity and Grace are not here today.
Sunday's their day off.

There is an uncomfortable silence.

§

Gravity and Grace are both here today.
Grace is wearing blue; Gravity is wearing black.

Idle, Grace smiles. Gravity is too busy
exploring the mechanics of liquids.

"Good mornin', ladies", I say.
"You weren't here yesterday", Gravity replies.

I think about it for a minute.

Catherine Daly
interviewed by Thomas Fink

Catherine Daly is the author of six poetry collections in print, most recently *Vauxhall* (Shearsman, 2008), as well as eBooks and chapbooks including *Secret Kitty* and *Kittenhood* (ahadadabooks.com). In addition to restoring historic homes in Los Angeles, she works as a teacher. Most recently, she was Visiting Assistant Professor / Writer-in-Residence at New College in Sarasota, the honors college of the UF system.

Thomas Fink: This interview is intended to focus on one of your various new books, *To Delite and Instruct* (West Hartford, CT & Espoo, Finland: blue lion books, 2006). Since some of our readers may be unfamiliar with it, I'll begin by citing the publisher's ad copy and then, assuming that you've approved of this text, I will ask you a few questions about it.

TO DELITE AND INSTRUCT is written toward a post-Zukofskian objectivism. The book is also absolutely perfect for course adoption in graduate programs which focus on creative writing pedagogy as well as creative writing workshops. Daly has led writing workshops for more than a decade, without focusing on exercise "chestnuts" that "yield" a poem. The book includes "the opposite" of Bernadette Mayer's infamous exercises, as well as mimeo worksheets turned into poetry writing exercises for the reader of 2D&I. The word hoard at the back, all the words again, sorted according to indo-european root, demonstrates that constraint from children's exercises travels a poetic terrain beyond BASIC. TO DELITE AND INSTRUCT asks the purpose and worth of the poetry exercise or experiment. It investigates pedagogy of reading, speaking, hearing, and writing. Beginning with poems containing definitions, problems, and a word box, that is, beginning with limiting statements, centered on poems relating to mimeo workbooks from the 1960s, ending with a word hoard of the words in the book with indo-european roots sorted according to those roots, TO DELITE AND INSTRUCT is a thoroughgoing poetry exercise with a self-limiting vocabulary, poetry written in answer to peculiar perception problems presented devoid of information and forming an exercise in perception: a book of poems. The book is available through blue lion books at café press.

Catherine, I'm interested in a particular prepositional phrase: the directional pronoun "toward" and its object, "a post-Zukofskian objectivism." How would you characterize the relationship between Zukofskian objectivism and what might succeed it temporally? In what ways does *To Delite and Instruct* enact such a movement "toward"? What value do you find in this movement?

Catherine Daly: It is hard to write one's own book descriptions, isn't it? The langpos, and many other adventurous poets of late, have treated the practices and messages of the Objectivist poets in their poetry and in their academic publications, "after" reading carefully and continually these writers. I would call this a post-Zukofskian Objectivism. I think, since the Objectivist poets were somewhat arbitrarily grouped under the label, it is fair to identify a particular poet, Louis Zukofsky, within the grouping for my focus in this book.
There are many ideas, such as treating words, poems, and books as objects, which are commonplace now, but which Zukofsky codified for himself in his essays, and these ways of thinking are now habits of poetics in evidence in

2D&I; I've also displayed my sense of mimeo heritage.

I purchased some of the source materials from a teachers' supply store we used to leave near. It had a back room stuffed with old mimeo masters and workbooks from the 1950s and 60s. Many served as props for *The Wonder Years*. Another source is the AWP "pedagogy papers" from the Associated Writing Programs conference in Palm Springs — they aren't papers at all, though I'm sure they appear that way on many a c.v. — they are writing exercises typed up on university letterhead, xeroxed and comb bound, and sold to conference participants. Another is the garbage from a house on the national register that I had the lock box combo for – the speech therapist who lived there for over fifty years had died and his books were in piles near the trash bins.

Many of the poems in 2D&I are sound poems, though they don't use sound in a particularly Zukofskian manner; some of these use voice recognition software and computer reading voices and tongue twisters. The idea of word hoard / sound-based word root, along with the idea of a word set a la BASIC English (not Gates' programming language, a simplified English), which Zukofsky experimented with, is also strong in the poems. By writing the poems, I had a sense of approaching some of these ideas, learning about them.

When I first wrote some of these poems, I thought they might become part of my big project, CONFITEOR, the second trilogy of which is entitled OOD: *Object-Oriented Design*. When DaDaDa became my first book in print, I started fitting Da3 into a larger rubric, and for a sequel to move from early modernism to high modernism, in my ideal survey of 20th century poetics. Anyway, *To Delite and Instruct* spun away from that, along with a set of fairly lengthy distaff projects. *Paper Craft* is another book that came from working on CONFITEOR poems.

TF: As you suggest, for Zukofsky, "the objectivist" is "a 'wordsman'" [sic], "a craftsman [sic] who puts words together into an object" ("Sincerity and Objectifications," Interview with L.S. Dembo, reprinted in *Louis Zukofsky: Man and Poet*, Ed. Carroll F. Terrell [Orono, ME: National Poetry Foundation, 1979], 268), and the Langpos as wordspeople have been especially interested in arguing that the palpability and performative aspects of language are more important for him than the representation of objects. Aside from the "word hoard," in the opening poems of *To Delite and Instruct*, you as a wordswoman put words in boxes. "Refining," which is saturated with art history, first features a list akin to set of a dictionary definitions, then a theoretical statement and a sentence involving procedure, then a double-columned list dominated by proper names and complicated by lines that allow for check-marks, multiple-choice linkages, or something else, a list of the names of Baroque painters from different countries, including the major woman artist of the area, and finally, the word box.

true, embossed, verax; that is, i.e.; exists, to be; akin to E. aver, avow, profess

Internal reading acts become synonymous with external discipline; their voyeuristic possibilities.

Arrangement in groups denoting numbers having a significant code.

very St. Jerome	_____	very Durer	_____
very Caravaggio	_____	very salonniere	_____
very La Tour	_____	very Voss	_____
very Candlelight School	_____	very Friedlander	_____
very *Discourse on Method*	_____	very lighght	_____

Guido Reni, Saraceni; Gentileschi; Honthorst; Terbrugghen; Velasquez; Zurbaren

Word Box

impenetrable	opacity	Dostoevsky's *The Gambler*
luminescent	Cartesian	to secret
l'Orangerie	emboss	intimate
lurious	insinuate	scrupulous

(2)

I am fascinated by how the play of allusion functions and/or refuses to function in "Refining," and I'd like to unpack some of this before getting to my question. One may practice "external discipline" to "refine" an "internal reading act," but whatever "significant code" might articulate a substantial pattern of relations among items on the list remains "impenetrable." For example, although "very Caravaggio" and "very La Tour" could join the six other Baroque painters in the two-line strophe, and "very *Discourse on Method*" goes well with "Cartesian" and some of the abstract language in different strophes, "Voss" might refer to a city in Norway, a World War One German fighting ace, or an engineering company; "very Friedlander" could refer to a noted modernist photographer, a contemporary poet/critic, or a Holocaust scholar. "Very Durer" and "l'Orangerie" lead the reader to very different eras than the Baroque period. "Candlelight School" seems to be a kind of school founded by Catholic organizations, but perhaps it refers to the tenebrous quality of a La Tour painting. As for the ascetic, exegete, translator, and encyclopedist St. Jerome, perhaps his efforts to "avow" and "profess" religious truth are supposed to be juxtaposed with those of Descartes, or else, he appears as a much painted subject. Finally, "very lighght" is an allusion to a one-word (or non-word) poem by Aram Saroyan that caused a furor by getting him an NEA Grant.

I hope you're sufficiently amused by what I've come up with and failed to come up with, and you're welcome to comment on my misprisions. But more importantly, can you go back to what you were thinking during the process of developing juxtapositions and "refining" this poem? Can you recuperate some aspects of your intentions and, perhaps, ways in which you resisted intention? And can you please talk about the functioning of the word box as a coda to the poem?

CD: The word boxes in these poems are, in a sense, the word hoard at the end of the book. But I don't think of the word hoard or any of the indices as codas. [Although ? a queue, a line.] The boxes prefigure the hoard; the opening games are a microcosm of the book and the word hoard is all the words in a "box." Because I wrote these games, instead of responding or attempting to transform mimeo language games as is my more usual mode in the book, I'm fond of them. They are a different sort of poem. This one, in general, is defining/describing light (a common ars for painting).

"Emboss"—I've got an anecdote about that. At a Black Sparrow reading at the (UCLA) Clark Library (home to the baroque library, fine press editions, among other collections—Bruce Whiteman, a Coach House poet, is Librarian), in my neighborhood, David Bromige put me up to asking Aram Saroyan about "lighght." Saroyan claims the repetition of the "gh" "embosses" the word. I.e., a special edition stamped into paper—totally unnecessary.

TF: OK, I understand that the word boxes generate possibility and should not be regarded as a new form of poetic closure. Great story about word as print-object!

Some readers are too curious for their own good, but could you illuminate the "very Voss" and "very Friedlander" references for me?

CD: Well they ARE closed, they're boxes. The word hoard provides closure, but the boxes (unlike the word hoard) have new words in them — they are apparently or formally both related and unrelated to the poem (are you getting the knowledge to use the word box — perhaps with the spaces in the middle section of the poem, to do anything? do you need any information to do anything with the words? are the words a poem or a section in a poem or the end of a poem?) Many of the words in the word boxes don't have Indo-European roots shared with the other words in the poem — maybe because I got to them a different way, they seem a little different from the rest of the words, which rely more on memory.

I was interested in attributions / authenticity for this poem. "Very" "embosses" the noun following, does truth? etc. Hermann Voss, who worked making de la Tour attributions and also curated one of the few Hitler art collections without plundered art was one Voss I had in mind. de La Tour because of the debate over *The Fortune Teller* at the Met being a forgery. Baroque — I was so interested with the Baroque / early modern in *DaDaDa*, especially with embedded word games and technology as word games. There's a local LA poet / steelworker named Fred Voss.

Friedlander is I think Paul Friedlander the Plato scholar, only a little the "other Paul Friedlander" (light artist), the photographer Lee Friedlander, or Ben Friedlander.

TF: Specifically in "To Put into Play. To Restrain" (80-4) and to some extent in the larger section "Pedagogy" (66-79), you take Bernadette Mayer's "Experiments" as a source text. The publicity for *To Delite and Instruct* emphasizes cases in which you write the "opposite" of her directions, but you often parody Mayer's language in a looser way, and you also seem at times to embrace her exploratory spirit, as do Charles Bernstein and Jonathan Mayhew in their revisions, as develop complex experiment that reflect your own particular interests — and some of the tasks presented are more or less carried out in other parts of this book. Further, you sometimes push the exercise to such an extreme that you appear to want to touch the limits of encouraging a contemporary *dulce et utile*: "Explore possibilities, where an act isn't news, isn't a/ message, isn't information, isn't a story, isn't/ imperative, isn't a prayer" (82);"Write something that will render yourself helpless as you write" (84). Here are some juxtapositions of your experiments with possible sources from Mayer [Bernadette Mayer & the Members of the St. Mark's Church Poetry

Project Writing Workshop, 1971-5, in *In the American Tree*, Ed. Ron Silliman (Orono, ME: National Poetry Foundation, 1986): 557-560.]:

Intentionally choose. Research the ideas and practices
    that surround that choice, even more than you did
    before making it. Pursue these. (Daly 80)

"Pick any word at random. . . : let mind play freely around it until a few ideas have passed through. Then seize on them, look at them, & record. . . . (Mayer 557)

Use a special vocabulary within that area the vocabulary
    Is commonly used. For example, while a "safe
    word" is normally a word out of context, use words
    in their original contexts. (Daly 81)

Take an already written work of your own & insert (somewhere at random, or by choice) a paragraph or section from, for example, a book on information theory or a catalogue. . . . Then study the possibilities of rearranging this work. . . . (Mayer 559)

Let animals write. Copy the sounds they make or the
    words they spell out as they move. (Daly 83)

Get a friend or two friends to write for you, pretending they are you. (Mayer 558)

In your teaching of creative writing, have you used Mayer's experiments? If so, how did that "work" or "fail" — or "work" and "fail"? As you set out to revisit, revamp, revise Mayer in this section, what were some of your goals? Did you learn anything new in the process of composition about your attitudes to these and similar exercises and how they are situated in experimental poetries and their cultural transmission? (For example, since Mayer's text and her St. Mark's workshop in the early seventies is a kind of crossroads between the New York School and Language Poetry, did this process have an impact on your poetic/critical investigation of the New York School and LangPo?) After finishing the section, did you notice particular effects of the language "deranging" or "rearranging" the conceptual apparatus?

CD: Horace's "dulce et utile"? how different from sweetness or pleasure is delite (I wanted to use the true spelling, not the one drawing a false parallel to "light", another thing indicated by the first poem, "Refining"), utility from instruction? More to the point of these questions, what do I think, for this book, of the utility of poetry; instruction in, around, about poetry; and instruction as a use or vice versa? What do I think exercises, reading, and writing have to do with ars poetica or retrofitting an author's ars poetica from her poems?

Related to these ideas, sweetness, delite, utility, instruction, ars poetica, are play, engagement, learning, knowledge, writing, reading. These are language games, and the sweetness of a game, delite, is engagement, involvement rather than "fun." But I suppose by instruction I mean something akin to constructing experience and knowledge through "game play" i.e., reading, writing, etc. Conceptual apparatus emerges from poems built from teaching games.

For the book, I used the free version of Mayer's Experiments at the Poetry Project Website. Because I originally read them from a poetry anthology, I have viewed them more as a poem or series than I might have done if I'd first seen them on a website.

In some courses I taught, I began by pelting potential students with a giant quantity of all sorts of writing exercises like Mayer's, and a jillion others online and in "creative writing workshop" books, forms, constraints that first course meeting — other instructors at that institution gave a writing exercise to use up time during the intro to workshop class meeting, and students expected somebody's "poem ideas" to "give" them poems. I frustrated that expectation. While form, constraint, or exercise can be applied to measure structure against desire, to "derange" habits of working, that hardly ever happens unless assignments come from the writer, or are accepted by the writer in order to pull or push one's practice a certain way. I wanted something to happen when teaching and when writing this book.

I have written this long book of poems which are also exercises and from exercises and turn the poem into an exercise.... While one of my purposes in writing the book was to exhaust the exercise, another was to flag the way readers play the language game when the exercise is an open one rather than one focused on producing a ... product ...

TF: Perhaps you are "flagging the way readers" can fail "to play the language game" in your "Six in the Mix" sections, which feature substantial passages, interspersed with English, in Russian, Greek, Hungarian, Finnish, German, and French, In "Hungry Mix" (102-3) the Hungarian one, it's easy to guess from the repetition of certain words and the number of words in each sentence that the

English is a translation of the Hungarian preceding it, and I confirmed this by looking up words in an online Hungarian-English dictionary; this also seems to be the case with the Finnish section (104-9), but I haven't done the same test. What expectations do you have of your readers? In other words, do you think that they should find a way to understand the passages in all the languages? Should non-Greek and non-Russian readers simply enjoy the aesthetic beauty of the Greek and Russian characters and/or register the material barrier to their comprehension? Should those who don't know Finnish or Hungarian just appreciate the mix of sound patterns? Should they try homolinguistic translation? Do you care less about how they approach the section than you do about how they might theorize epistemological and social implications of the polyglot collage that you have provided for their instruction and delite?

CD: The Finnish section and Hungarian sections are machine translations from these languages without Indo-European roots. The Word Hoard is all the (English) words sorted according to Indo-European root. The standard collections of online translation tools don't include languages with different alphabets or roots. [I did a few projects for an internationalization — or i18n — firm that translated software into other languages. We used machine translations for estimating line lengths and costs. I still have an incomplete project of translating Locket, a book of love poems, into all of the Romance languages.]

My Uncle, Neal Skowbo, gave me the Language CDs he used to learn a bit of Hungarian before he and his wife Judith went to Hungary, in celebration of the book release.

From "Odds" I filtered only certain numbered passages through the machines, and the sections of tongue twisters I filtered through different machines (voice recognition and reading software) which ship in Microsoft desktop software in French, German, and English.

Part of the blue lion mission is to publish works which are exhaustive, which run with concepts and their ramifications as away as possible. One of my long term ideas is to use the possibilities of desktop software almost everyone works with every day for poetry. Another, for this book, is exploring assumptions about languages and knowledge. For example, advanced knowledge of modern French and German is required of most graduate students in English; this used to be a required knowledge of Latin and ancient Greek across all disciplines. So I am, and many in my audience are, "supposed" to be able to "read" many of the languages in the book.

Why not read the passages with wonder? They are a jumble of suppositions which don't hold, nonsense, and the almost-intelligible. One ars poetica...

TF: Since I have a PhD in English, you'll note that I didn't ask you about the French and German. But the farther away most English professors get from their graduate days and the more they have to focus on the contexts of teaching, research, committee service, etc., the less time they often feel able to spend on keeping their knowledge of foreign languages viable.

In various statements on your blog and elsewhere, you have underscored your advocacy for women writers and the centrality of feminism to your work. (Sometimes, you emphasized the word "distaff.") Here is "Explanation of the Idioms":

> The female poet died down, she rolled off the
> anthologies like a log. The excitement which came
> about as a result of her break down broke down,
> disintegrated. Had she used the words to stand out,
> to get ahead? Was she intransitive? It's not that
> memory fell through or some other poet got aorund
> the rules. She couldn't hold on; she showed up, but
> no one caught on or got the gist of it—they just
> looked on. We settled down to wait for someone
> who'd persist. (193)

In the fourth sentence, the substitution of "intransitive" for "intransigent" is especially interesting. This passage seems to be a critique of a patriarchally-inflected complacency and indifference to women's suffering and to "where the meanings are" for women poets. In what ways is *To Delite and Instruct* informed by your feminist concerns and aims?

CD: Since I don't have a PhD in English or in anything else... or a job....

For a female poet, especially a more experimental female poet, questions about women writers and feminism are also questions about identity and more specifically the place of identity in poetry. This book is about knowledge, perception verging into experience and knowledge yielding a certain sort of being alongside- or before-the-poems identity. It isn't a feminist project per se. But, the poems spring from the female-dominated profession of teaching. Authority is most often female in the workbooks. Female educators wrote most of the source materials, which I think is interesting — the authorship of subsidiary materials. I think feminism makes a nice presentation of the mind body problem, too.

TF: I'm interested in your idea that *To Delite and Instruct* "is about . . . knowledge yielding a certain sort of being alongside- or before-the-poems identity." Could you unpack that a bit and give an example or two to illustrate it? Finally, as a way of ending this interview with a sense of the larger context, how does this book fit into your big project, **CONFITEOR**?

CD: Well, I think I remarked elsewhere that one of the surprises in the poems — a prose poem in stanzas written from a page of clip art is the dominant format in the book — is their commercialism, brandedness. One of the reasons for this is that the clip art is line drawings of objects; the perception exercises are based on "reading" these towards reading and hearing language. Another is the brand names in the Microsoft dictionaries — these emerge once one starts using voice recognition software. But also our education — here, learning to speak, read, and write — trained us as consumers in a specific way. So the junk that emerges when one measures a memory against such an exercise is amazing.

Women are still consumers more than men are; we tend to be in charge of the bulk of household consumption.

I wanted to design a project that would test sound and memory as I was using it; *File 'Em* and *Phylum* were rearrangements of *My Life*. Sound objects not lyrics. The whole procedure around the sound poems reminded me of taping Jimi Hendrix albums I checked out from the Decatur Public Library from the record player I got from my parents for Christmas for promising I would use it to play French 10 inch language LPs (given to me by the same Uncle, Neal Skowbo) using Dad's portable cassette player and 25 cent tapes. Our parrot, Po, is invariably in the room when I get a few hours to do something like have a foreign-language avatar read tongue twisters into voice recognition software using the tiny microphone that comes with a desktop computer. Po had no idea what was going on, but wanted to make some noise too. So he is in there as a writer.

While answering these questions, I started working more in earnest to attempt to figure out an identity theft project I've had on the back burner since my identity was stolen over Christmas 2003, after *Da3* came out and Ron and I were married (odd, just as any American woman is particularly bereft of an independent identity). It seems Cartesian being has mobile or multiple identities based on varying objects of perception, if one views perception of objects to precede abstraction.

I have a collection of catalogs I received from stores where the fake Catherine Daly purchased tens of thousands of dollars of items. She went down Fifth Avenue (I worked on Park Ave. for many years) with my credit card and a fake driver's license, applying for new store cards and charging the limits. Bendel's, Saks, Bergdorf Goodman all thought I was a very special customer.

The heart of 2D&I was written around 1999-2001-ish, and then for a while in 2003 it looked like the beginning of *OOD*: *Object-Oriented Design*, the sequel to *DaDaDa*, which is enough unfinished for it not to be painful that it is not moving toward publication.

DaDaDa moves from finding a way inside the canon to finding philosophies and personal stories inside women's writing, ending in a legendary of women artists. OOD moves from singular stories to abstracting objects out of ideas or reducing them to binaries in a series. Dea has a section tentatively entitled All the Angels and Saints, and it also has a section of Catherines fairly indebted to the martyrology. That and Addendum aren't even close to being finished.

The reason *2D&I* is not in there is that it works oppositely. *Paper Craft* works oppositely as well. I call them distaff — on the surface they go together, but philosophically, they are mirror images of Confiteor.

The Confiteor is the confessional, mea culpa, or statement of faith:

I confess to Almighty God
And to you my brothers and sisters,
That I have sinned through my own fault,
In my thoughts and in my words,
In what I have done, and what I have failed to do.
I ask Blessed Mary, ever virgin,
And all the angels and saints,
And you, my brothers and sisters,
To pray for me to the Lord our God.

The project is to simultaneously survey 20th Century poetics, women's writing, the form of the Confiteor and its ideas from confession to prayer, the reformation idea that a confessional is also a statement excluding and including various groups, and to be my poetry.

Dance Dictionary: Directions for Bodies & Feet

Flic-Flac

a crack, as a whip
flicking or lashing movement
bar center
whip through positions two to five

En Dedans

After opening
on the earth, raise
working leg
horizontally,
toe parallel hip,
a perfect half-height.
Whip
foot down,
bending knee.
Brush the ball
of your foot against the floor.
Pointed toe crossed,
facing the audience as you
your face
throw that foot out to them
(don't brush the floor).
Fling it down
brushing the floor,
pointed toe behind you,
away, beyond sur le cou-de-pied.
Open to the second position in the air
perfectly half-height.

En Dehors

Second position
in the air
whip
foot down,
bend your knee, that knee, brush
the ball of your foot against the floor.
Pass through fifth position
pointed toe poised, crossed, away,
farther away from them...
whip
facing, pointed, to them.

En Tournant

flic foot flac half-point
the turn itself en dedans or en dehors
supporting leg
rise on help point
full turn while
working foot, open slightly, brushes
across the floor to cross
supporting leg
in back in front, in front in back
working leg thrown to second position, half-height

Assemblage

Unlike reading (in my language, left to right), from back / to front, not in
order assembled or arranged but in the order glued to paper (not two, not
three dimensions, both), so, along the ground then launched into the air,
returning inevitably to the ground. Two, higher, half, beats according to a
rhythm, beats made with calves; from one foot, or behind, in front,
different from back, underneath, over; / continuously together, darting
backward, forward, different from downstage, upstage. A big, carried turn
or sustained traveling turning which way and on the points.

Attitude

knee higher than foot
attitudes - ballet to me
despite the positions -
modeled on a statue
old photos, portly actresses/danceuses
ballerina twists and turns
pivots on a music box
as plastic on a spring

Battement

beat the band
beat the ground with your legs, your feet
stretched, disengaged, struck
stretched-and-lifted
raise the working
moving
other leg
(with apparent ease)
outstretched, level with hip
an exercise, the movement to the field
sudden, strong, a beat
only this — leg joining that —
the body, else at rest
in one sweeping movement, and then, and then, and then.

Eligible

"A balloon, my dear, would take us higher."
—Barbara Guest

I. (what has died)
generations, waves, clouds of gnats, mites, no see 'ems,
rose from their roots in mud, on water, near the latrines,
sprouted wings, swarmed, mated, fell,
in subsequent weeks predator, prey, fertilizer,
links in a chain, a cycle, an illustration, a reason for a belief
(we could no longer misunderstand but apprehend the founding
        misconception).
Scavengers in the slime left us twitching, itching, human.
[We are like mongeese or mongooses. Mon goose de mongoose?]
The ropes did not morph into snakes, nor vice versa,
and we were not quite afraid, which doesn't prove anything.
What has died? Our examples,
desiccated, dried, we dissect.
II. (which are eligible)
Persists. This restless pursuit of airships,
heaven for the failures of fiendish imaginations,
realm of gods and goddesses, garishly colored and sickly sweet,
horror tale told by the victim, anthropomorphic science fiction,
get well card
at least earth leads if only to the end
oh, to see a therapist in outer space,
where is closure and boundary
outside of oxygen or gravity,
death and drift
III. (where is this room)
dirigible
poetry, where is this room
three sided, not pyramidical
a snake swallows its tail
a crayfish eats its shell
hells have fallen,
letters, lifted,
we are sad sacks of sand

Score

Amelia Simmons, *American Cookery*

and tolerable   in soups and stuffings   ring beans,
Penny   used in Turkeys.
fields
and
young, is   and in   hell
Sweet Thyme cultivated. yellowish Bean, and early
                    more   no pole
board Bean, is easier   is off, shelled   the *Horse*
Frost   — must be poled. the richest   excellent may be
Six   *Bean*   *Windsor Bean*, is an earlier, winter   speck or eye   of
          Bean, is tough,   *Bean*, is rich   export
                                yellow small bush
English Bean what *they*   in cookery, and
profitable, easily cultivated
be raised by boys, I can   **Peas – Green**   purple and white
The   could be set in light
          take   in point aromatic
          of the vines,   from   feet   more
Calivanse,   *White Bean*,   only, or they run
tasteless, and
          Crown Pea, is second in richness   flavor   most useful and best
*The Crow*in the sea   is large and
on the
sand   and is large, easily   is produce   *Summer Savory*
Early   the pods are tender   *Sage*, is used in Cheese
Marrow Pea, requires a strong   and salted   good in
                    spring   collected, are good
Sugar Pea,   but not generally   and butter in
Spanish Manratto garnish roast Beef, excellent shell Bean
All Peas   as soon equal   herb in old
and   water   a   they are and used in
Herbs   *in Cookery.*   cookery.

ard and tolerable *Penny* fields y and med

yellowish Bean and early born

more ex no pole

Bean is easie is off shelled

Frost Be   Shell must be poled   he richest   ite the *Horse B*

ad excellent   ay be glp

Six 1   *Beat Bean is* an earlier   com

for winter   speck or eye   L

ean is toughean is rich bu   ear export

yellow small bush in cookery and scar

glish Bean what *they* profitable easily cultivated 7 be raised by boys I car

Calivanse White Bean tasteless

in soups and stuffings

used in Turkeys

and in F   jell x1y cultivated

Peas-Green

purple and white   set in light

ring beans

perial take   in point   Aromatic

if the vines w i l l   from feet   general only or they run

Pea is second in rich flavor   most useful and best

in the seas o *Idehaval* large and   on the

sand   large easily o producummer Savory

Earth push the pods are tender and

Sage is used

Marrow pea requires a strop and salted   good in

ring   collected good

fully **but not generally**

Sugar Pea

Spanish Mauratte   *garnish roast Beef* excellent

shell Bean

butt_r in

All Peas *P*   ick   equal

used

in old

and   out water a sponta   diately they are

fla   tivated

Herbs   *in Cookery*

n cookery

Score

ard, and tolerable. 　　od in soups and stuffings. 　　　tring beans,

Penn﹐
fields, y
and medi﹍ 　　　is used in Turkeys. 　　　er﹍

　　en young, is 　　　and in S 　　　ell.
Sweet Thyme, is ﹍nds; ﹍ 　uly cultivated. 　　　ie﹍ ellowish Bean, and early b.

　　　orn ou﹍
　　　e more ex﹍ eds no pole.

Cr﹍
　　　board Bean, is easie﹍ is off, shelled 　　　ate the *Horse B*
Frost Be 　. shell--must be poled. 　 the richest 　　ay be gro﹍
　　　　　　　　　　　　　nd excellent. 　　　　co﹍
Six ﹍ Bean, ﹍ndsor Bean, is an earlier, g﹍ 　for winte﹍ k speck or eye﹍ a﹍ 　uvation of
　　　　　　　　　　　　　　　　ear export﹍
I﹍ ﹍ean, is tough, ﹍ean, is rich, bu﹍ yellow small bush,
　　　　　　　　　　　　urth in cookery, and sca﹍
﹍glish Bean what they de﹍d﹍
﹍rofitable, easily cultivated, 　　　　*Peas--Green* ﹍ ﹍n, purple and white 　　﹍
﹍ be raised by boys, I car 　　　　　　　ould be set in light
The ﹍ 　　　　﹍perial, take﹍ k in point ﹍ ﹍ey 　　　﹍romatic,
　　　　　　　of the vines, wi﹍ ﹍ from 　﹍e feet h﹍ ﹍nore genera﹍
Calivanse, ﹍hite Bean, i﹍ ﹍ only, or they run ﹍ ﹍r﹍ ﹍s.
tasteless, an﹍
　　　﹍ ﹍ ﹍rown Pea, is second in richn﹍ ﹍lavor. 　　　most useful and best a﹍
　　　　﹍

The Crou﹍ ﹍ in the seaso﹍ ﹍ndehaval, is large and ﹍ ﹍arjora﹍
on the
sand 　﹍ ﹍, and is large, easily ﹍n, is produc﹍ ﹍ummer Savory, d﹍ ﹍od.

Earl﹍ ﹍ush, the pods are tender and ﹍ ﹍er 　*Sage*, is used in Chees﹍ ﹍vated, ﹍ 　　　﹍rk.

Marrow ﹍﹍ *Pea*, requires a stron﹍ and salted b﹍ ﹍rsley, good in ﹍ 　　　　﹍
　　　　　　　　　　　　﹍pring﹍ ﹍ collected, are good ﹍
Sugar Pea, nee﹍ ﹍fully fr﹍ ﹍, but not generally app﹍ 　　　　　﹍d and butter in
　　　　　﹍bo﹍
Spanish Manratt﹍ ﹍ *garnish roast Beef*, excellent 　　﹍ ﹍r shell Bean.

All Peas s﹍ ﹍icke﹍ 　　　﹍nes as soon a﹍ ﹍ved equal t﹍ ﹍ ﹍nerb in old ﹍hed
and cl﹍ ﹍out water, 　﹍ediately; they are 　　　﹍ns, and used in ﹍ry
fla﹍ 　　　　　　　﹍tivated in

　　　Herbs, 　　﹍ul in Cookery. 　　　　　　﹍ cookery.

Julienne

Christian Isobel Johnstone, *The Cook and Housewife's Manual*, "Peregrine Touchwood's Address" in *Women's Writing 1778-1838 An Anthology*, Fiona Robertson ed.

is found, it may be assumed as an axiom, this his progress in
Gentlemen, -- Man is a cooking animal and in whatever situation
writers of those ages making large account of an art, from which
common sense in all
crane, the lordly swan, the full-plumaged peacock, borne into the
      vassals to the flourish of trumpets, warlike
found no sanctuary either in the riotous household of the jolly
feudal hall, man and a fasting; and, finally, It is the main business
instruments, marrow-bones and cleavers. ('Bravo!' cried
     art, contributing to the comfort and luxury of
head; the latter, as the poet has it, eager to   England before the
     our seats of learning. Oxford watched over the culinary flame with
Reformation zeal proportioned
attained in the science of gastronomy.
     digging his roots with his claws, to the refined
     His best and dearest friend, plum-porridge;
     The meddling person likes
to have a finger in the pie; -- Meat
cavalier, or in the gloomy abode of the
     ('Only hear till him!' whispered Meg.)
     eat them; -- The churl
invites a guest, and sticks him with the spit; -- The belly bloody
     carcass to the modern *gourmet*,
apportioning his ingredients, and blending his essences, a pretty mess; -- A
half loaf is better than not bread; -- There goes reason to the roasting
of an egg; -- Fools make feasts
the former broaching his hogshead of October, and roasting a whole
     wreathed front in Britain; and
has kept exact pace with the degree not yet elightened worshippers.'
of Rome and Greece, and confine myself to the Gothic and Celtic
     emerged what I call the chivalrous
advance in England, when the Reformation not only
arrested its "—Fall out with mince-meat, and disparage
the dinners, -- the proof of the pudding is in the eating.'
     for what he called 'the bigotry of
feudal age of cookery, -- the wild boar roasted whole, the stately
     violently expelled from monasteries and
     borrows its most striking
Roman; from the ferocious hunter, gnawing the half
collop, torn from the The rash man gets into a stew and cooks
pastoral, as the last was that of the hunter. Here we have sinoke, mild
     woods,
     banquet of the Greek, or the sumptuous entertainment
complete! *First,* We have the brutalized digger of rootsl then the sly
entrapper of the finny tribes; and next the fierce foul feeder, devour-
ing his ensnared prey, fat, blood, and muscle!
man's master; -- He who will not fight for his meat, what will he fight
for? – A hungry man is an angry man
smoldered for a time. Gastronomy once more raised her parsley-
     than elegant.
"But, gentlemen, the genial spark was still secretly cherished

Julienne

is found. it may be assumed as an axiom, that his progress in civiliza

Gentlemen, — Man is a cooking animal,* and in whatever situation h:
writers of those ages making large account of an art, from which
common sense in all
crane, the lordly swan, the full-plumaged peacock, borne into the

leges, found no sanctuary either in the riotous household of the jolly
feudal hall man and a fasting, and, finally. It is the main business of
instruments, marrow-bones and cleavers. ('Bravo!' cried

head; the latter, as the poet has it, eager to in England before the

our seats of learning. Oxford watched over the culinary flame with
Reformation: wh zeal
attained in the science or gastronomy.
digging his roots with his claws, to the refined
His best and dearest friend, plum porridge."*

to have a finger in the pie; — Meat and mass h
cavalier, or in the gloomy abode of the lank, pinched-visaged
strangles ('Only hear till him!' whispered Mes \ El,
invites a guest, and sticks him with the spit,* — The belly is

reeking carcass, to the modern *gourmet*,
apportioning his ingredients, and blending his essences, the
half-loaf is better than no bread; — There goes reason to the roasting
of an egg.* — Fools make feasts and wise

the former broaching his hogshead of October,* and roasting a whole
wreathed front in Britain, and daily
tion has kept exact pace with the degree not yet enlightened worshippers
of Rome and Greece, and confine myself to the Gothic and Celtic
gradually emerged what I call the chivalrous
siderable advance in England, when the Reformation not only
arrested its prog

Reign,
Fall out with mince-meat, and disparage
the dinners, — the proof of the pudding is the eating.'
tribes, among disdain for what he called the
feudal age of cookery, — the wild boar roasted whole, the stately
fire Gastronomy violently expelled from monasteries and col-
countries, borrows its most striking illustr
tions and
Roman; from the ferocious hunter, gnawing the half-bro
collop,* torn from the The rash man gets into a stew and cooks him
Touchwood had a high disdain the bigotry of

the kettles. The next age of cookery, gentlemen,
pastoral, as the last was that of the hunter.* Here are have simple, mild
Cookery as a woods, genu
private life, had made considerable progress banquet of the Greek, or the sumptuous entertainment of
complete! *First*, We have the brutalized digger of roots; then the sly
entrapper of the finny tribes; and next the fierce fowl feeder, devour-
ing his ensnared prey, fat, blood, and muscle! ('What a style o' la
man's master; — He who will not fight for his meat, what will he fight
for? — A hungry man is an angry man

smouldered for a time. Gastronomy once more raised her parsley-
ox, in the exercise of a hospitality far more liberal than elegant.
'But, gentlemen, the genial spark was still secretly cherished in

Karri Kokko
interviewed by Tom Beckett

Karri Kokko is a Finnish poet living in Helsinki whose recent work includes a set of 1024 newly minted combined Finnish words, collected in *Avokyyhky, lattiaheroiini* (Open Dove, Floor Heroin) and published in 2007 by ntamo, a press specializing in avant-garde poetry run by poet Leevi Lehto. He maintains several blogs, among them Lyhyttavaraliike, a poetry blog in Finnish, and Sanaruno, a blog for Pwoermds.

Tom Beckett: Where did/does poetry begin for you?

Karri Kokko: Well, I can give you an exact date, for one. I wrote my first poem December 2, 1962, when I was seven years old. I had started school a few months earlier, but I'd been able to both read and write since I was three. The poem, though, is the first piece of my early scribblings to survive, and certainly the first and only poem. I don't have a clear memory of how the poem came about, or what ignited the will to write it. There was an urgency to do it, I'm sure. I remember asking my mother for a pen and some paper, with a definite intention to write a poem, only a poem, and nothing but a poem. It wasn't about expressing myself; it was about performing an act. This is, of course, pure speculation, since neither I, nor my mother, have any recollection of that moment. What we have, is the document, a tiny, yellowed piece of paper that my ma ripped off a notebook or something. When I was done writing, my mother signed it with my first name and added the date. At the end, she also wrote my age, seven and a half.

I can tell you this because I still have it, the manuscript of my first poem. What's remarkable, is that my mother had the wisdom, or the foresight, to save it. Not my early drawings, but the poem. She kept it through the decades and gave it to me a few years ago. I don't know why she chose to save it, but somehow she knew it was special. Not the result, but the feat. Not my age, but the determination.

The poem speaks for itself. The title reads "A Child." After that, twelve words (or possibly two hay(na)ku!). Here's the prose translation: "I am a small, helpless child, but when I pray to the Lord, it helps me." Not great, but not bad for a seven-year-old, either, huh? A few things of note, though. The poem reads more a statement than an invocation, and it's not even a prayer as such, but a *defense* of prayer. I'm sure there is a linage for that, straight from St. Augustine and on, so you might say I hit the hard stuff right off the bat. This is even more significant because, although religion was present in my family, it wasn't something that governed our daily life. And it certainly didn't equal art or poetry. It was me who made that connection. It wasn't about expression; it was about having something to say and the willingness to say it. There's the telling "it" in the last sentence; although my syntax and grammar might've been faltering, the evidence says clearly: It's the praying, not the Lord that helps. What's more, I'm using only block letters. My spelling is correct and there seems to be no double takes or revisions. There's a rhyme of sorts, but there's only a vague sense of breaking the text into lines. I'm also trying for a meter, which is evident because I'm using both inversion and abbreviation. In short,

I'm right away dealing with both form *and* content.

So, where did my intuitive sense of making poetry come from? Short of listening to nursery rhymes and pop songs, a boy of that age had better things to do, and I certainly had not yet read any poetry. There were few books in our house, and my parents weren't in any way "bookish" — far from that. But my mother, who had dropped out of high school, loved poetry. She had the Iliad and the Odyssey, in Finnish translation, and she had read them, too. (The books are in my possession now, and I can tell by the things she has written in their margins.) She had a few other books as well. They were collected works by classics from the first half of the 1900's, the golden era of Finnish poetry and well before modernism. On occasion, but not often, she used to recite poems from memory. She can still remember a few of them. I'm not saying this was out of the ordinary; this was before television, and people, literary or not, were supposed to know the classics. We used to sing a lot, too, the whole family, especially on car trips. There was song in the house.

I'm not sure if the above has any actuality in it. But I'd like to give credit to my mother. She left school when she was fifteen or sixteen, and never had any formal schooling after that. Yet, now that I think of it, she always talked books. She still does. She loves Nabokov. A few years ago, around the time she turned seventy, she picked up Proust and never looked back. That's all she reads. The other day, she told me she'd just started her fourth round of *Lost Time*. Then there are the rumours that she has notebook after notebook after notebook full of her own memoirs hidden away somewhere. My sisters should know more about that. There are also a couple of minor writers and an artist from my mothers side, with a new one coming up: my cousin, Lauri, a twenty-something, just published his first collection of short stories. Then, of course, there's my sister, Meiju, who's written a series of childrens' books... What I'm saying is that although it took almost ten years for me to write my *second* poem, I always knew I was going to become a poet. My mother, or my father, never pushed, nor pulled, me into it or away from it; it was just there, written in whatever.

I didn't start writing poetry seriously until my early twenties, but I made a few stabs at it in my teens, of course. My main influences came from your country, namely, the Beats. Reading *On the Road* at the age of fifteen was a major turn; though it wasn't until a year later I learned it told about actual, living people. All I wanted was to go to America. My wish materialized in 1972, when I became an exchange student, spending a year in Parsippany, New Jersey, some forty miles west from New York City. I wonder if I wrote any lines during that year; I was too busy shooting beer at the reservoir and going to Grateful Dead concerts. Saw Zappa, too, and Captain Beefheart. All of whom I had heard about and listened to *before* I left home. Not your typical exchange student, I can tell ya. The last episode of this phase was played out in the eighties, when I met both Ginsberg and Burroughs, respectively. Ginsberg was here with Peter Orlovsky, and I got to spend a couple of days with them, acting as their guide. It was January, with minus degrees, and Peter walked around town in just his Bermuda shorts and sandals, virtually barefooted. Nothing to it. We even shared the same stage: Allen wanted me to read the Finnish translation of "America," line by line, after him. This was in early 1983, and I'd just published my first book of poems. I translated one of them into English, and asked Allen to take a look at it. Sitting at the back seat of our ride, he went through the poem and made a few revisions. "Now, you got it," he said and handed me the piece of paper. You bet I wish I still had it, but I don't. I wonder what happened to it. Maybe my mother has it stashed somewhere. (**Editor's note**: Later Found. See next page.) Burroughs, then, came over a few years later. He was over seventy already, but brilliant as ever. I remember sitting back stage with him, sipping screw drivers out of plastic cups. Accidentally, I tripped mine on the table. What happens: Burroughs — Old Bull Lee, for Chrissakes — gets up, finds a rag somewhere and sweeps the table, taking care of the mess, the mess I had made.

Tom, you want me to go on answering the second part of your question?

TB: Please do.

KK: Okay, I'll do that in a minute. But there's a round-about way to it. What I'd like to do is drop a few more names. I mean, although one has the natural gift or inclination to become a poet, one's not going to do it alone. There are the books, the tradition, and then there are the people that come your way and make a difference.

My first mentor was a Finnish conceptual artist and critic, J. O. Mallander. I met him around 1973, when he ran an art gallery in Helsinki, called Cheap Thrills. I was eighteen at the time and I started going to the shows that exhibited both Finnish and international conceptual and avant-garde artists. I hang around the gallery and we started talking. Mallander was into Fluxus and American Abstract Expressionism, especially Jasper Johns. He introduced me to mail art and the work of Joseph Beuys and Nam June Paik. He had close connections to the Swedish art scene of the sixties and seventies, artists like Öyvind Fahlström and Carl-Erik Reuterswärd. The Moderna Museet in

Coney Island

1. The only time I really ~~was gonna~~ nearly died
   was when ~~I got seated~~ beside a lady who
   ~~sat weighed~~ 200 lbs.,
   on the maddest ~~twirlin~~ cyclone ride ~~machine~~ in Coney Island.
   ~~whirling~~ //Cyclone

2. That happens to me always ~~always~~, and nobody heard me
   ~~when I either was got~~ chrushed against the car side
   ~~or yelled~~ screaming stop from the ~~bottom~~ of my heart.
   The man on the machine he just went on reading his paper,
   ~~and~~ Big grown ups men rode the tiny cars deep in their thoughts.

3. In the picture I stand with hot dog and Bud in hand,
   ~~afterwards,~~ but not even the colors photo reveals
   the black ~~mark~~ bruise on my side underneath my shirt.
   At the shooting gallery I won a golden Buddha
   and a golden fish, ~~but~~ that died on our way home.

4. The amusement park was getting ready for the winter
   it was too cold to fuck underneath the boardwalk.
   To get black jack you need twenty ~~and~~ one, worry
   have to play it at least two, that I learned.

To Allen in Havis Amandq
Helsinki 28th of Jan. 1983
from Karri Kokko

Stockholm, Sweden, was a haven for all these avant-garde artists and acted as the Internet of the time, so to speak. People all over just gravitated to it, in need of acceptance and influence. I myself got the tail end of it, of course, since I was of a younger generation. But meeting Mallander and reading him and listening to him talk about art was an important part of my early education, none the less.

Fast forward to the early eighties. By that time, I'd finally picked up a pen and started writing poetry. But in spite of my introduction to the avant-gardes of art and poetry, I had little clue as to the means of incorporating the ideas into my own work. At the time, the mainstream of Finnish poetry was concerned with anything but the things I was into. There'd been a time, in the early sixties, when a few people had experimented with concrete poetry and other non-conformist poetries, but by the time I happened on the scene that tradition was all but dead. All Finnish poetry, or at least the poetry that got published, read alike and looked alike. There were a couple of reasons to it. First, at the time, free-verse Finnish modernism was only thirty years old. Second, the only opposition that it got was a leftist, political opposition, not an artistic one. I'm simplifying things here, but what I'm trying to say is that you either complied and fit in or you didn't exist at all.

As it happens, my first collection of poems, *Uno Boy*, was published by a major publishing house, in 1982, when I was twenty-seven years old. In hindsight, I wonder why they took it. A lot of the stuff was written the way poetry at the time was supposed to be written. Then again, there were other things: a poem written in the form of a cross-word puzzle, for example, or a verse for verse reversal of the Genesis. The reviews were positive and reassuring, but then, something happened. The custom here is that once you get published you keep sending in manuscripts at a steady clip. To establish yourself as a serious writer you have to publish something at least biannually. My next two or three manuscripts were turned down, however. They didn't give any specific reasons as to why; they just didn't buy my stuff. I'm in no position to second guess their judgement, but I take it that our poetics just didn't meet. A few years passed, and after trying a few other houses, without any avail, I just quit.

Although I never stopped writing completely, I walked away from poetry for almost fifteen years. I wasn't mad or sore or bitter; I just accepted it. Now that I think of it, I suppose I felt alienated and alone, without any peers and without a supporting network. Then, after a decade of out-of-poetry activities and inspirational connections, Leevi Lehto happened. Leevi, who is four years my senior, published his first work at seventeen and was well off into a career as a poet and translator, when he, too, for various reasons, some other than mine, some exactly the same, left the scene for a long time. His "second coming," as he calls it, realized in the late nineties, with a collection of "programmed" sonnets, called *Lake Onega*. I was working as a journalist at the time and just happened to notice a news article of its publication. Something clicked and I called him right away and asked his permission to be interviewed. He complied, and we met. Finally, finally I had somebody with whom I could talk poetry.

After that initial meeting, Leevi and I met and talked occasionally, but it wasn't until a few years later that I got the notion and courage to write poetry again. In late May 2004, Leevi happened to mention Ron Silliman and his poetry blog. I visited it and within minutes I had started my own first blog, Muistikirja. When starting it, I didn't have a clear notion as to what to do with it. The name of the blog, "A Notebook," points to the idea of a poet's public notebook, though. So, for a few months, my entries were "about" poetry, not poetry as such. I didn't have the guts to produce my own stuff, yet.

The next few weeks and months proved pivotal. Surfing the sites I found on Silliman's blog roll, I soon found people and poetries that touched me deeply and whose example, eventually, encouraged me to start writing again. A few of them were from faraway places, people I would never have encountered if not for the Net. People with whom I soon struck a conversation and a friendship: Mark Young, Geof Huth, Anny Ballardini, Eileen Tabios, Jean Vengua, and Tom Beckett, to name a few. Sometime later I was collaborating with harry k stammer! Oh man, I felt lucky and blessed.

One of the household names I soon stumbled into was, of course, the one and only Jukka-Pekka Kervinen, a fellow Finn who everybody was raving about, but of whom nobody knew about in Finland. Turns out, he lived, still does, a few miles down the road from me. Soon enough we met and have been talking ever since. He's even published my work. Our daughters converse with each other on the Instant Messenger. His genius, and example, proved unmatched. I needed him, I needed *somebody* to tell me: Just do it!

There would be others. In August that same magical summer, Kenneth Goldsmith was here, invited by Leevi. We met and right away recognized each other as long-estranged brothers, if you may. His Warholian approach to everything affected me like the sweetest of drugs. No rules, no limits. Soon enough, I had three or four blogs going at the same time. I was writing poetry backwards and making text collages. I was making visual stuff, doing things I had dreamt of doing my whole life. A week after Kenny, Charles Bernstein flew over for a few days, again at Leevi's invitation. We talked poetry and baseball. I was starting to believe in miracles. Miracles as in other people, that is.

This has been a long and winding answer to your question, Tom, but I had to do it. I had to do it, because I think poetry for me starts with two things. There's the given, and then there's the thing you do with it. You take heed, and then you do your own thing. You are on your own, but there are also others who are there, if needed, to sweep after you.

TB: You blog, speak, think in Finnish and English. Would you speak to how that affects your practice as a poet?

KK: Again, lots of things there, Tom. First, I'd like to say that, although I write a mean occasional hay(na)ku or pwoermd in English, I don't think my skills allow me to consider any serious writing in that language. English is a mistress I like to play with, is all. Not that I don't love her; I really do. But producing a bulk of original work, nah. Anyway, it would require moving over and really committing myself to that, and I'm too old for that now. That said, I *will* continue being unfaithful to the missus and fool around on the side whenever I feel like it.

Thinking, or working, in two or more languages certainly affects my practice as a poet. We might look at it from an angle. When a poet writes, he's getting into all kinds of languages, not only the first one he picked up. That's what poets do; they get into words and try to find out what they mean. Again, poetry is only partly about self-expression; it's about learning what the words themselves have to say. Every word has a history; in fact, they are laden with baggage.

My English is based on mimicry. I have a good ear for it, and when I think or write in English, I try to imitate the phrases and choices of words I've read or heard somewhere. That's all there is to it, and that is also why I don't think I'd be able to *create* anything new with it. From nine to sixteen years of age, I was taught British English. Then I spent a year in the States and switched over to American English. For many years, I listened to Bob Dylan a lot. What I learned from him, really listening to him, was not merely paying attention to the words, imagery or ideas of the songs, but the *sound* he was putting forth. The meaning or importance of sound. The meaning and importance of expressing something that's beyond and above the initial surface of language. And not only that. What Dylan taught me is that there are no constants, nothing is fixed. Listening to the endless renditions of his own songs, bending and shaping them time and again into something new, always something new, now that was a revelation. Writing poetry is about something else than what's right there. It's about *poiesis*, making something new. Or like Jasper Johns, the painter, puts it: "Do something, do something to that, and then do something to that."

Other than Dylan, I've read a lot of Elmore Leonard, the true master of the colloquial American English. I've read all of his books a half a dozen times, and I still can't come up with a spoiler for any of them. That's me, the poet. I look at language from an angle other than the practical or the conventional one. Now, if that's because I know or use other languages, then so be it. It sure makes working with words all the more interesting. I think an extra language, any language other than your own, is always an advantage. That is why I envy those who know Classic Greek or Latin and maybe few others to go with them. I have to do with English, Swedish and a little French.

TB: Who do you think of as your poetic forebears?

KK: They are mostly non-writers. Miles Davis, Cy Twombly, Keith Jarrett, Mark Rothko, to name a few. For me, writing poetry is painting with a thin brush, doing water colors, making small print. What I'd love to do, quite literally, is going for the big picture. I know I can't, but I'd love to. I just love the rich sound of Miles Davis and the endless possibilities that are there in his different combos and stylistic phases. I love his refusal to stay with one thing. I love the absolute beauty of Jarrett's solo work. Like the Dead, he's not afraid of letting it all hang out, without a safety net. These guys don't shy away from the horror and the risks that are there in the business of looking into one's soul and making something out of it. I love the broad canvas, the big brush. I envy the painter, all painters. They don't have to stick with the linear, the reason of language. That is also why I love the collage, the mixing of different media, in the works of, say, Kurt Schwitters and Robert Rauschenberg. I'd love to write poetry that you can just look at, without the need to read it line by line, from left to right, the way you are *supposed* to read anything that's written.

Even so, I consider all of them as my poetic forebears, artists that have influenced my aesthetics as a poet. This has much to do with a personal problem. As a writer, I have extremely great difficulties to rid myself of the linearity, the syntax, and the meaning of the written language. Making poetry, that is. My preferences are towards the non-linear, the absolutely free, but it seems it's very hard for me to shake the authority of the language police deeply imbedded in my system. I guess this is why my work is greatly divided. There's your traditional short poem, mostly elegiac stuff about love, nature, or the human condition. Then there's this other stuff. Things produced by shameless appropriation, collages put together from various sources, computer-generated artefacts, and visual poetry where the elements of language are almost completely erased. That's me, right there. I'd love to be able to compose original, absolutely free poetry straight from within, but I can't. When I look inside myself, I find either nothing or pathetic conventionalities. At least, that's how I feel. So, to come up with anything worthy, I have to use all these artificial, or adopted, means of creation.

This doesn't mean I don't have any poets that I consider exemplary or meaningful to my development as a poet. Two early reading experiences come to mind, both from the time I was fifteen. The first one was Jarkko Laine, a Finnish poet in the Underground or Beat tradition. I picked up his early work the way I eagerly picked up anything with a Mothers of Invention or a hippie flare to it. With a friend of mine we read his work in front of class and caused a mild sensation. Right away I knew I was onto something serious and fun. The other one was Eliot's "Waste Land" in Finnish translation, a definitely serious and unfunny work if there ever was one. Now, why Eliot, among all the Fugs and Japhy Ryders? Again, you have to keep in mind the late appearance of our modernist tradition, and bringing the basic modernist work into Finnish had been an essential part of the project. So, "Waste Land" was the thing to read if you wanted to introduce yourself to "new" poetry. Anyway, I was impressed, and in my young heart, I felt I was onto something "great." There's the dichotomy again: tradition and the present, convention and non-conformism, square and hip, messing with and shaping my virgin mind.

Later on, others would come by, of course. My Finnish readers know who the Finnish ones are, and I won't bother you mentioning any of them here. All I will say is that I'm an eclectic: I'll take anything from any time or any tradition — as long as it's both serious *and* fun.

TB: Do you think that a poet has any unique social responsibilities?

KK: Responsibilities, yes; unique, not so sure. First of all, I don't think writing political stuff or promoting radical ideas to raise social awareness is an obligation; it's a matter of personal choice and temperament. We are a heterogeneous bunch, and there are a variety of ways to do it. Think Sheila E. Murphy, Mark Young, or yourself, for example. Intimacy and issues, all rolled into one.

Doing our thing, we are connected in many ways and not only to our readers or the reading public in general. There are all kinds of people we work with: peers, colleagues, editors, publishers, printers, artists, journalists, critics, and what not. Besides writing, many of us teach or work as editors or publishers. That's a lot of social responsibilities, right there. In fact, it's hard for us to *avoid* them. I mean, I think a poet's responsibilities, if any, are rather towards the people he actually makes contact with, works with, and lives with, not towards an abstract readership. Call me naïve, but I reckon the adage "think globally, act locally" applies to the poet also. (With the advent of the Internet, we have to redefine "local," of course.) What I'm saying is that a poet's social respons-ibilities don't differ that much from the next guy. Why do people tune up Harleys or make Sushi rolls for a living? Not because they're supposed to, but because they can and will.

The difference is, of course, that we think poetry is, as writing, "communi-cative," and thus "social." Is what a poet does by default, we say. Well, that's true, but I can also think of poets and artists whose work is elitist and in no means "communicative," and yet we deserve them.

For me personally this means two simple things. I take my writing very seriously and I try to do everything in my power to help my peers in every which way I can. The first part covers my responsibilities both as a preservationist of the Finnish language and a tax payer. The other's the real thing, love in making.

TB: Let me put it a little differently. What, my friend, do you want poetry to do? Why does it matter?

KK: What do *I* want? You just keep throwing high heat, Tommy dear. To try for an answer, let me recount the story of Giotto, the early Renaissance painter from Florence, of Tuscany. As a young boy Giotto worked as a shepherd, and to pass the long hours out there in the hills he used to spend his time drawing. For lack of proper materials, he drew on rocks or made his pictures right there in the sand with a stick. One day Cimabue, the most famous painter of his time, walks by and sees young Giotto's drawings. He's impressed by the boy's apparent skills and asks him to join him as a student. Giotto accepts (actually his father does) and the rest is history. Even today, seven centuries later, millions of people from all over flock to see the raw beauty of the former shepherd's images in the cathedrals of Italy.

Now, I think what we have here is analogous to all art, including poetry. We have this talent and the willingness to use it, no matter what happens. We write our poems, no matter if the wind or the rain washes it off before anybody actually sees it. Then one day maybe, just maybe, a Cimabue happens along the way to help us. And if we are talented enough, and persistent enough, maybe we find an audience. And if we're lucky, really lucky, maybe we get to touch a few people's hearts.

So, asking what we want poetry to do for us is really asking what we're willing to do for poetry.

I mean, we do write for a purpose, don't we? Think of Giotto, here. Very few reach up to his level, of course, but I'm sure we can all share his urgency. His dedication to making art even at a very early age, even before he could have had any ideas about meaning, content, or purpose. That's how I see it. We really can't, or shouldn't, worry too much about the doings of poetry. We just do our bit and keep on doing it.

What happens after that is anybody's guess. Let's see. It's certainly not just one thing. Okay, here goes: If people find it worth their while to learn by heart lines that they don't quite grip but rather make their heads spin and hearts jump — do we need any more evidence as to why poetry matters?

TB: What do you find most encouraging/discouraging about the current poetry scene(s)?

KK: I see mostly positives. On a personal level, I have very few complaints, if any. The last few years, the Muses have been good to me, and although I'd love to write poetry full time, at least I get to work, collaborate, and converse with a host of other poets.

In many ways, my position is quite unique. As poetry editor of *Parnasso*, the leading mainstream literary magazine in Finland, I have access to just about everybody, and what's even more important, I can help new and up-coming poets have their work published. As a middle-aged poet in his early fifties, I know practically everybody in the Finnish literary scene: poets, writers, editors, publishers, translators, critics — many of whom I consider personal friends. Some of these wonderful people were born in the 1920's, some are *in* their twenties. I feel like a true intermediary, if there ever was one.

As it happens, few of these people live in far-away places like Australia, Italy,

New York, Schenectady, Ohio, and California, most of whom I've only met through the Internet and none of whom I'd have any connections with if it weren't for the Internet. For poets of the world, I think, the net is a god-send. I'm not saying everybody should be blogging or having their work published in the net, but after cheap Internet connections became a common-place, you were out of excuses. It didn't make you write better poetry (or any poetry, for that matter), but you and your work didn't stand isolated from the rest of the world, either, whether you lived in Akron, Ohio, or in Espoo, Finland. You could read just about everybody; you could find any fact; you could reach any person. Think U. of Buffalo; think Ubu Web. Think Silliman's Blog, As/Is, Jacket. Think publishers like E. Tabios, J-P Kervinen, or M. Young. Take Poet's Corner. Take E-Values. Networking hasn't made any of us rich, but without it we'd certainly feel a lot poorer, a lot less worthy. A lot more lonely.

It's a new thing and there's no telling what's become of it. I'd say there will be a lot of "inter"-everything. I mean, really, what language is poetry? I see a lot of people working in two or more languages. It's what poets do. I'm not saying we'll all be writing in this or that language; all I'm saying is that each and every one of us will benefit from this interaction, these multiple possibilities.

That said, I'd like to add a few words about the Finnish poetry scene or Finnish poetry in general. A few facts: I write in a language that is spoken by less than six million. I write in a language that was first written less than five centuries ago. I write in a language that is very different from Indo-European languages, a language that is more suited to describing a seal hunt, or a walk in the woods, than complex ideas or philosophical concepts. The first novel written in Finnish was published in 1870. Finnish as a medium of poetic expression became of age only a hundred years ago. Our modernism is less than sixty years old.

To become a poet and to live as a poet in Finland is a mixed blessing. More often than not poets get their first collections published when still in their twenties. (The idea being, to seed out future novelists; that is, writers who can eventually make a profit for the publishing houses.) After two or three published works (say, in less than five years) you could receive a grant (either by state or privately owned funds) of monthly allowances that lets you concentrate on your writing for a year. Then three years. And, eventually, five years. This is in no means automatic, and only applies to a handful of people, but what I'm saying is that compared to many other countries, writers, poets, and artists are very well taken care of here. As a poet, you won't be able to buy a house, but most of the problems that we have you would consider a luxury.

Most poetry books will only sell a couple hundred copies, though. That total could rise to a thousand if the majority of our public libraries decide to add it to their collections. A decade or two ago, that was a given, but not anymore since the money allotted to our library system has plummeted these past few years, one of the victims being poetry, of course. Why poetry? I can only cite the obvious. Because the value of poetry cannot really be weighed. Poetry is not collateral.

In other words, I could go on complaining about small sales, uninterested publishers, stupid media, lack of meaningful criticism, closing down of libraries, the struggle to survive of small Finno-Ugric languages, or whatever. But I won't, because although I think poets work in close connection with all these activities, although poets do have a role in the social fabric that is Finland or anywhere in the world, poetry is still confined to the margin. It *is* the margin.

being more than naked words
words being more than naked
naked more than being words
words naked more than being
being words more than naked
words more than naked being
more being than naked words
naked words more than being
words more than being naked
being naked more than words
more than words being naked
naked being more than words

list'n

h'ear

Comp as Expl

(G. Stein abbreviated into foursomes & sixsomes)

ther
sing diff
exce gene comp

beca
inte cons
long conn thin

depe
desc comp
conf like chan

rema
deci prep
degr pain occu

with
arou happ
part crea refu

acce
ente mode
spea impo unex

defi
auth clas
outl bett ther

cont
shou live
anyw indo quot

quit
cert nati
acti thre leas

seve
sati chan
star conc extr

quot
quit cert
like leas seve

sati
ther cont
shou conf deci

diff
beca depe
extr ther extr

conn
gene cons
long desc mode

spea
chan star
happ part chan

indo
thre ther
cont shou pain

gene
crea ther
refu acce ente

unex
defi auth
nati acti rema

refu
acce ente
sing thin happ

part
sing conn
pain comp thin

mode
spea exce
unex defi auth

impo
rema beca
conc occu with

arou
live anyw
like degr degr

prep
conf conc
diff desc inte

bett
quot quit
cert live anyw

thre
exce clas
outl clas outl

comp
bett prep
deci indo cons

long
impo chan
star depe occu

with
arou comp
comp crea chan

leas
seve sati
inte nati acti

prep
chan depe
degr pain conn

clas
outl crea
mode spea extr

ther
desc nati
acti thin conc

indo
bett occu
with arou chan

star
conf exce
impo unex defi

auth
desc leas
seve sati crea

Kaksi runoa kokoelmasta *Vapaat kädet* **(ntamo, 2007)**

Montako hiekkajyvää tarvitaan jotta voimme puhua
hiekasta, montako hiusta jotta saadaan hiukset päähän,
erilaisia tapoja sopia siitä, mihin kiinnittää huomio,
mitä ajatella, muistaa, ennakoida, miten toimia, ehkä.
Se, vastaavatko merkit tosiasioita, ei kuulu tähän,
teksti lepää katsottavana ja ääneti, vähän niin kuin uni
tai puut jotka tulevat mieleen aina kun katsoo puita
tai hirsi joka tähän vedettynä muistaa unen ja kuoleman.
Näytä minulle läjä pisaroita ja minä kerron mikä niistä
kuuluu mereen josta kuu heijastuu puun tai oksien läpi,
mutta sitä en tiedä montako sataa pisaraa tarvitaan,
jotta vesi olisi meri eikä maata viistävä pilvi eli sumu.
Pisarat, niiden kosteus, on toistettava sanelun mukaan,
toisin kuin sade, joka niin sanotusti putoaa taivaasta.

§

Mitä sitten jos nainen onkin maalattu silmä äänettömässä
runossa, tarkemmin sanottuna sen vasemmassa reunassa.
Toinen uittaa surunsa unessa, toinen huokaa näkökykyään,
ikään kuin hänkään muuta olisi kuin tyhjä muistitikkunsa.

Omenaisen puun saa hurmattua kielellä, poikakivi kipittää
tyttökiven perässä vaikka ylämäkeen, jos lähtevä tai tuleva
viesti on viehkeä nännin tai kallon alueella, siksi juuri olen
laittautunut kauniiksi: haluan mennä kauniina kauniin luo.

Mutta meidän ei ole syytä väheksyä rakkauden harhoja
parantavaa voimaa, olen hullu koska olen rakastunut, vaan
en hullu siksi, että pystyn lirkuttamaan sen nöpöläiselleni
kuin minkä tahansa kreikkalaisilta periytyvän käsitteen.

Hankaavine alkuineen ja soljuvine vokaaleineen sana lisää
nautintoon, josta se kertoo: nautin yhtymisestä suussani.

Two poems from *Vapaat kädet* (*Hands-Free*; ntamo, 2007)

How many grains of sand do we need to talk about sand,
how many hairs to make it up to a full body of hair,
the many ways to decide as to where to lay one's eyes,
to think, remember, anticipate, or to act, perhaps?
Whether the signs match the facts is not at stake here,
the text just lays there for you to see, silent, like a dream
or trees that pop into mind every time you look at trees,
like the log here remembers death and dreaming.
Show me a bunch of water drops and I'll tell you which ones
belong to the sea, reflecting the moon through the trees,
but I do not know how many drops it takes to make a sea,
nor a cloud hanging close to the ground, known also as fog.
The drops, their very humidity, need to be repeated as prescribed,
unlike the rain that falls from the sky, they say, just like that.

§

So what if the woman is a made-up eye in a silent
poem, in the upper left-hand corner, to be exact?
What are we, an empty flash memory, bathing
our woes in dreams but finding fault in eyesight?

We may charm an apple tree with a tongue, even
a he-stone will roll uphill after a she-stone if the signal
is appealing in the region of the nipple or the skull.
To the feasts of the good the good unbidden go.

But who are we to belittle the cure of love against love's
illusions. I am mad because I am in love, but I'm not mad
because I can whisper in her ear sweet nothings better
than any concept dreamt up by the ancient Greeks.

The spirant frictions and gliding vowels of the word
add to the pleasure it conveys: I love it in the mouth.

translated by the author

phewture

riverb

loverb

lamen't

seecret

visious

taughture

Jill Jones

interviewed by Tom Beckett

Jill Jones won the 2003 Kenneth Slessor Poetry Prize for *Screens, Jets, Heaven: New and Selected Poems* and the 1993 Mary Gilmore Award for her first book of poetry, *The Mask and the Jagged Star*. Her latest full-length book, *Broken/Open*, was short-listed for The Age Book of the Year 2005 and the 2006 Kenneth Slessor Poetry Prize. Her work has been widely published in Australia as well as in a number of print magazines in New Zealand, Canada, the USA, Britain and India. In 2007 she took part in the 23rd Festival International de la Poésie in Trois-Rivières, Quebec, Canada and her poems have been translated into Chinese, Dutch, French, Italian and Spanish. She is also widely published online. She has collaborated with photographer Annette Willis on a number of projects. Her day jobs have included film reviewer, journalist, law book editor, events manager and arts administrator. For nearly seven years she was Program Manager with the Literature Board of the Australia Council for the Arts. She took up a position teaching at the University of Adelaide in May 2008.

Tom Beckett: Where did/does poetry begin for you?

Jill Jones: There are many ways I can answer that and here are some of them.

Poetry begins in a space. Not one I can define. It is often apparent, however, when I'm walking. But even before that, it is in the body's space, and pace, its energy.

There's always birds in it, and light.

Often I can begin with the sound of words, a phrase, in the jingle jangle brain. No sentences but in strings. Secretly, I wanted to be a rock star way back when. And I am very influenced. How could I not be? No word is mine anyway. There's a list of influences I could go on with but they change over time.

Another beginning. I tried to make a book when I was about eight years old. It wasn't poetry and it was crap, of course. I'm a child of the suburbs, those blank, sunny stretches I remember that held nothing but boredom for certain kids, like myself. In my story I "escaped", to the supposedly more cosmo-politan, semi-bohemian inner city of Sydney. It was from there I started, eventually, to write. In my mind I was merely writing about "what I knew". My experiences of "nature", "environment", "place" were all metropolitan or suburban and any art that approached these was like a great invitation to me. I got with those lines from Wordsworth that I first learned in early high school: "This city doth, like a garment, wear/ The beauty of the morning; silent, bare,/ Ships towers, domes theatres, and temples lie/ Open unto the fields, and to the sky. ..."

Nowadays, of course, you're not supposed to admit to reading Wordsworth, but it was all part of my experience as a reader and would-be writer at the age of, ooh, fourteen, and I can't be bothered repudiating it at this late stage.

Of course my reading expanded. What Australian high school kid didn't read Slessor back then? Well, I did at least, and poems such as "William Street" and "Five Bells" entered my consciousness, and if "Five Bells" isn't about Sydney, then I don't know what is. It's interesting to read Slessor's own notes on "William Street", in the preface to his Selected, where he says, "The general reason for the poem remains, since it was intended as a defence of metropolitan fascinations against those who considered the city 'ugly' and found beauty only in the outback". The poem's first stanza, and its well-known refrain reads: "The red globes of light, the liquor-green,/ The pulsing arrows and the running fire/ Spilt on the stones, go deeper than a stream;/ You find this ugly, I find it lovely."

OK, it's not one of the world's great poems, in hindsight, but I'm talking beginnings here, what a kid embarking on poetry thought might be possible. And despite that, I was a very late beginner, in one sense. I started writing poetry, badly, in my teens, then stopped and didn't get going till way way later. The poetry of Adrienne Rich helped a lot in that second beginning, now some 25 odd years later. Sort of obvious, I suppose, looking at the changes in my life.

Beginnings are difficult. Poems seemed magical once (still do at times, but I'm talking about "then"). Words were magical. And poetry never ends even when it is difficult. I think it will be difficult to end.

Sometimes I don't know I'm beginning. Stuff happens with words. One way of beginning is like a tuning in — you hear a dog barking, or someone says something, you see an angle in the street and a word associates itself with it for a moment. It's associative, or accretive. It goes or it doesn't. Good old hindsight might do the intellectual grunt on the whys and wherefores afterwards. It's a little like the problem of how to "exist in language", to borrow a phrase from Nicole Brossard. Sometimes it seems like too much hard work. And never to forget, writing comes from the body. I've thought of it as a complex of physical activity that's pretty obvious, like the hand typing or pushing the pen or the eye reading the words being written, as well as what's less easy to document, what someone else I can't remember called "felt sense", a bodily awareness of feelings that come out of words, ideas, images. But it all requires energy to generate this activity.

I sometimes have a problem with energy, or I certainly did some years ago. Perhaps it was simply tiredness — not just on the physical level but that of depleted possibilities, a kind of millennial exhaustion. I would turn it around, something like Gerard Genette said (I was reading him a bit some years ago and got stuck on it, so I have the quote to hand), "Perhaps the best thing would be ... never to 'finish', which is, in one sense, never to start".

But these days I often write to order, or use other ways to make poems: reading someone else to kick start, making lists, noodling on the net, using constraints. That can work. I am naturally a last minuter so being 'made' to do something is useful. There are, in fact, lots of possibilities.

TB: You mentioned thinking poetry comes out of the body. What's your sense of how bodies figure in your work?

JJ: The body in the poem is, among other things, its rhythm. The other things include the senses, including all forms of sonics, and sound relationships, what I get through my ears as well as the sound felt and heard in my body. And even the feeling of not being able to say, the words I don't have words for, how that feels. There's a famous quote from Mayakovsky, I think, about walking and mumbling, of sounded rhythm getting to the word of the poem. Perhaps it's like chanting.

Walking, and moving is a key for some poets. Didn't Coleridge and Wordsworth talk about their different styles of walking as part of their composing a certain kind of poem? Let alone Baudelaire and his flaneurie. I don't drive, so I walk and also use public transport a lot, which has its own rhythms - how you see as things pass, what you hear and don't hear due to noise factors, as well as the actual physical feeling of the train or bus. Buses are much harder to write on (on? in?), or Sydney buses are. I can't write in cars. I don't know why. But you can see that a lot of my writing does start en plein air, so to speak. But not just in observational mode. What you do. Not that hearing and seeing isn't 'doing'. But it may explain why some of my poems have a kind of broken or collaged kind of narrative, Changing trains, changing travel modes, the coming and going of bodies, voices, weathers. You can see a lot of this in the sequence 'Struggle and Radiance' or the snapshot poems I was writing on the poetryetc list for a time.

Poems are made of language, obviously, and language is material, it has a physical presence (including its technological modality - and is it weird to say I sometimes touch my screen to follow something). The material is never static. Then there's words on the page, the look of it as well, the visual rhythm I can get going.

The sounds of words and their 'feel' are important to me. I go sometimes with rhyme and have written the occasional poem with a traditional rhyme and metric scheme. Some of the sonnets in the sequence 'Traverse' approach that. The stresses and rhythms are obvious in metrical verse, of course, but irregular stress is also rhythmic or tends to rhythms that aren't iambic. I don't know how much I get it right but I am conscious of a wish to get a poem to 'swing' somehow. (I realise this is a jazz kind of terminology.) Timing is important (and turning), the swing between the binaries, the alternations, however irregular they may be, how the poem moves, how it becomes. I sometimes write poems to songs or pieces of music, even movements from symphonies. For instance, the poem 'The Skim' from Broken/Open is based on the rhythm of a song 'The Spark' by The Roots. The end result is hardly ever something you'd pick, but I know where it started.

I don't write lot of poems about bodies or the body in the sense that, say, a lot of poems were written out of feminist ideas from around the 1970s and early 80s. It's not a kind of project that ever sat easily with me. I don't think it's a theoretical position, I am just uneasy about it, for me. Of course, I do write love poems, they are about bodies.

I do write about, as well as out of, the senses and the rhythms of the body and people tell me my work is 'sensual'. I mention breath a lot in my poems. As well as obvious connections to 'breath unit' and such, it also connects to my own breathlessness. I'm not an asthmatic but I am very close to its possibility. I am very conscious of my own breathing. I am also seem to be sensitive to sounds at a certain low level. I feel them. I also suffer from a kind of vertigo and feel bodily a kind of state of 'between-ness' when I've experienced an episode of vertigo. It's not necessarily pleasant, mind you. But I am my body and it's what I do, so it is part of my process, a techne of the body, so to speak. It's taken me a while to realise this was something I was doing in my work. There are always these little mysteries about the making, the secrets one keeps from oneself at times.

TB: What do you want from a poem? Why does poetry matter?

JJ: Well, Tom, these look like two very different questions to me, though maybe not. Let's see. I'll answer the second one first. Though I'm not sure it's up to me to say why poetry matters. But, OK, to me, yes, it matters. It's what I do, in a way that defines me, unlike a lot of other things. It's also how I think a lot of the time, in that I experience a poem I make as also a way of thinking. I mean this in the broadest possible sense — emotional thinking, the thinking of skin and nerve.

So - what matters? The power of language. That it's full of possibilities. By that I don't mean the new, necessarily. There's plenty of bad new things. And what's new to me may be old to my neighbour. So, I'm not talking about progress. The power — that it can say the unsayable, the not yet knowable. By me.

There's a lot of poetry around these days, so it matters to a lot of people. The

77

poetry itself may or may not be what presses my or your buttons. But people seem to believe there's a magic there. Poetry does something for them, clearly, as it does for me. It makes up the world, a world. Often it's a world we know, so it shores it up or, at times, embellishes it. But sometimes it makes a different world. Maybe that's the 'new' that's interesting, pleasurable, disruptive. Stepping outside yourself, your construct.

I see poems as landscapes (though I'm not fond of that word), the horizons go on, they are only fixed when you're still (and even then, who is ever still). They have weather, which is unpredictable. One of my favourite quotes, which I've lost the reference for, is something John Ashbery said, along the lines of there being only three great themes of poetry, love, death and the weather. The weather really is the matter at the moment, I think.

At times I do wonder where the necessity of poetry has gone, here, in this place. A little anecdote — and not an ego thing. I was in Shanghai a few years ago and we were "assigned" a Chinese guide (who we managed to dodge out on mostly) ... but when she found out I was "a poet" she became all impressed and a touch deferential. Which I found discomforting and embarrassing, especially as I had nothing to offer or show for it, in the context of a language and culture in which I was a tourist. So it was nothing to do with me, this "poet" thing. Especially as, back home in Sydney, I knew that if I mentioned I was a poet people would move away from me as though I'd farted, or berate me that "it doesn't rhyme" or that I was "a wanker" or an "ay-leet-ist". I don't know if it's the same in your neck of the woods, Tom. And I wonder what this idea of "poet" meant to this Chinese woman, about whom I knew nothing.

I'm not sure I've answered this question at all. So, before I get to grips with "what do I want from a poem?", I need to clarify, is it me as a reader or a writer of "a poem"? Or maybe there's an answer to that in what I've said so far.

I can say that I respond to poems that are locales, a space somewhere. I want change, ground and air, in the form's thingness, it's landscape, as well as the poem's aboutness. I always jib at the "about" word, though it's a useful word if you don't get too hung up on it. I think of it in the sense of "round and about", a sort of peripatetic meaning.

OK, looks as though I'm forging on with an answer. I'm into a poem's ecology, if you will, its own dynamics, its topography (own yr own metaphor, eh). I'm interested in equivalences, correspondences, rather than representations. I want to be moved somewhere rather than smoothed in place. I like it when a poem appears to click onto something, then doesn't because it's headed elsewhere, then maybe it clicks again, and then ... etc. Language as resource, not a program, that's not too stuck in its own devices, either, nor too proud of its meanings and ego investments. Though there's no point in pretending that "I" ain't there but I is only a relation, to others, the othernesses — flowers, dirt, horses, history, robots, clouds, human beings, storms, bugs etc. No I but in the world. And as for desire, then the poem allowing desire, making space for it, not just sucking it up. So, what goes around isn't exactly what comes around at all.

The question also begs the question of poems v. poetry. I'm a poetry kind of person. I see I'm writing poetry, rather than lots of poems. And then there's the other question. What does a poem want from us? And I obviously can't answer for the poem.

TB: Would you take me through one of your poems (your choice which) and speak to the occasion of its making? I'm looking for a concrete example of your compositional process/practice.

JJ: Ah, this one could go anywhere. First of all, my process in general is on the fly, whatever I can do in between a full-time job and a life. I used to be much more social but now I tend to work at poetry on weekends to keep up with writing and associated tasks, including blogging. I am at risk of becoming a boring person. I write on the train, en route essentially, as well as in cafes, even in meetings. There's a poem of mine which partially consists of notes made during a meeting about risk management and data collection, called 'How would you say risk management?'. In fact, the original draft became two poems after a suggestion from someone to break the original down. I'm always open to suggestion. I can be a tad precious at times about my work but not that precious.

I've got notebooks all over the place and I think it'd be fair to say I have a bit of a stationery fetish. I like French and Japanese-made notebooks because the paper seems good enough for all kinds of pens, including roller balls and fountain pens. Artist's visual diaries also work, and those Moleskine thingies, but they're not cheap. Most Australian notebooks allow ink to bleed too much and are mostly spiral-bound which is OK but can be irritating when the poorly-manufactured ones unravel and get caught on things and the paper rips. I can pick up good Japanese-made notebooks reasonably cheaply here in Asian stationery stores — Kokoyu and Maruman are good brands. I got some good things in Hong Kong once, as well, inexpensive and great for what I wanted.

And if I'm ever in Paris, which isn't often (as in four times, ever, but the fifth is planned), I will stock up on Rhodia or Clairefontaine, which are cheap there, but exxy or completely unavailable here. I live at the arse-end of the world, you must remember. And I will write on anything, including the back of an envelope, if needs. Mustn't waste things.

But, yes — pulls back from the fetish precipice — notebooks ... which aren't that well-organised, but I take everywhere, that I use and preserve. They get filled up with observations including weather conditions, my own turns of phrase, overheard conversations or things I think I hear, things I see written down, on walls, in someone's newspaper. etc. It can get a bit pervy, but a lot of art practice is like that, I suspect. Sometimes an almost fully-formed poem is formed quickly on the run. I'm sure this isn't news for most poets.

So that's one way I work, from what is written out of a situation, locale, the nonce, through a soup of words, phrases, towards a poem or poems. I may still stick to a pen or pencil in a first rewrite, putting together the notes into something. Then I'll move to the computer and begin the re-drafts. That could take hours, days, months, or years.

Another way I work is more from or with the screen from the start. I may do a bit of flarfing, though I haven't for a while. The poem 'Clouds To Powder' in Broken/Open is based on a Google search on the phrase, 'morning rattles clouds'.

I will pull apart old drafts and move lines and stanzas around arbitrarily, just to see, or sometimes put dead poems through a babel translator and see if the progress of words and phrases through various inversions of languages works a transformation I like. Sometimes, I like.

I use the screen to work more quickly with reformatting, and reformatting can often lead to a different, sometimes better poem. The look of a poem is important.

I may set up restraints. They could be formal, eg setting up line endings/ rhymes before the poem is written or determining a poem will contain a certain number of words or lines (sonnets and hay(na)ku fall into that category). Others are conceptual, poems based around or containing a certain idea, or based on some other kind of writing, or another at form (ie, ekphrasis, which I've worked a lot with). That can be done on paper or on screen. I plan better on paper, you know, circles and arrows ... etc.

And a lot of what I do moves in and around all these kinds of writing practice. I'm not sure, again, if it's any great secret. It's work, making. The mysteries are in your head and body and in language, and when the making works out right. I mean, there's magic in the process but the material description of it, I dunno, does it reveal anything? It's why there's relatively few decent films directly about writers and writing. Who wants to watch someone writing?

So, some examples. The final (so far) version of this poem, 'While All This is Going On' is available on line at the New Zealand electronic poetry centre. The origins of the poem lie in a poem I wrote quite some years ago, around 2001, which was essentially a disjunctive succession of lines, observations, overheard phrases and happenings in my street, in my house, ending up with 'the poet' working. They were all pretty factual. Some of the lines included 'Drugs pass across the road from hand to hand' and 'no-one on the radio, the door of the nation closed/ and poets make words of little boats'. This was a reference to refugees being excluded from this country, the so-called and shameful Pacific solution. The poem's original title is lost to me but one working title was 'But Who Is My Enemy?'. It began around a time I was re-reading Shelley, the political Shelley, and there's a reference to a portion of 'Ode To the West Wind' in it, "from whose unseen presence the leaves dead/ Are driven". I played around with the poem for some time, maybe a couple of years, on and off. I may have even submitted it somewhere, not sure. It was never right, A bit too much detail not doing a lot, and it looked lumpy on the page. But there were things in it I liked. A couple of years later I wrote a series of lines in a large notebook. It was around the time of the last Australian Federal election in the spring of 2004, that is October (just days before my birthday, as it happened), and I was 'not happy, Jan, not happy'. There are lines such as 'Somehow we're all starting to sound like the shadow', which is the first line in the notebook, or 'It's elbows and interest rates and the beautiful soft furnishing of night programs', or 'Windows blink, murmuring diamonds, cast-off sounds twist into my dreams'. Looking at this now, I think I may have been watching TV as I wrote it. I see from the notes at the bottom of the page that I planned to write something titled many things but including '101 footnotes to a lost text on war'. Somehow, in a move I don't quite recall, I decided these lines and the other poem, and a few other orphan bits and pieces, might work into something. I wrote '101 lines on a spring campaign', I think I called it, mixing up the lines, getting together 101 of them. I was trying to get the poem to move between the very particulars of a place to the over-arching political state of a country. But it was always a bit uncooked, over-reaching or under-reaching, I don't know. I did send it off somewhere but it got the inevitable arse. It became '62 Footnotes For a Lost Text on the Spring Campaign' for a short time. I left it for a bit. Then, one day, playing with it on screen, I ran it all together as a paragraph. It seemed to work with much, much pruning. The currawong in the last line became a raven (an Australian raven) because I suspect that's what it had been all along, a big black raven. I sent it off to nzepc for their FUGACITY 05 anthology and it came out in three paragraphs. I don't know if that was something to do with a coding error or whether someone there re-edited it like that. But I kind of liked it and so it stands. For the moment.

Another other more concise example. Breath, the hours is a text and visual work, essentially ekphrastic, that I wrote 'to' photographs taken by my partner Annette Willis. I had been offered the opportunity to do this by Rebecca Seiferle, editor of The Drunken Boat. I had an idea about 'journey', pretty broad, eh. But Annette and I had been on journeys together. We're both interested in street textures, in shadow and light. We picked out some photo-graphs of hers and I sat with them, and put something together around them, then we talked some more. It was a dialogic process, between the two people involved and the two practices, as well as the dialogue in the work, line by line, including the repetitions. The form is my adaptation of hay(na)ku. I'd origin-ally thought of using that form but the project really required a different movement, an eddy and flow, so I came up with the idea of using a longer line with a shorter line as a lever, in other words, a six word line being a hay(na)ku written in a straight line instead of a stepped stanza, followed by a three word line. I find that 'things of three' can mesh together yet move along. The words of the poem were reworked from a number of existing fragments I'd written over the last few years, most of them had been written during journeys and towards something but had never quite settled.

But the poems are definitely made up of my preoccupations, place and weather.

TB: Who do you see as the poets, peers, contemporaries most affecting you now?

JJ: To some extent whoever is in front me will affect me, one way or another. I don't have to like something for it to affect or influence me. I'm ornery enough to go in the exactly the opposite direction from whatever may be in front of me. I sometimes make a point of reading poets whose work is nowhere near what I write, is more, say, conservative. So long as they don't greatly irritate me, I can plot my own way by setting a course pushing away from what they do whilst getting some good ideas as well as enjoying the ride. So I don't have a reading program, ie I don't just read certain people, or just talk to a certain group. I am aware of 'schools', very much so, we've had our own poetry wars in Australia, but I find that kind of thinking very limiting for my own work. I can't do gangs. That's largely the kinda gal I am. I'll read anything, the back of a chip packet or beer can. You'll always find something of interest.

As for now, my poet friends affect me, of course. If I can have a natter to them over a drink about what they're reading, or share a bit of gossip, or talk about a good plan for poems or poetry, although they may or may not influence my work, they will affect how I feel about poetry.

I know you're probably after names. All I can do is pull some books from my shelves and see which of them have meant something to me recently.

OK, so here's Peter Minter's *Blue Grass* sitting atop of Peter Gizzi's *Some Views of Landscape and Weather*. In another pile, Ange Mlinko's *Starred Wire*, Mary Rising Higgins *O'Clock*, and Michele Leggott's *Milk and Honey* and *As Far as I can See*, all of them very differently shaped books, and containing different poetries. Or Jose Kozer's *Stet: Selected Poems*, a bilingual version translated by Mark Weiss, who kindly sent me this copy, and so full of energy and marvels, though I read no Spanish. These are some books that have made an impression on me recently. There are many more.

I could also include the people I've met via blogging and email lists. The internet has made a great difference to me. In the mid to late 1990s I had withdrawn from poetry circles. I got near to giving it away, it was one of those rather twitter and bisted phases a lot of poets seem to go through, though there were other reasons. Then I started exploring the internet and joined a few lists such as the UK-based poetryetc and and US based wompo. What this did, for a poet sitting pretty much on her Pat Malone here in Sydney, normally reliant on whatever books from overseas you could get your hands on and the very occasional visit by someone fri'fully teddibly important, was to open up a whole new world. What was ACTUALLY HAPPENING RIGHT NOW in places other than Australia. I know that sounds kind of naff these days but, by golly jingo, back then it made a real difference to me. For a while it allowed me to blow off all that need, to be part of the poetry gang here. I discovered traditions I barely knew about (and still barely know a lot about). I could get access to texts I'd never even dreamed of either free or through the online bookshops. And I could be part of conversations, and be accepted as part of conversations, with people who were typing on a mid-winter evening while snow was falling in the English Midlands or New York or Iceland while I was up getting ready for work in a lather of late summer vile humidity. I was getting dates again, so to speak, people wanted to read my work. For a while I felt a bit disconnected from my own scene. That changed quite some years back, and now I get about with some of the old gang and some of the new gang in real time and space and we have plenty to talk about. But my contacts online are pretty important and central, and they affect my work. Though a preponderance of that would be USAmerican poetries of the kind that get labels such as post-avant or experimental or what have you, mainly due to the sheer weight of numbers online, I also look to the UK, Europe, Canada, New Zealand, Asia, anywhere really, if it's available. There are gifts out there every day, and also real exchanges of books, chapbooks, mags between the rest of the world (and the rest of Australia) and a gal in suburban Sydney. Seriously, and I suppose obviously, I wouldn't be doing this now if not for all that. And my poetry book shelves would be a lot less packed as well.

There are the early influences, and the forebears, as it were, but you're not asking me about them. But I do think, even now, there's a lot of dead folks who affect me. Funny, I don't think about them as dead. They are also contemporaries if I am reading the words they wrote right now. That's contemporary.

I'm also affected by music so titles and first lines are important to me, and atmosphere and tone, sonically, like you might get in some funk, nu-jazz (or old jazz) or electronica. I've done mashups of my own work and others. And films and visuals of various kinds. My partner is a photographer and we work together and talk together about light and shadows and words. She taught little kids many years ago, she taught them poetry and that is so, so important. To sound or sing or clap out words and poems. To get the body moving with language. I'm pretty shy but in my room I can move it as well, and no-one needs to know.

TB: I guess that I need to know, Jill. And you told me!

A final question: what do you find most encouraging/discouraging about the current poetry scene(s)?

JJ: What I find most encouraging is partly in the answer above - a kind of loose global community these days, where I find access, feedback, friendship, knowledge. But I do wonder that many of my fellow Australian poets aren't part of the dialogue out there. There are relatively few Australian poets even with websites, let alone blogs. There's not huge numbers of them active on email lists. Australian poetry publishers or organisations don't have a true web presence that much. (A web page that isn't updated in a month of Sundays let alone a blue moon isn't worth bothering with. And a badly designed web page, sheesh!). John Tranter's Jacket magazine is what you might call a benchmark, a real leader in presenting poetry online, but hardly anyone in this country has followed.

In another direction, I am discouraged by writing that is too in love with itself. Or skips over other traditions a bit lightly (you could do it by tripping gaily, I guess). Also, I do wonder why a lot of poets spend so much time trying to make things look "fresh and natural"? I still see a lot of this in my own scene here. I find it unsatisfying. It's hard for me to respond to this kind of "naturalised" poem anymore. It seems so forced. But so does a lot of experimental work, so-called, by definition, it seems. So, I appear to be arguing against myself.

What is also discouraging are too many quick judgments and opinions. The gold star review instead of biding one's time with work, of judging work based on the worker's supposed stance or tendency rather than the poetry.

That's related to my own dissatisfaction at being caught between, and it's why I couldn't really answer your previous question satisfactorily, Tom. What I find discouraging is that so many people like to put you in a box, a school, a gang, whereas I go in between. But ultimately the poetry wars are boring rather than discouraging. They continue here, sometimes raging, other times as guerrilla skirmishes. The discouraging bit is when someone tries to "get" you in a review. It's happened to me, and plenty of others. Critique and real discussion of poetry, rather than just reviewing, is almost non-existent in Australia. There have been so few books of poetics published, when compared to the States, for instance. There's the odd glib newspaper article that purports to summarise what's currently going on or tries to give a historical perspective but it's usually mainstream or conservative stuff. Or there's a "grumpy old poet" type article. I don't like that kind of negativity, especially when I detect it in myself.

But really, I am much more encouraged than discouraged. Though what really discourages me is my own lack of time and space to stretch out as a poet, what encourages me is that there's so much going on, so many possibilities. There are many poetries and many ways they keep happening, especially across the wide range of technologies from the old-fashioned DIY to the new. It seems that poets have to keep doing it for themselves, but I don't see that as a bad thing, it's just part of the way.

It is always good to discover new poets everywhere, the up-and-coming as well as to rediscover the neglected or those you ought to have known but never did, the stars of other traditions. It's good to know that you don't really know that much.

And what is encouraging is that I can talk like this over oceans and miles and time. So, many thanks Tom for the opportunity.

TB: Jill, it's been a pleasure.

My Ruined Lyrics

"You forget whole years, and not necessarily the least important ones."
— Javier Marías, ***The Dark Back of Time***

1. Hold On

The song isn't as loud
as you think it should be

It accompanies the road
nonetheless

You hear it in the rain

Hang on, even a cicada has got
its dream rhythm

That walks with you
through the door

After you've crossed the river
look back, it's passed you

The notes trail

Its attributes are lies and truth
the clash of pasts

2. I'm Coming

I can't give you any more
although the weir overflows

And here in my pockets
another flow

Of cellophane, an old musket
a slide rule, seed catalogues, powers

The river rises
in the hundred year flood

There's something planetary
in the moan of levees

I lay my hands on
evidence changing gears

My logbook is full of
sneaky miles

The lie is of the tongue

And I would kiss you with it
when I come

3. Fields of Wheat

The hour is a vast frontier
moving into day.
In it I spent a year
and then a decade
moving you all around.

It was all down to
bad timing at a desk
the design of borders
a lack of motivation and petrol
and now the Russians have come
with gold lamé g-strings
and a kind of unattractive
comedy
that beats queuing.

I know these are dreams of salvage
and dawn the rescue hour
climbing stairs into duties.
But the orders are confused
and nothing seems to grow.

I ask the Russians for true grain
and a giant sleigh
but it's become too warm
and foghorns tumble.

It is each according to need
and the sun strikes up the band.

4. Bird on the Run

Somewhere the war
is outside my window
showing on a graph
heart-shaped
and inevitable.
But I do not roar in pain
yet.

I am waiting for the birds
then I'll know.
They are not a chorus.
They do not know
how to come home.
They no longer bear
the message.

Which is why

    I jump the sill
    I jump the rocket launcher.

    I jump the map

and it bears me.

      Hear my wings!

5. Flesh and Spark

And when I came
to you
it was raining

We had to be covered
in something other
than ink-black night

The guitars had all drifted
in their boats
animals were nervous

If we don't get access
there's still
recall, its open moment

Along the curled map
of seeds
and their prices

Among the shot
the falling lead
and winged cartography

There, let us have
our doubts
we grave them secret skins

Though covered
they tell flesh
and spark

6. Unusual

The air fills with
petrichor
after rain on sandstone.

It's unusual, and we must
speak it
this drought, this daring.

It will be fire.
It will be cord and rope.
We'll sing it long.

The war wasn't a lie.
The bombs dropped ... so.
And near where you told me.

Trace it on the sheet
and this once
dream it on the beach.

Then outside awakened
again we walk in the depth
of field.

Thirteen Particulars

Birds
Clouds make sky
into other spaces
glad for clearness?
Remember the birds
particulars

Flux
The material gathers
flocks premises degrees
of flux plastic
and vibrant bruised
easily

Heat
Temperatures
like emails continued
heat in the hard drive
a love song
businesslike

Minutes
I earn, you
earn, we sometimes
stand and watch
minutes without labour
gathering

Air
A little breathless
in the sexualized
the conditioned and
the happy sad
air

Leaves
Undermined
by service delivery
do you get it? Leaves
tenuous in late
autumn

Old Walls
Hill, road, river
the moisture wish
tangle rusts in
the old wall
resistance

Organism
A salty pull
expiration forecasts time
that carelessly hangs
habit is greedy
tasted

Music
Noise moves through
rooms, cars, fences
huge chords reporting
the lost sun
music

Breath
A walking breath
from a map
pinging the stratosphere
that invisible blue
trellis

Beat
Chlorophyll wind beat
vegetable sprung growth
wages of distance
to the crumbling
ground

Silvereyes
Something drops through
air the silvereyes
work of birds
where money never
lands

I Must Be With You in the Cold Time

I've lost my sensitivity, you say.
That was always possible
along with a fear of breathing.
As though this was intentional.

I watch as bucket loads drop
then slowly decrease.
I go into work tasting of externals.
I've wished an end, nevertheless.

Elasticity is way round ascension
after a time of emptiness.
A world is stored in whole numbers.
I agree, my absentee moves too hard.

Fear at night blanks inner recovery.
Each word is sent without meaning.
Conceit's attributes rupture in body.
Psycho-technology witnesses my sketchiness.

I'm hungry with these skinny solutions.
My sweat thickens the walls of an hour.
Even the packages are vanilla wrapped.
I wish for response rather than a flip-phone.

Who Can Say When Her Time Is?

This is a song of the white.
The multitude or the pattern.
The rose or the wind.
A woman who begins,
a woman who disappears.
a woman drinking blossom's shadow.

There's a taste that becomes
with spring's movement,
its dreaming is intense. She knows
her secret virtue can be seen in
the water moon that must be (surely)
lying low, somewhere near.

Her body composes its treasures
beyond all the experts in confusion.
Her burdens lightly gather round —
the pure land or fever dreams,
plumes or rejected solutions,
the many-in-one or chaos.

She's never alone among memories.
What's supposed to occur now
is incidental to what happens.
Rising from the grass are fences
and clouds, those little brothers
playing games with the instant.

The moon takes its time.

- *after Sidney Nolan, Rosa Mutabilis, 1945*

Javant Biarujia
interviewed by Sheila E. Murphy

Javant Biarujia is a poet, essayist and playwright born in Melbourne in 1955, of mixed Celtic and Mediterranean descent. Between 1982 and 1996, he ran a small literary press called Nosukumo, devoted to "poetry on the margins", publishing twenty titles. Also under Nosukumo's aegis, he edited *The Carrionflower Writ*, a literary broadsheet publishing Charles Bernstein, Betty Danon, Scott Helmes and dan raphael, among others, and *taboo jadoo*, a journal for "multilinguistics, amphigory *lettrisme, zaum*" and other experimental literary genres. His work has appeared in journals such as *Bombay Gin, Boxkite, Chain, Generator, nrg, Otoliths, Raddle Moon, SALT, SCORE*, Geof Huth's *Subtle Journal of Raw Coinage, Tyuonyi* and *XTANT,* and in over twenty anthologies, among them *Patterns / Context / Time: A Symposium on Contemporary Poetry*, edited by Phillip Foss and Charles Bernstein in 1990, and *The Best Australian Poetry 2005*, edited by Peter Porter. In the past five years, he has published three books of poetry, most recently a New & Selected titled *pointcounterpoint*. (Salt Publishing: Cambridge, 2007). His lifelong project on hermetic poetics and private language, Taneraic, with its own entry in *A Dictionary of Avant Gardes* by Richard Kostelanetz, now has a site on the Internet, and he is currently working toward publishing a comprehensive dictionary of the whole project.

Sheila E. Murphy: It is a privilege to conduct this online interview with you, Javant. You are widely known as poet, playwright, editor, and inventor of the hermetic language, Taneraic, in 1968. At this moment in the calendar, how do these various roles inter-relate to comprise your poetic vision?

Javant Biarujia: Thank you. The pleasure — and privilege — is all mine. After all, being an Australian writer with limited exposure in the US, and when compared to your extensive publishing history, it seems an odd choice to have me as interviewee! But I'm entering into the spirit of it all, and now, having finally moved into my new home, I am able to sit in my new office and devote myself to the task, after a hiatus of five very frustrating months. (I was taken aback when the builder said to me one day I was feeling this way because I was missing my "environment". He had astutely recognised that, with all my books still in boxes, I was living in an exile of sorts.)

You have neatly encapsulated the observation that I am a writer. Period. I am also a prolific correspondent — the old-fashioned way, on paper sent through the post. I started as a poet, but also published essays, and then a decade or so ago I wrote a couple of plays, both of which won prizes. The second went on to be translated into Dutch and performed in The Hague, developing an independent life of its own. Something you don't see so much with poetry. I've worked most my life as a writer, but I've always needed other jobs from time to time, to make ends meet. I started my working life in a Persian rug shop, which I ended up managing, after dropping out of university to do so (and to travel). I mention this because the "Persian experience", and especially the tutelage I received from its proprietor, Alison Vala, as well as my travels to Japan and South-East Asia, and my life and loves on the island of Java, have become a great source of creative pabulum in my life's work.

My hermetic language (or, *"langue close"*, as I call it, calquing the term on *maison close*, French for brothel!), **Taneraic**, has been with me since I was thirteen. I wanted to be able to write a diary, but without the fear of its being read by prying eyes. (I come from a large family!) A lock would easily be picked, and a hidie-hole would soon be discovered. (Do you say "hidie-hole" in America? That's my Scottish side coming out in me.) Although Taneraic began its life in a mathematics class, while studying codes, my private language blossomed as I discovered a talent for languages, as well as language. I was studying French at school, but Russian at home at the time, and later, at university, Indonesian. However, it was when my French teacher introduced me to Esperanto that Taneraic really came into its own. I began my diary four days shy of my fifteenth birthday, and have kept it continuously ever since. I wrote it faithfully in Taneraic for seven years, until I considered I had written thousands of pages in a language no one else could understand, and yet I considered myself a writer, whose aim it is to communicate with a public. When I returned from a year's sojourn on Java in the late 1970s, I put aside my Taneraic dictionaries and started to write my diary in English. By that time, I was living in my own apartment, and no longer felt any fear of discovery. I wrote in English from then on, over most of my writing and publishing career (I ran a small press called Nosukumo for fourteen years with my sister Susan Rachmann and my life partner, Ian Biarujia.) After a decade or so, I found that if I neglected Taneraic any longer, it was in danger of becoming lost even to me. I set about reconstructing the language, for I had burned the original handwritten dictionaries, and, with the aid of a computer, writing a comprehensive Taneraic–English dictionary, which I plan to publish in 2008, Taneraic's fortieth anniversary. Also, starting with Volume 80, I have returned to Taneraic as my language of choice for the diary. So, it is alive and well again! It has also developed a life of its own: a friend has devoted a Web site to it; I correspond in it with poet and linguist Michael Helsem, for whom I prepared a series of lessons; and it has come to a wider audience through such efforts as those of Charles Bernstein, who, calling Taneraic a "poetic experiment", quoted a dream in Taneraic in *My Way, Speeches and Poems* (University of Chicago Press, 1999), adding that while "[n]o more a poet of the Americas than Bunting or MacDiarmid, Javant Biarujia, an Australian poet, has embarked on the most systematically and literally idiolectical poetry of which I am aware" (p. 135).

I went further. In 1978, I legally changed my whole name by deedpoll, encapsulating the essence of Taneraic into my new name, and almost immediately, in this new guise, I found the courage to send my work out to publishers. Within six months of having adopted my new persona, three poems I had written on Kenneth Anger and Anaïs Nin were accepted for publication in Sydney's main gay monthly magazine. What's more, I was paid for my very first appearance in print (five dollars a poem!), which spoiled me for the many years of unpaid publication to come. Of course, people are intrigued by my name for its very exoticism. Needless to say, no one can guess at my nationality or ethnic heritage, for it doesn't quite fit anything people are familiar with. On the other hand, I have never tried to conceal the origins of my name, or tried to jump on the multicultural bandwagon.

None of this, however, has really answered your question, for, *au fond*, I don't know myself how these disparate entities interrelate. David Bowie, after changing direction in the late 1970s with his largely instrumental work, *Low* (my favorite), called himself a "generalist". I think this word best describes me, too, for I don't think I can be pinned down. I've written and published poetry for twenty-five years, yet an Australian reviewer a few years ago dismissed me as a "visual language" or "concrete" poet. Juliana Spahr compared my use of Taneraic in a long "bilingual" poem with the "fake language" poetry of David Melnick. The City Library here in Melbourne issued my book *Calques* with its own, unique Dewey category, for they couldn't recognise the contents as poetry. And theatre reviewers have no idea who I am. I do see these instances as external problems — my creative vision, such as it is, is unhindered by other people's notions of assignment or classification. Although I would have to say poetry is my first love, it is interesting to note that my play *Comfort* has been the most financially rewarding, earning me the right to call myself a professional writer. Yet I have written just two plays, one of them quite short. I have translated a novel from the French and adapted it for the theatre, but directors are not banging down my door! In fact, now in my fiftieth year, I no longer feel driven to succeed, when, in strictly commercial terms, I have failed. A *succès d'estime*, never a put-down in France, no longer feels that way to me here, at the bottom of the world, in Melbourne, Australia.

SEM: Attaining the stature of unclassifiability seems to me to be the highest compliment, but one that brings with it complications, as you clearly point out. The potential for missed understanding by others is considerably higher. You referenced correspondence of the old-fashioned kind. Can you talk a bit about letter writing and its importance as art, or am I taking this point too far?

JB: My friends all look for the quill when they come to visit, but that is to misunderstand my *resistance* to the brusquerie of so-called modern communication and preference for what you call "correspondence of the old-fashioned kind". Now, I am treating this interview in the form of a letter, not only because of its being an online interview, but also because I find the style more congenial — I'm not out to proclaim any truths, to unearth any profundities, or as, O'Hara himself said in his manifesto, to "improve" anyone.

So, if you want to know more about letters, I suggest you search the attics! That seems to be where the best letters are, mouldering away like Hart Crane's grandmother's love letters or the ones Rozanov found. Rozanov declared that the "postmaster who peeped at private letters (in Gogol's *Inspector General*) was a man of good literary taste." And a few lines on (Rozanov: *Fallen Leaves*, p. 64): "Writers' letters are on the whole tedious, colourless. Like misers, they keep the 'bouquets' for print, and their letters are faded, dim, without 'speech'. They ought not to be published. But private people's letters are indeed remarkable." Though what Mayakovsky undoubtedly cherished about letters was the freedom in which he could write whatever he liked without having to consciously think of style or the demands of the public, I must say I find his poetry far more interesting than his love letters to Lili Brik.

Writing letters is an act of friendship, not a literary activity. Often, it's the intermediaries — editors, executors, the Bachelors of Arts — who strip the bride bare by publishing even the most insipid of letters. For profit, of course. (Vian satirises writers' hunger for publishing and publishers' hunger for profits beautifully in *Froth on the Daydream* [an oblique way of translating *L'Écume des jours*].) Delacroix, painter, writer, diarist and correspondent, believed in the value of letter writing as a critical tool for his painting, where he could range, discourse and evaluate his visual art with others as much for himself. There is a close relationship between writing and painting, word and image. And there are bleeding edges, where art gives way to craft and both are imbricated with the activities of the non-artist, hobbyist or amateur. It is the untutored eloquence of Van Gogh's letters to Theo that puts them on a par with his painting. Both his writing and his letters, it seems to me, qualify as great art — I never cease to weep before *Starry Night*, and I read his letters with tears in my eyes for the solitude, the misunderstanding, the depression that lie *au fond*. Miller wrote, reinforcing Rozanov's case, that "Van Gogh, without having any literary pretensions whatever, wrote one of the great books of our time, and without knowing that he was writing a *book*" (Miller: *The Books in My Life*, p. 35; emphasis in original).[1] Correspondence is a confession to others, whereas a

---

[1] *Haiku Review* have just loaded up my essay on Dessaix's first book ("Dessaix in Venice. The homotextual dissimulation of Robert Dessaix in *Night Letters*"), which opens with a quote from Miller's "Letter to Lafayette" and goes on to comment on the nature of published letters:

" 'It's like a grand sickness,' said Dudley, speaking of the Letter which he had at last begun. 'I want to wash up my own life and literature too. The book opens with a nightmare, an evacuation, a *complete waste of images*' " [quoted in Henry Miller, *The Air-Conditioned Nightmare*, 1947; p. 153; emphasis in original] *Night Letters*, too, opens with a nightmare. In many ways, dreams — or nightmares — resemble letters: be they destined for a private drawer, publication or the waste-paper basket, letters constitute the least structured genre of writing, often the least professional; they are free-flowing, unformed, held together merely by a thread of arbitrary memories, thoughts and associations, full of non-sequiturs and blind alleys. In literature, however, all the non-alphabete idiosyncrasies — the loops, the curlicues, the dashes, the scrawls, the cross-outs, the exaggerated exclamations — are cancelled out on

diary is a confession to oneself. (Like Miller, however, I could never manage to get past the first few pages of Rousseau's *Confessions*. By the way, Miller also pointed out that deception was more likely to occur in letters than diaries, for lying to yourself is surely a sign of madness. He meant deliberate lies — as, according to Vidal, in Nin's *Diaries*, both edited and unexpurgated — not self-deception, or an evolving understanding of oneself, which may occasion contradictions, contrary revelations and reversals of belief.)

It all boils down to what O'Hara called Personism (which I'm inclined to misquote as "Personalism", a complete "missed understanding" of what O'Hara was on about).†² The letters I write are private, not literary, though many of them are addressed to other writers. And they are usually addressed to one person. I don't consider structure or rhythm or field when I write letters (unlike Olson's *Letters for Origin*, which acts as a bridge between his poetry and prose), but, unlike my poetry, I am concerned about their reception. I never write Letters to the Editor (well, I did a few times when younger, on points of grammar), but I love reading them in *The Age*. Such letters give a democratic voice to people who might otherwise have no avenue open to them.
I've got about forty books of letters still on the bookshelves — but it was this category I thinned out the most when I moved house last year (Blake, Butor, Cézanne, Pound, Shaw, Mead, Plath, Simenon, Symonds, Weill, etc. — all products of a young enquiring but undisciplined mind). For I had moved *on*. That said, correspondence permeates our literature, our psyche, from biblical epistles to a plethora of *Collected Letters* down through the ages. There are

---

the printed page. For this reason, printed books of letters should be viewed with the same scepticism reserved for memoirs and diaries: that is to say, with utmost suspicion.

² A *note bene*, before leaving this Question, on "missed understanding" — an obvious pun on "misunderstanding", but so effective, nonetheless. It allows for a new interpretation of an old complaint. I like that. I take it that it was yours. I have a keen ear for idiolect, especially that which transmigrates beyond borders and continents. For example, it was not until riffling my French dictionary the other day that I came across an American definition of "pabulum", which I used to mean nourishment of the mind in my answer to your first question — as "mindless pap"! I understand how dangerous dictionaries can be in leading us astray, so I don't know if my Robert has deceived me or not. I love what mishearing ("missed hearing"!) can do. I listed a few of my own in "HomO'Hara", my poem on Frank O'Hara, and have even written a poem round a "mondagreen" of mine of a David Bowie song.

letters as letters, and then there are letters as artefacts. Letters may act as catalysts, generators, architects, prime movers. Peruse any library's shelves and you'll find works titled "Letter(s) to, from, of or by …" or "Correspondence with …" (e.g., "Carrier Letter", *Letters to Unfinished J.*, *Four Unposted Letters to Catherine*, *Letters to a Young Poet*, etc.; you'll find my own "Letter X", a parodic cut-up, online at *slope*'s Web site). For that reason alone, letters form a major part of our appreciation of art, if not art itself, though it now comes to mind that Nin saw letters as an *intrusion*: the choice was to write letters or write novels. (This from someone who slavishly wrote letters back to people who wrote to her, even when she was ill with cancer, for she mentioned often how hurt she felt when she wrote Djuna Barnes an admiring letter early on in her own career, only to be met with silence. Vidal sent Nin's "weakness" up in *Two Sisters* (p. 14): "her pen-pals now range across the earth and her fame increases with each passing year". Nin, it is to be noted, also started her voluminous *Diary* as a letter to her absent father. And O'Hara variously referred to his "manifesto" and "statements" as a letter or "little diary". It all gets mixed up!)

The whole basis of the "Mosque Masque" section in *Low/Life* was based on love letters written to me by a young Muslim girl trapped in a traditional family overseas — put as vulgarly as possible, I think she saw me as a "ticket" to the West. But that is not to deny the depth of her feelings, or the pathos of her letters. In one letter, she spoke of a dream she had, which, unbelievably, I found almost image for image in Loti's *Désenchantées* (I am not so cynical as to think she fabricated her dream after coincidentally reading the same book!), and this sparked a whole series of poetry for me. But apart from that, and "Letter X", turning letters into poems has proved a failure for me — I think for the reason that you don't find very much of *me* in my poetry. I am not an "I" poet as such, and have always favored abstraction. O'Hara called it the "choice between 'the nostalgia *of* the infinite' and 'the nostalgia *for* the infinite' " (O'Hara: *Collected Poems of Frank O'Hara*, p. 498; emphasis in original). His "Personism" was for the latter and against the former, but I'm very small-c catholic when it comes to prepositions. That's what I meant by being a "generalist".

Sorry, I have to leave off here — I've got letters to write!

SEM: You've led us perfectly into a discussion of the books *Low Life* and *Calques*. Please talk about these in context of the larger scheme of what you are doing and discovering.

JB: That's to presume I know what I'm doing! As a high-school student, I thought I was an existentialist, and so I envisaged my future books to be *spare* — as in Flaubert's desire to write a book about nothing. Hardly did I know it then that Larry David and Jerry Seinfeld would surpass anything I — or Flaubert — could have imagined with "Seinfeld", the quintessence of our era. Warhol started the clock ticking, but as Vidal said (paraphrasing Socrates), "A life untelevised is a life not worth living."

I soon found out, despite clinical depression in my youth, that my outlook on life errs on the side of optimism; existentialists' gravitas was not for me. (I couldn't possibly write a book called *The Plague* without satire.) Voltaire's *Candide* is one of my favorite books, which I have in the original, as well as in English, Indonesian and Italian, and reread every year. Its alternative subtitle is *Optimism*, not the everyday optimism I just mentioned, but Leibnizian, which I'm not about to get into, except to say that Voltaire's tool of choice was satire, and it was this genre of criticism that greatly appealed to me. That said, I try not to descend into burlesque or caricature, but to concentrate on the ludic elements of satire in my work. This quest has led me to Pataphysics, OuLiPo (Ouvroir de Littérature Potentielle, or potential literature workshop) and Italian and Russian Futurism, culminating in my small magazine for such, *taboo jadoo* (1989–1984), a "journal for multilinguistics amphigory interlinguistics écriture d'ombres langue close lettrisme zaum kubofuturizm (both written in Cyrillic) jasyan kachathatapagajadhadaba (a Sanskrit word written in devanagari, defined as *'an example of a meaningless word'* [Macdonell])".

Calques, for the benefit of those who don't know it, is a book of poems of "pataphysical interpretations" of Queneau (Q), Éluard (E) and Derrida (D) — Q.E.D., the result of a line from Zukofsky(s): "mulled in my mind it's velleity or levity" ("Catullus 72: *Dicebas quondam*"; the pluralising "s" on Zukofsky here is to signify Celia as well as Louis as authors of their "translations" of Catullus, for she is almost always left unacknowledged.)[3] As I said in a Note at the beginning of *Calques*, "I have gone beyond translation, through the various ploys/plays of amphigory, paronomasia, mistranslation, dislocation, collage, etymology and 'extravagation' (i.e., wandering beyond proper bounds), in order to test poetry". (Australian poet Chris Edwards has recently done the

---

[3] A friend of mine cited a deluxe limited edition of an early twentieth-century poetry book in an antiquarian bookshop in Paris recently, titled *Calques*. (She was going to buy it for me, until she saw the price!) All she remembers is that it was poetry with illustrations of a famous artist of the period. I've made enquiries — even visiting the bookshop in question — but have drawn a blank. So, if anyone can solve this little mystery, I'd be most grateful.

same — marvellously — with *A Fluke: A mistranslation of Stéphane Mallarmé's* [reputably untranslatable] *"Un coup de dés".*) I gave credit to Zukofsky at the time of publication, in 2002, but if I had thought about it, Prévert, one of my earliest influences, who led me to poetry as I write it and whom I epigraph in *Low/Life*, could be said to be behind *Calques* as well.

Calques has an as yet unpublished companion, *Confexions* (another French word, this time for "making" — especially off-the-rack — rather than for "tracing"; the irregular spelling is to ward off monoglot English speakers from associating the title with confectionary, that is, chocolate or candy). In it are found poems, readymades, cut-ups (like "Letter X") and constructions, such as *"plus ça change"*, composed entirely of newspaper headlines, like Wright's "Hearst Headline Blues", except my *dada* is not revolution or racism but the headlining of homosexuality over the past twenty-five years, starting with the year America recorded its first official case of AIDS, in 1981 (the same year Ian and I met — we celebrate our silver anniversary in June). If there's a message, it's in the title: *The more things change (plus ça change), the more they stay the same.* (Whalen made this point forty-six years ago in *Like I Say*!)

Normally, I turn away from "message" poetry, bald manifestos, propaganda politics. Perhaps it's because protest poetry does not have the kind of history in Australia as it does in other parts of the world. Certainly in many non-English-speaking cultures, art is elevated to such an influential level in society that artists have helped to change society (and even become presidents; think of Vaclav Havel's "velvet revolution" in Czechoslovakia). The rights movement in the US, with troopers killing students on campuses, Martin Luther King, the Black Panther movement, Stonewall, etc., simply has no equivalent in Australia. (To give a current example, while George W. Bush is taking more and more flak over America's invasion of Iraq, Australia's prime minister, recently given a reception in Washington fit for royalty, has emerged completely unscathed from any criticism, much less condemnation, from his Australian constituents for his wholehearted commitment to the "Coalition of the Willing". Even Tony Blair is envious.) It would take a lot more than poetry to wake most Australians up. Voices that do speak up are quickly marginalised by the Murdoch press empire here, that controls most of the country's media. (Remember, Rupert Murdoch was an Australian before changing his nationality for tax purposes.) So we don't have a tradition of Ginsbergs or Reeds or Joplins — or even Dickinsons or Whitmans — here. So, when political commentary or sexual politics has entered my work, I try to imbue the language with complexities, to give depth to it, in order to "spread the word". Occasionally, however, I find starkness beautiful, as in the dispersed-field arrangement of the anagram "atom bomb", "a tomb", in "let om bhodi land", in *Calques*. (And no one but me would probably guess that my Joycean pastiche, "nisi prius shem about the prima facie", also in *Calques*, is a censuring of our conservative government's scuttling of the 1999 referendum on becoming a republic — our head of state is the Queen of England, you know!) So I subvert the political in my poetry. In a recent chapbook, *Anagoge of Fire*, I printed my poem on René Crevel, titled "crève-Crevel" (*crever* is very informal for *tuer*, to kill, while a *crève-cœur* is a heartbreak and a *crève-la-faim* is a miserable wretch), in which I expose how blind politics and prejudice corrupted surrealism; it ends:

LANGUAGE, THAT GRAND, IRRATIONAL, AUTONOMOUS, EXPLOSIVE, COLLECTIVE, SUBVERSIVE, CAMP, UNRECONSTRUCTED SOUL! FAR FROM BEING A COMMUNICATING VESSEL, HOWEVER, BRETON WAS TO RENÉ AN *EMPTY VESSEL*, AS HE WITNESSED HIM ASSAULT SOVIET GUEST WRITER ILYA EHRENBURG AT THE WRITERS' FESTIVAL (ANOTHER PUNCH-UP!), FOR REFERRING TO SURREALISM [THAT IS, FAKE REVOLUTIONARY FRENCH LITERATURE] AS "PAEDERASTIC ACTIVITY".

Ginsberg could get away with stark declamatory verse because America — and the world — needed to hear/heed what he had to say. The sheer nakedness of the poetry (and sometimes the poet!) was transforming and transcended much of the Beat production. (Bukowski, for instance, was just *nostalgie de la Bouekowski*.) Waldman's *Iovis*, too, is transcendental. For me, too much of the L=A=N=G=U=A=G=E School is marred by cant and rant, which is okay in a conscious work of art but unforgivable in rhetoric. At least Bernstein knows how to combat "official verse culture" and win; he is inventive, satirical, witty, insightful and a pleasure to read. The danger is in "counter-official verse culture", which can be stolid and indigestible. Jolas' *transition*'s Proclamation is valid, because it confines itself to language, and the S.C.U.M. Manifesto was only effective against Warhol, but what do we make of the Second Manifesto of Surrealism's "dashing down into the street, pistol in hand, and firing blindly, as fast as you can pull the trigger, into the crowd"? This may have been the apotheosis of Ern Malley's "Culture forsooth! Albert, get my gun!", itself a paraphrase from Hanns Jost — and appropriated by Hermann Goering — but in the light of current events, its *literary* provocativeness is lost. Too many times artists have been hijacked by politicians. Just ask Nietzsche.

So I shun causes and categories. Having said that, *Low/Life* contains some of my most politically aware work, with poems on recent political events in Indonesia and East Timor, distant terror in Italy and a long "romanticised" suite of poems on Islam (a commingling of my Indonesian life and Persian influence). But, as I wrote to Michael Farrell a couple of years ago, when he sent me a poem on domestic politics: "I feel direct political messages have only worked for a handful of poets (Neruda, Mayakovsky perhaps); political pieces without the persona(l) of the poet date fairly quickly. That's just my bias, I guess. I still feel quite uncomfortable about my 'overtly' political poem on East Timor ["island of blood island of marrow"], which I think stems from the fact that I ignored my own deeper feeling".

Therefore, if not to politics (the external realm), I look to beauty (the internal realm, psychology's interior). Russian exile and artist John Graham, who privileged the unconscious in his work and writings, wrote that there were two necessary elements of beauty: "perfection of form and surprise or rarity." My work is far from perfect, and my form is "unmeasured", not measured as in most poets' work, but I intuitively understand what Graham is aiming at. It must come down to defining what I — we — mean by beauty. The word "beauty" is an empty vessel — as all words in and of themselves necessarily are — and so, as I said in a letter to Italian lettriste Betty Danon, we must infuse words with meaning through our actions, thoughts and states of being. "I have experimented with a whole language of 'empty vessels'," I wrote in my letter to her, "and sought to fill them with meaning in my life. I wrote in 'baqain/purges' [in *Calques*] that it's not a necessarily certain or known path — '*Vego, antareudiyo ai veqomaqaizetten*' ('Perhaps it was mislaid in translation') — we can become confused or lost". It may seem strange for an atheist to talk like this, for many people have the mistaken belief that atheism equates to an absence of values and ethics. "God (*tat*)," I wrote in an essay once, "may have created the world but *it* — yes, lower case and neuter — did not create the word."[4] I went on to say that it "is no paradox that Taneraic radicals have no *intrinsic* meaning — how could they, when they have been 'created from nothing at all' [linguist Johannes Aavik asserted this when he created 'new' words in Estonian for modern-day exigencies, such as 'crime']? No word has intrinsic value. When I am asked where the vocabulary for Taneraic comes from, I answer, 'From beauty'. Epeolatry supplies the sounds and maybe a little

---

[4] "*Tat* is 'godhead' in Taneraic but demonstrative 'that' in Sanskrit, which Barthes says 'suggests the gesture of the child pointing his finger at something and saying: *that, there it is, lo!* but says nothing else' [Roland Barthes: *Camera Lucida* (p. 5)]. That is indeed *tat*, which has said nothing since it was invented" [from my essay "A + B = Essence", *HEAT* # 4, 1997].

algebra (topology), too, but I am speculating."

Now, just as I feel about politics, so, too, I feel about religion. I don't go along with the assertion that the world today wouldn't have the architectural, sculptural and art masterpieces — or that the world would be a lawless and unethical place — if it weren't for Christianity, Islam, Judaism, Hinduism, Buddhism and the rest. Humanism, as Goodman described it, would have produced those same masterpieces — and our best laws. I am suspicious of artists who wear their religion or their cause on their sleeves — and I'm even more suspicious of people who co-opt artists to bolster their own arguments for them. It's the Voltaire in me, I suppose. (I should also mention I'm a sceptic. Tzara, for instance, was supposed to have come up with the name Dada by randomly opening the dictionary and hitting upon the word. I thought I'd try the same with my own Littré, but somehow Dodécaèdre doesn't have the same brio.) That Australia's supposedly greatest living poet, Les A. Murray, for instance, should circumscribe himself as a "Christian poet" simply points up his limitations as a poet of any abidingness, in my opinion. (But I am grateful to him for his early promotion of John Kinsella, whose integration of Australia's tradition of pastoralism with postmodernism has created a new identifiably Australian poetry.) I think attributives are limiting to an artist — so terms like "Christian poet" or "gay poet" or "protest poet" have no appeal for me. I would never call myself an "atheist poet" or a "gay poet" or an anything poet, except, perhaps, an "Australian poet", in the biographical notes at the end of a foreign anthology. (I suppose I should mention here that although I am Australian by birth, Australia is *completely* absent from my work, at least consciously, and if unconsciously it's present, it's also unrecognisable. My landscapes are other, foreign or interior.)

Notwithstanding *Calques* — and Barthes and Breton and Crevel and Derrida and Eluard and Prévert and Queneau and Tzara et al. — I am not a theoretician as such, and eschew isms, mainly because I largely fail to comprehend them.[5] I

---

[5] Barthes' *Pleasure of the Text* brought me back to Flaubert, discarded since high school:

"Flaubert: a way of cutting, of perforating discourse *without rendering it meaningless*. Of course, rhetoric recognizes discontinuities in construction (anacoluthons) and in subordination (asyndetons); but with Flaubert, for the first time, discontinuity is no longer exceptional, sporadic, brilliant, set in the base matter of common utterance: there is no longer a language *on the other side* of these figures (which means, in another sense: there is no longer anything but

confuse O'Hara's personism with Mounier's personalism; I'm still coming to grips with what epistemology and phenomenology are; heurism evades me as much as mysticism; I misinterpreted existentialism; semelology, semiology and semiotics have sown their seeds of doubt; and hermeneutics is an on-going process. I do love instinctively the interiority of surrealism (though repugn its machism[o]), oulipoetics (the games poets play), and, contradictorily, I prefer the mortar-board academicians' dadaism to just plain *dada,* which is, after all, a hobby-horse that's been flogged to death (*un cheval crevé*).

This is perhaps what I satirise in a lot of my work. The refrain "I have mislaid my documentation" in "*baqain*/purges" — itself a "comment" on paralleling texts in different languages — pointedly shows up artists more interested in being "written up" than in creating their own work, or in laboring on grant applications with funding bodies controlled by the "official verse culture". It is why I found pataphysics — and the oulipian tradition — the perfect vehicle. Play is essential to my work. I am what Huizinga called a "homo ludens" (well, a homo, anyway!). So I've coined my own ism for it: Ludicism (not lucidism, which would be its antithesis; and certainly not Luciferism, which brings to mind a certain nun, who wrote to me when I published Pete Spence's *5 Poems,* back in 1986, telling me in all seriousness it was the work of the devil). *Tyuonyi*'s anthology *Patterns/Context/Time* (1990) was perhaps my earliest exposure in America of my brand of ludicism, with the (part) publication of "The Logos Discursus", with prose poems titled "pattense" (the conflation of pattern and tense), "in the status of texts (hubris)" (echoic of Houston, Texas), "hope spurs etypic" (you know!) and the rest. What I look for in other poets is their ludic play, and heartily recommend James Taylor's *Smoke Proofs,* Peter Minter's *Empty Texas,* Geraldine McKenzie's *Duty,* John Kinsella's *New Arcadia,* Michael Farrell's *ode ode,* Chris Edwards' *utensils in a landscape* and *A Fluke,* and Berni Janssen's *Mangon* (I know I've forgotten to mention others here), which should all be available in America but probably aren't. (With the exception of Kinsella, who's published by W. W. Norton — a major publisher for a major work.) To sum up ludicism in a catchphrase: Through levity to levitation.

And so my Marseillaise is, if I must march to the beat of a drum: *L'Art Pour l'Art!,* in this world lurching to extremes....

---

language); a generalized asyndeton seizes the entire utterance, so that this very readable discourse is *underhandedly* one of the craziest imaginable: all the logical small change is in the interstices" [pp 8–9; emphasis in original].

SEM: Your work is replete with sophistication, fluency and pleasure in language and thought occurring at progressive levels of depth within intervals that subdivide into what seems the definitive infinity. I am interested in learning what you perceive to be the most interesting current trends in any of the arts you may care to mention.

JB: I don't know how to answer this question. You have revealed an inability in me for recognising such things as trails to the future, which is another way of saying "trends". (By the way, I really like your term "definitive infinity", not only for its echoic qualities, but also for its contradictoriness, a form of antisyzygy where sparks may fly.) I recently saw an interview on television with a much loved Australian author, best known for *Storm Boy*, Colin Thiele, who died in early September, 2006 (around the same time as Naguib Mahfouz), who replied to a similar question put to him by the presenter: "That's one of the lovely things about human beings: you can't predict what they'll come up with [next]."

While the future (prediction) is slightly different from the present (current trends), you will agree they are inextricably bound. I have simply gone my own way ... blindly. I do not see myself as a modern or postmodernist; I don't care about the pursuit of the "new", as innovation or revolution. Nor do I care about any prevailing thought or imagination-catching theory, for I have always written only with private considerations in mind. I am like a jellyfish ensnaring passing plankton purely by chance and just by being there. On my bleaker days, I would say I write in a void — another name for Australia, for the English republic of letters is decidedly transatlantic. I am not at all obsessed with death, either of the self or the established order. I do wrestle with my conscience, which is another way of saying I am a poet of the interior. (It is interesting to note that the words "ambience" and "ambition" derive from the same Latin root.) And I read blindly, too, everything from Gide's *Fruits of the Earth* (my favorite prose poem) to Tanizaki's *In Praise of Shadows*. The current I found that carried me away was Bachelard's *Poetics of Space*, Steiner's *After Babel* (though not all his views), Barthes's *Camera Lucida*, Breton's *Communicating Vessels* (though the man is repugnant), Pasolini (essays and films — surely I am the only customer to have bought an Italian light fitting simply because it was called *Teorema*!), Daumal, Davenport (poetry and essays), Derrida, Sontag, Mabille, Tournier, Huizinga's *Homo Ludens* (from which I coined "ludicism"), the Fluxus and Oulipo experimenters, and so forth. Not to mention poets!

The presiding *mood*, though, if not a trend, is millennialist, apocalyptic, the end-is-nihilist (religion again!). Arthur Danto wrote a book called *After the End of Art*, for instance, while Frank Lentricchia and Jody McAuliffe capture the current mood in *Crimes of Art + Terror*, which appeared a couple of years after — and perhaps in response to — the atrocities of September 11, 2001, in America. For living memory, we have lived with the notion of *the end of...*, and especially since we as a species have become aware of our power to destroy all life.

Currents can be dangerous; there are undertows and rips that can be fatal. And it's so easy to get it wrong. I couldn't believe that McAlmon ridiculed a writer "who believed himself the modern of moderns, because he filled five pages of his last novel with x's, line after line of xxxxxxxxxxxxxxxx, as a symbol of dead soldiers and their graves" [*Being Geniuses Together*, p. 191 (original 1938 edition)]. This is the conflation of personality into disposition. Personally, I find such repetitious symbology as poignant as Prévert's "Familiale", Owen's "Anthem for Doomed Youth" or Levi's "Buna". (McAlmon must have had a selectively low opinion of the avant-garde of the day, for, seemingly contrarily, he published Mina Loy, William Carlos Williams, Gertrude Stein, Djuna Barnes, H. D. and others through his Contact Publishing. Or perhaps he just didn't like the "heavy-witted" author of all those Xs. On the other hand, I can't imagine McAlmon deriding Sterne for his solid black page at the end of Chapter 12 of the First Book of *Tristram Shandy*, a little bit of avant-gardism two hundred years before McAlmon's — and *definitely* before Sterne's — time.)

The art I would have liked to mention is architecture, for it has always been of great interest to me, and it, perhaps more than any other art, has a power over us great enough not just to stir the emotions and engender opinion but to affect the quality of our lives in a material way (no pun intended). It is the only art which has a purpose, a use. An art which is also a technology and a science (as opposed to art which aims at incorporating science or technology into it, or art born of technology). But I don't know that I have anything useful or interesting to contribute on the subject. Besides, no matter what I do say, it's of no consequence — and I think such inconsequentiality works as an impediment. (Oh dear, another pun!) One thing I do know, and that is: the margin cannot be anywhere else but on the margin, for any shift (seism) is to change its nature (seity).

SEM: As a final question, Javant, please share one or more artistic projects you plan or anticipate taking on in the short- or long-term future.

JB: A deceptively easy question — that may explain why it has taken me so long to answer it — on such a complex issue as the future. I'm not even sure there is such a thing as the future, just a perennial present. But here goes:

This year, Salt Publications has brought out *pointcounterpoint: new and selected poems*, edited by John Kinsella, that will introduce my work to new audiences in Britain, where my work is unknown, and promulgate it in Australia and North America. I look forward to this book very much, which brings together the various strands of my work over the past two decades, from the romanticism of *Thalassa Thalassa* of 1983 (critiqued in Tim Rood's 2004 book on the famous cry of the Ten Thousand) to the absurdist, Oulipo-inspired *Calques* of 2002.

Now, *Calques* brings me to the other MSS languishing in the desk drawer, for I have at least two companion works in mind: *Confexions*, a book of readymades, and *Reprises*, a book of "covers", in the sense of Bowie's *Pin-Ups*, or, closer to poetical home, Lowell's *Imitations*. *Confexions* is all but done — as are the other three MSS (I can't put the finishing touches on them until I have a publisher; it would be too hard to bear otherwise) — but *Reprises* is still germinating as an idea of interpreting my favorite poems by favorite poets, starting with Mallarmé. However, such a project brings with it the vexed questions of imitation, mimesis and even plagiarism; suffice to say I haven't worked it all out in my mind yet.

The other MSS at various stages of completion are *Warrior Dolls*, a Whitman-esque reworking and enlargement of my 1981 book, credited by Paul Knobel as the first "openly gay" book of poems in Australia; *Imaginary Lines*, an "oneiricon" or book of dreams written as prose poems (something between, say, Burroughs' *My Education* and Leiris' *Nights As Day, Days As Night*); *Virilities*, for which I received a writer's grant for one year from the Australia Council, our equivalent of America's National Endowment for the Arts (a Sydney publisher requested the MS. two years ago, albeit unfinished, and I'm still waiting to hear back if they're going to publish or not — what other professional could be pushed around so much as the artist, he asks in a disabused tone?); and *Logos Discursus*, which started out as a contribution to *Tyuonyi*'s Symposium on Contemporary Poetry, in 1990, but which has since developed into a book of prose and poetry. I also bandy about *Linea Alba*, a collection of homoerotic poems taken from my other books (the dark line of hair that snakes down from the navel to the pubes is called *linea alba*; paradoxically, a white line) and *Calculus Incult*, which was *Calques* originally, or something like it. And I'd like the whole box and dice (the "Complete Works") to appear under the umbrella title, *Vivimus Vivamus*, perhaps with its two Vs somehow interlocking Perec-style on the frontispiece. In full, the Latin phrase is *dum vivimus, vivamus*, let's live while we're living, a phrase I first used in a poem I wrote when I was 19, but reprised for a poem in *Low/Life* almost twenty years later. Then there's *Tabula Rasa: Uncollected Poems*. This is not a project at all, but just a dream. I just like the title, and I like Arvo Pärt's composition of the same name (which I'm now going to put on the turntable, if you'll forgive the anachronism).

I have another life as a playwright, too. *Comfort*, my 1996 play about the plight of a comfort woman interned on Java during the Second World War is about to have another season, in a provincial but artistic town in New South Wales. (It was pure serendipity the issue should hit the headlines again so prominently, with the Congressional Hearing in Washington, and Japan's public intransigency on the matter.) I've written two plays so far (the first, *Afternoon of a Fawn Cardigan*, a short radio play on AIDS, was actually banned in Queensland), and I'm expected to write more. Perhaps a comedy. I put ideas down at the back of my diary. At the back of Volume 79 (2002–2003), for instance, I noted plans for three (short, à la O'Hara) plays: *Fair Enough* (based loosely on Georgina Beyer, the first transsexual in the world to be voted into a nation's — New Zealand — parliament); *Merton & Morton* (based on a friend whose two favorite authors are Thomas Merton and H. V. Morton); and *Crux* (based on a ballet dancer). I see I also penned a paragraph on *Imaginary Lines*:

BOOK: *Imaginary Lines: Oneirocritical poems.* A grammarian in Trajan's and Hadrian's time, Hermippus, wrote a work of five books titled *Oneirocritica....* Like Leiris, I think of my dreams as poetry — but a book of dreams; is that the book of an old man? I envisage a note on the back of the book: "When Javant Biarujia, as a young man, was asked to describe himself in just four words (a word game in which the participants conventionally listed off four adjectives), he replied without hesitation: 'Dreams are my perfumes'."

Plus I have numerous ideas for literary essays, which I enjoy writing. (In fact, my last essay on Anaïs Nin, "Potential Paradises", at just under 39,000 words, is a good chunk of what could become a critical work on Nin — it would have more chance of a wide audience than poetry, I'm sad to say.) And for a decade or more now, I've pondered the question of choice, which I've come to see more and more as an illusion, and definitely a propaganda tool of capitalism. Choice has increasingly become a weapon against someone's sensibilities or a way of absolving oneself of responsibility ("That's your choice!"). On page 14,238 of Volume 78 of my diary, I sketch the following note: "What I react to, when everyone nowadays is saying 'I chose' this or that action, this or that way of life, is their living on the surface. Making choices for every waking moment, is to live on the conscious level, all the while denying the unconscious." I haven't written the essay yet, for it strays from the literary to the philosophical and psychological, for which I'm not qualified, and I may just be wrong. (For example, I saw on television the other day how an MRI scan of a Buddhist's brain "showed" that he could will — or choose — happiness as a state of being.)

Before I close my diary, I note I once had another idea for a book to be called *Addictionary*, a sort of poetical Ambrose Bierce. I don't think I ever got beyond the entry for "**prose poetry**": "The same as for **electricity**. Without the meter. (*Cf.,.* Volt[aire]; *vid.* Baud[elaire].)" No … wait! In Volume 68, which covers late 1997, I just found two others: "**asymptote** *n.* Rule of thumb at the end of a draughtsman's (rain)bow. **orator** *n.* Someone who gives talking head.") It's not me — too cute by half. Not me at all.

And this is not to mention my life's work, my *langue close*, Taneraic. I had hoped to publish next year, on the occasion of the private language's fortieth anniversary, the definitive *Nainougacyou* (dictionary), but I'm hopelessly behind in my work. Like most lexicographers (if you'll permit me that term), I'll be dead and buried before the task is done.

So, you see, I've got my work cut out for me! I don't know how much of the above, if any of it, will see the light of day. It doesn't really matter. It is the work I live for, contrary to what I hear most workers say. I live for this work, for it is the work of my imagination, poured out onto paper. I've long ago shrugged off the fact that I'm never going to be a success, that most of my work will never be published, that I'm cursed with that lovely Baudelairean word *guignon* (what my friend Johnny Kesselschmidt, the subject of my most oft republished essay, "The Colossus of Melbourne", calls *shlemazelkeyt* or *unglick*). Self-doubt looms always, as Rorem said (I'm currently reading *his* interviews, after having read his diaries). Perhaps Burroughs, in his book of dreams, sums it up best: "Writers tend to be bad luck. No trouble … no story." Or poem. Or play. Who knows how long we have or what the future holds? Mallarmé said somewhere (I read it as an epigraph in Balakian's book on the poet): "To end up in a beautiful book, that's what the world was made for." *Ain't that the truth!*

Sasi srou qu gasta sasi beijiscya

[*Lear*]

Sasi srou qu qabda laqiavi gasta sasi
Beijiscya daqiru celini areso bihari;

Yos yolesubatti nuri ledicia e yes e aica
Nar nuyole alinmoutatqa ai zi nari.

Sasi srou qu douqirdi zalas jame,
Busai yoda taruh biranda,

„Ou busí beijiscya, ou beijiscya dayole qussa,
Ou beijiscya, ge bucelinda,
Celinda,
Celinda!
Ou beijiscya, ge bucelinda!"

Sasi beijiscya yenda yoyariso: „Sasi roguis,
Ge abui zevus das haleqa esouqira!
Ni svai, busí srou, busediada e avi qancuis?
Cye nu raida eher jescyubdi palout?"

Peu daroceya haunta marnu lunata e aiveya,
Sqedeyar iher qepiqa ga sou beduq das asyan;
gan liaibebatti giri — ayoi bajaq das qiri,
Cye zioro palout das lasqan,
Lasqan,
Lasqan,
Cye zioro palout das lasqan.

„Giriscya, ni tunai arí mas avi didi
Abui palout?" Nuni giri yenda gon: „Qeman."
Ji cengagun uzaiveto mas qancudiyo espeveto.
Ayoi giranisqou qancu ayoi jicyadi jalan.

Yodajuda pula damiavo yole qarainda sayavo,
Busai hangirdi sirosyi niape aiban;

Evon e peu vayole besiu yoirauda bigí bigiu
Oma seduscyi ema iyohi aisyan,

Aisyan,
Aisyan,
Oma seduscyi ema iyohi aisyan.

(For Ian Biarujia. Literal translation of the Taneraic: "The Owl and the Pussy-cat: Mr Owl goes to sea with Mr Pussycat in a beautiful boat painted blue. / They both take some honey as well as coins which are wrapped in a bill. // Mr Owl meditates on the stars, / And sings while playing music, // 'Oh, dearest Pussycat; oh, Pussycat who is my love, / Oh, Pussycat, how beautiful you are, / Are beautiful, / Are beautiful! / Oh, Pussycat, how beautiful you are!' // Mr Pussycat says to the singer: 'Mr noble one', / How your voice has [such] elegance! / Would you like, dear bird, to become my partner? / But what to do to get a ring?' // A life of boldness for one year and a day, / Sailing unto the land where the quince-tree has appeal; / There, they encounter a pig — his ears are pricked up, / But on his nose a ring hangs down, / Hangs down, / Hangs down, / But on his nose a ring hangs down. // 'Piggy, would you be willing to sell us cheaply / Your ring?' That pig then says: 'Agreed.' // Therefore, a turkey the next day casually marries them. / Their wedding ceremony gives them pleasure. // They dine on pomegranate which grows on the banks, / And they use a strange dessert spoon; // Then, as life is a mystery they dance arm in arm. / Along the beach in the moon's light, / Light, / Light, / Along the beach in the moon's light.")

Commando Tidbits Make Me Amorous

[A Zukofskyan "translation" of Catullus]

Commando tidbits make me amorous
Aurelius when peckers or pudenda
don't remedy the quintessence of your animal cupidity
could cast them out of pizzles and into Crisco
conserving puerile milk puddings
not spotted dicks in agar agar: Nigel where are you
idiot key in the facts the mood here is "fashion sux"
in repentant suet occupation:
wear them as my toque cocks
infest Malibu boys
quite qualitatively you lube it you shove it
manioc quantum leaps over its voracious parachute:
hunk undo my prepuce but needs must enter
would see tomorrow men fuck or quiver their corps
in such impolite celestial atlases of cum
but the nostrum inside your head is laced with
atomic serum my sperm licks facial
cream attractive paederast on the bus patently obvious by the door
through current rapists wit

Icoglan

... je trouvai sur le soir un jeune icoglan très bien fait.

Is this an encounter by chance for the narrator (the Baron, Cunégonde's brother), or by design, contrived by an amorous longing? Voltaire presents the reader with an eighteenth-century account of cruising. The evening, a favorite time for cruisers, doubles as a literary code for passion. The foreign, barely assimilated, Byzantinism of "icoglan" is a psychoanalytic, if not poetic, inference of taboo, a forbidden *trouvaille*. In Littré's *Dictionnaire de la langue française*, "icoglan" reads: Page du Grand Seigneur, along with a different quote from Voltaire (*Ode* 16 — was the quotation from *Candide* too speculative for Littré?). The word (*s. m.*, not found in *Harrap's New Shorter French and English Dictionary*) derives from a corruption of the Turkish *itch-oghlan* (Littré's orthography): "interior" and "young page". Turkish dictionaries are succinct but revealing: *oglan*, 1 boy. 2 catamite. 3 (cards) jack. The entry continues with a naïve candor: *oglanci*, paederast. A garçonymede jackoff! The pleonasm of *très bien fait* does the work of the simple Turkish dictionary: it reveals what is apparent in the *ici* of desire, unspoken in Parisian society but celebrated in Constantinople.

Icoglan alludes to the Occidental perception of the *deviant* Oriental ("a woman is for procreation, a boy for pleasure, and a melon for sheer delight" — so says the "Arab" proverb). Moreover, *icoglan* assumes the *toga virilis* of a Proper Noun in the eyes of the fetishist: A Handsome Young Icoglan; youth fulfils the same fantasies engendered by Tadzio; *la brama d'un ragazzo senza colpa*. However, the ico[gla]nography of *personality* is not developed, for complexity gives way to an introjection of the *fante* (a sema[n]tic configuration). Icoglan has no biography to speak of; he is nothing but a conduit for orgasm.

A moment's paronomasia generates *itchy couillons, gland d'écot, langue tout de go, il cogne des anges*, slightly indecent, all of them; appalling puns redolent of latrine walls or patients stricken with witzelsucht. Littré's *itch* is the essence, the *élan vital*, of ignorant desire.

Il faisait fort chaud: le jeune homme voulut se baigner; je pris cette occasion de me baigner aussi.

Preludes. A sign of venery — for virginity has long since been stripped bare. The narrator is *acting out* an autoerotic continuum to paroxysm (how many times has the narrator imagined this scene [scenario] and masturbated in measure to it?). Seduction superimposes itself on place, and makes of it an insinuating tryst. Who has not heard of the concupiscent pleasures of the

Turkish bath? The gay sauna descends from this syzygy of pipes and plumbing. A mutation (or *flow*) is effected at this unspecified location of water (a stream, a water-mill, a watering-*hole*?), for the reflexive may double, when the opportunity arises, as the reciprocal.

Je ne savais pas que ce fût un crime capital pour un chrétien d'être trouvé tout nu avec un jeune musulman.

A concordance reveals youth is accentuated in the proposition of each of the three sentences: the predicate of one becomes the subject of the next, and so forth.

Splash! The confession of a transgressive state (if not a transgressive act) which is, paradoxically, boastful, for the reader may infer possession was lubriciously consummated. The narrator articulates the subversion of meaning in a double ledger, one of which is counterfeit.

Christianity in Voltaire's world establishes the norm or stereotype; Islam, the exotic, forbidden, anti-Christ. From the dominant profane rank of cruiser (the hunter), the narrator appears now in the passive position of a dominated subject (the hunted), subject to [the] infidel[ities].

What the narrator *finds* on his evening stroll is a *discovery* (internal action); when the Baron is *found* [out], he is brought before the courts in a case of "*excovery*" or exposure (external reaction). The anxiety the cryptohomosexual has of being caught and held up to public humiliation is, nevertheless, subordinate to his revelatory desire, in this case, to penetrate. Furthermore, the *crime capital* is no less than having to live one's life in a metonymic world, a metonymic nakedness; a duplicative world in which the prattle of celibacy serves as a channelling of encounters. How rapidly the degeneration of the narrator's pleasure is marked in the text! Voltaire scarcely disguises his equivocation in these three sentences, for it serves his purpose in his ridicule of the Leibnitzian "best of all possible worlds" — after all, he more or less asks, who would want to be queer?

Letter X
a media cut-up

Paris

X dear:

   In Hyperluxurious English, all the "tabLloyd's" letters from: cut-above-the-rest sister & bad-mouthing brother, & we have certainly enters, above all others, give the supplest eyewash of Diana (my loveFist in her knuckling). They Methuselah to hear about her beaux & the parties past hair *d'or* & resourceful eyes. Isn't that the one? Well, he wasn't symptomatic — if that's what you mean. He hasn't changed a bit since I was in kilts' virilities. Do Miss from Engl& . . . I was a fully developed alcoolic — organigrammes I can replace — I suppose now when he just could not be bothered with fleshless women, which was NietzscheGoethe&Cologne on your début; next year, I can chaperone you. The Ritz(whereas I live in a garret & eat *aspirine*). The day was imperceptible, white, unreluctant & silver as a pizzle-whistle! He is tall with the idea, but I will no doubt feel simply amorous. I am symbolist junior that you have the Minerva to touch lepers. I suppose the Queen Mother has read you my letters by taxi on the streets of Paris, &c. She was taken to the megaphone life as we all in mourning now, but I chanted the litanies, not very well Mediterranean. I knew her in so much to? see&do, there never seemed to be an end of no end of blue. You are, X dear, the world's most adorable Marks&Spencerwoman. I had a pearl of your body in Lungfish. I wondered whether Dido was but did not see the yacht. You could really have spent "spittoon-jacking" efforts to get him into the lifeless mainstream of about a million luncheons, which were all very much alike, the nothing-to-write-home-about canards (DID DODI DO DI?, the cut of her evening gown, *etc.*) could easily have had the greediest pictures, statues & mosaics — but each one has tunnelled home to roost in most unpleasant ways later on, when life of these — like Mother T.'s, which was built below paradox.ures, civic "kingdomofheaven" to Calcutta in a vision & told her to BAN THE BLONDE BOMBSHELL where & many others, should first give US all our pretty girls who naked, worth a million statues of Aphro Ditto tobesure. Completely breathless with some legend the god hard in the *dégueulasse* ruffian-*fin*. Suicide perhaps. After tea.

   It was on her gay trip to Paris that she was spun over, *clair de lune* moustachometer at Zenith, the bluest of blue eyes, & the moanful: stiff & no introducing; deliriumdreams of warm cocktails & nothing or forever about him. Cut live to the scene.

Well, it was a pleasant & beautiful ride up to Longlish & lovely looking, & we slept, peacefully & informally, but I tried to keep awake to see all I could of the Lapsang Souchong Tea.

There is one thing about an English cabinet that intrigues me, is that I ran off & left my bones (?) without saying a goodbye, . . . I was in bed . . . salt of the earth down a single address or telephone number; & now I really do feel badly about Dukes & high dignitaries so nice to me on the boat & I know he does not know a soul in divorce. English divorces have always been difficult to get: difficulter than silent numbers. God knows.

The PrinçofGulls eschews "men's nights", as he is in love. With a subprincess I ever hope to put my eyes on, & nice, & . . . larger one diamonds & looking like a little old turkey gobbler, & none other than our outrageous Lady Pip-pip! Who do you think is first-rate? Prussic:acid,Poison. Kensington must bivouac to the cut flowers of those promissory lands, before we all go to the paytoilet's AmericAbsolute (11, rue Scribe): we & our constituent prophets & dervishes. But a large cocktail party. Mind you, all this time I had not been home even to clean up after the Twenty dollars.

To go back to the cocktail party, we were all drinking *dédains du regret*; a perfectly indignant memberofthAcademy developed syphilis. Nevermind! I cried&cried. Never is an inconvenience; world of poverty & oblivion, where most of my friends have to clean. She picked up clothes off the floor, & decided what used to come at flowering intervals — for what, I really don't know; separated; I found her again with another family, friends of ours, except that she did with them in beds that our immaculate status was looking as *muguet* & Crusoelike as ever, with just a touch of the Abyssinian Desert. Finally, our (S)he picked up Edward, black & h&some. He used to take my mother in our house, had very famous friends of ours, & there she was with them over East End — really greatly reduced but comm&Ed by his cummings&goings on his days off for his weddingactbasketpiece cod. Liz, dressed in her black gloves, never touched anything, of course.

From that moment on, in the life of that cocktail party, I was still in the dark! with Edward. Though young, I sat in the back seat, but he & I always had very lively *micmac* looking as grammatical & *trictrac* that children should never be born to any parents but those tictac toe &c. There was a long shoot. Cut! This is a wrap. Who was it said (imitating), "A *ca'amite*'s a chiggen-hawk's fingger-lickin' what'sbeenfixedup y'knowha' a mean E'on 'Arrow bloomin' Winchista boy"? I was still in the dark! pressing your beautiful h&made & grammalogued underwear: abaslezaristos.com.uk.

I left off last Monday, at the cocktail party where I met the Harrodans! Tuesday, we went down a stupendous weathercock! It really HAD belonged to England, hadn't it?

This she-he was an interesting character, having been your main reason or whether perhaps it was Edward, after all. You had the onebrown eyes? Isn't that the one? Well, he didn't rain on my paradoxical really; not very well *stuffed*.

Have fun, & Mahatma g&er to Jack off to joy to! Isn't it strange? I can't endure what love is now that "Malice doesn't live 'ere ennymo." I never know my animus from the bang-bang banging with DNA (like a Tironian sign).

I have effigies, not bouffants. I am completely fascinated by cocktails concentric as snow – even more intricate than I expected — s'pose it *was* adultery, & he was forced into husb&ry — he will be a muftiMonarch spendthrift, to his great joy & Queen if he wanted to *Camille* himself in mufti in Paris for $34 — with her face suspencered from his fly. On him — huge old Queens demobilised he has no grip to wear his schism "at the three-quarter" desire.

Take care of that hard wee hung "oh-ing" & "aah-bitching" tour ettEiffel Palin syndrome (Lafayette's rout) miserable *ooglup* hard-assed thrushbitch — & lodes of Pater Art's kisses to you all.

Affuctionately,
Y.

Tôtekiko

```
by  sno   this  mou
   w  il      a  nt
   T    l    e n  ing
he  aves of sand h    s
          a   v   al    t
s        ll  e ma     r
h and s  of   s mOiré o
y         b     ng   n
       day    be e s  g
garde         low ripples
s n               a  r
   ow  is T     l   c
   r     a his     a  thE
   raKe   n   tw   nd
d    d  ho me    ward j
             n  is    o
t    ea   e        s ur
wo     ve       stone na
       s highly     as l
c                  al   o
al       be    tr  so   n
    led       low  u
                th    in
       r      c  r
ip    ol  aK  t    whi
pli    o   e   w    te
   ng     r  d  colOrs
```

Kyôto

Barry Schwabsky
interviewed by Tom Beckett

Barry Schwabsky was born in Paterson, New Jersey, and presently lives in London. He studied at Haverford College and Yale University and has taught at Yale as well as at New York University, the School of Visual Arts, Pratt Institute, and Goldsmiths College, University of London. His poetry has been published in *Opera: Poems 1981-2002* (Meritage Press, 2003) and *Book Left Open in the Rain* (Black Square Editions, 2008) and in chapbooks published by Tamarisk Press, Burning Deck, Artsonje Center/Meritage Press, Seeing Eye Books, and Black Square Editions and limited edition artist's books with artwork by Jessica Stockholder, Luisa Rabbia, Suzanne McClelland, Katharina Grosse, and KK Kozik. As an art critic he writes regularly for Artforum, The Nation, and other publications and has contributed to books and exhibition catalogues on artists including Henri Matisse, Alighiero Boetti, Betty Woodman, and Gillian Wearing; his essays have been collected in *The Widening Circle: Consequences of Modernism in Contemporary Art* (Cambridge University Press, 1997).

Tom Beckett: Where did/does poetry begin for you?

Barry Schwabsky: Your giving me a choice of tenses seems to offer me a choice between, let's say, developmental and ontological types of answers. To give an answer of the first type, I could say that it began when I was, I think, a sophomore in high school. Somehow I read or someone told me that someone had written a book-length poem about my town. I was so flabbergasted that anyone would want to do such a thing that I went to the library in order to find a copy and see for myself: So I came to *Paterson* by William Carlos Williams. Fascinated by what I read, I looked for more Williams; Williams led me to Pound, and after that I just read anything I could put my hands on (sometimes even, I'm sorry to say, shoplift) that was published by New Directions. That publishing house was my education.

But of course I already had a sense of poetry before I had an inkling of modern poetry as the House of Laughlin taught it. My father had never been to college—something I believe he'd lived as a deep injury as a young man—but my mother had had a single year at Brooklyn College before she'd had to go to work. From that year she'd kept a fat black poetry anthology that she'd had for an English course. It was one of the more prominent items in our tiny bookcase, and it always fascinated me, even before I could understand much of anything in it. And of course back beyond that there were all the children's rhymes and chants with their verbal magic.

But there were also beginnings after that, for instance, the moment when my eye was drawn to an interesting dust jacket spine in the Paterson library and I took out John Bernard Myers' *Poets of the New York School*—a huge beginning for me. I remember how John Ashbery's "Clepsydra" appeared to me as an impenetrable wall of words. I thought I would scale it some day, and eventually did. But O'Hara, Koch, and Elmslie, for instance, were more immediately rewarding.

And what about retroactive beginnings? A few years ago, I took my daughter to see Cocteau's *Orpheus*—a film I'd loved as a young man and seen several times but not for at least twenty-five years. Re-seeing it, I realized that this film had given me a certain image of a poetic vocation that had stayed with me long after I'd stopped thinking about the film itself: as the desperate effort to transcribe enigmatic transmissions on a radio that no one else can hear. Obviously there were reasons why, when I later read Jack Spicer for the first time, he made perfect sense to me.

TB: Where does your poetry come from?

BS: That's the question, isn't it? Because it does come from somewhere. When I read something I've written, and it seems good, then I think, "Damn, this is good! I wish I could write like that!" So I don't believe it comes from me. (Although I'm happy to take the credit anyway.) When there is something in it that dissatisfies me, something that is only approximate, that something is what I recognize as coming from me, just me—my haste, my lack of nerve, whatever. My job is to try and spare the poetry from all that. Frank Stella once said, "I try and keep the paint as good on the canvas as it was on the can." Likewise, I try and keep the language as good on the page as it was in the air, where my antennae picked it up.

TB:Your response reminds me of these words from the title poem in your book Opera:

> The poet who thinks for me
> detests the writer who bears my name.

You are a professional art critic. I'm wondering how you think that activity influences your practice as a poet.

BS: People always ask me that! Well, for one thing, it takes time away from poetry—but then so does every job. On the other hand it gives me a lot to think about. Art that inspires me gives as much to my poetry as poetry that inspires me does, or music, or whatever. When I was younger I think it was very important for me to see how artists use materials. It gave me the sense that I could use language as a material too—almost sculpturally. Rather than mainly in its relation to interiority, which might have been a debilitatingly strong tendency on my part otherwise.

As an art critic, I hone a craft of writing that is different from but related to the writing of poetry. I keep trying to become a better writer and I think I'm succeeding. My increasing mastery of prose must have some effect on my writing as a poet.

There's another thing: The art world is a much more "worldly" world than the poetry world. A lot of money flows through it, even though a critic never gets very close to that much of it. People in the art world dress so much better than most poets do! I think there's something quite instructive about being a tad closer to capital, which after all remains the bedrock reality of our social existence.

TB: I earn my living as a Health Inspector. I crawl around bedrock realities a lot. It gets messy.

One thing I always try to draw poets out on, with varying results, is their felt relationship to social reality. Do you think you as a poet have any special social responsibilities?

BS: I think doing one's work well—doing it for what it is in itself without subordinating it to one's own ego, for instance—is a big responsibility that everyone has, no matter what kind of work they do. It's also important not to propagate falsehood, which for me means that there are certain kinds of manipulative rhetoric that are foreign to my writing. On the other hand I don't expect my poems to make people's lives better in any other way than to provide thought and pleasure. That's as for responsibility. As for social reality, the work comes from that reality and is permeated by it. I don't need to make any special effort to include it. It's there, willy-nilly. But funny enough, the whole question of social responsibility is very subjective. What does it mean to you? Somehow I have the idea that a health inspector must have a much more concrete sense of it than an art critic.

TB: I work in a number of different environmental programs. It's a small department. One has to be a generalist and have a tolerance for dealing with garbage, human waste, insects, rodents and angry people. The bulk of my time is spent doing housing and food service inspections. The job can be physically demanding and is not without risks. I've been assaulted and I've had a gun held to my head, not to mention some frightening encounters with dogs. I've learned to listen hard and to look at things carefully.

The incidents just alluded to occurred during housing inspections. One never knows what one is going to find when one walks into someone else's dwelling. Once I entered the living room of a single-family rental property. The tenant was sitting on a recliner which rested on a hardwood floor. The floor was riddled with perfectly cut round holes, each about 10 inches in diameter, which were spaced at, oh, three or four foot intervals. I had to step over several of them to approach the gentleman in the recliner.

"Sir," I said, "there are a lot of holes in the floor. What's the story?" He: "The furnace isn't working. Thought it might improve the circulation of air." He was serious. His problem (not enough heat) hadn't been addressed by his landlord, so he attempted to solve the problem with his own limited knowledge — and power tools! Only to make the situation worse.

Many of the issues I see in the course of my work day are the result of greed, laziness, ignorance, inattentiveness or mental illness. It can be very difficult to cut through at times. That said, I believe it to be worth the effort. I think the responsibility of every human being, but especially an artist, is to cultivate the ability to attend and respond.

BS: A big question would be the relation between "attending" and "responding." Some people respond precipitously — they haven't allowed themselves to attend sufficiently before responding. Others have the opposite problem — too diffident about responding to what they have perceived. It's hard to get the right balance. I'm surely in the second category, among the diffident, unfortunately.

TB: I am often in the second category as well, Barry. But I think about these issues less in terms of balance than I do in terms of risk. I've often repeated my thought that a poem is akin to an unsolicited kiss. Poems and unexpected kisses evoke similar ranges of response. What's at risk for you in a poem?

BS: Watch out you don't get accused of lyrical harassment one of these days.

There are all sorts of social decorum one might be afraid of violating in a poem. Sometimes I'm afraid of sounding sentimental, for instance. It's a question of knowing whether your rule of thumb — "Avoid sentimentality" is probably a good one — is helping you stick closer to what the poem should be or whether in this instance your rule is in fact preventing you from realizing that. On some occasions a poem will be falsified if you don't allow it a necessary senti-mentality. That's just one example. Another: Because most of my poems are short, I have to watch out for my fear that they are insubstantial: Am I perhaps trying to make a poem longer because I suspect a short one is less impressive? Or on the contrary, is the poem short because I haven't pushed myself enough to develop it as it might be? Another worry: Is the poem too hermetic? The list could go on....

Then there's the risk that the whole effort is null — that I am completely on the wrong track. A while back, I read something that Matisse wrote, where he said that early on, when his work was finding little acceptance, he would say to himself, "If Cézanne was right, then I'm right." I was touched by the need to cleave to a precursor, not for any sort of specific "influence," but simply to take courage. I say something of the sort to myself when I need courage, though some people might find in this comparison merely a proof of my inflated ego: "If Paul Celan was right, then I'm right." It would be so easy to say almost every choice of his was wrong—and that's part of his greatness, that he made it all so right.

TB: What gets you going, makes you want to write?

BS: It could be anything, really. Sometimes it's just something that I hear, or read, that strikes me as strange and somehow of poetic interest. I might start repeating that thing in my head, and as I do, it starts to attract more language to it—more things I notice. And so a poems starts to crystallize. Other poems start in a much more deliberate manner, when there is some particular linguistic field I want to delve into. For instance, there was one point—this was quite a long while ago, but it makes a clear example—when I had it in mind that I wanted to write some hymns. But it was hard to get into the right spirit for it. So I started by making a poem entirely out of pieces of language taken from Thomas Traherne's "Centuries"—a prose book, not a book of hymns, but which I thought had the right kind of rhythm and cadence to help bring to this hymnlike state of mind. After that I was able to write a hymn that wasn't dependent on a specific source. But only just one.

What never comes into it is that the poems never begin with some topic that I want to address. They are not discursive in that way—though some of them might be about discursivity. They really tend to come either from concrete bits of language, or from a certain linguistic terrain, and with the feelings that revolve around that. I don't want you to think that because I speak of language rather than subjects that I am dealing with words in a somehow objective manner. I don't think that's the case. I am dealing with language but what gives the poem its form is always, I hope, the emotional thread that runs through it, maybe almost invisibly but nonetheless essential for that.

TB: I know what you mean about proceeding from concrete bits of language. I've often thought about it in terms of establishing *constellations* of language or vocabulary. Do you often work from source texts? And what are your thoughts about appropriation in terms of your work?

BS: I have periodically written pieces that are in some form or another, usually partly, derived from a specific source text. Not only literary sources. My first chapbook, *The New Lessons*, was derived from a vocabulary book. I'm still quite attached to that work. Another poem came from a typing manual. In those cases, as with the Traherne poem, I literally collaged bits of language from the sources. I haven't done anything like that for a long time, though. Somehow I can't be bothered to work so systematically any more. I need to work in a more mercurial fashion. Still, some more recent things are more loosely derived from a specific source—in some more subjective way, without literally extracting and recontextualizing existing material. For instance, "Opera" comes from an Italian poem *Il Fiore*, which has (wrongly, I'm sure) been attributed to Dante and is in turn a version of the French *Roman de la Rose*. I couldn't even tell you how the poem is related to its source—I don't remember! But it definitely comes from that. I was always interested in Burroughs' cut-up methods as a sort of secular divination. These days, though, the idea of doing anything very methodically makes me feel very tired. Somehow I prefer the idea that the poem emerges against the background of a certain resistance to it, rather than from a concerted effort to make it appear.

TB: I'm interested in exploring that notion of resistance in the composition of a poem. Could you flesh it out a bit?

BS: Shouldn't one somehow be a bit skeptical? The Canadian poet Rob McLennan recently asked on his blog, "Who (in their right mind, I wonder) *chooses* poetry?" Well, someone once said that you don't choose poetry, poetry chooses you. So why not play a little hard to get? Let poetry make a little effort. At least that way you see whether it has a certain minimum of force. Plus it should become more concentrated through the process of working against the resistance.

You know, some poets—including some of the best—seem to find it important to simply produce a certain quantity of material that is recognizably theirs. Possibly this is because they see themselves as professional poets, and the point of a profession is to practice it. Whereas I'd rather prevent a certain quantity of run-of-the-mill work from coming into existence. Which may have something to do with the fact that I don't see myself as a professional poet, and furthermore I don't even see poetry as a profession. There are certain times and places where it can be a profession but I don't believe that ours is one of them. In my lifetime in America, probably the only true professional poets have been Allen Ginsberg and, eventually, John Ashbery. Otherwise, there are professional professors of poetry, but that's not quite the same thing—though it's probably one of the factors that encourages overproduction.

On the other hand, some people would simply say that I am "retentive" or "repressed." Overly controlled or constrained. Maybe I am. But you know, you can't make poetry out of who you should be, you can only make it out of who you are.

TB: Why do you write poetry?

BS: Out of a fascination with language. And a surmise—it's almost embarrassing to say this today, but I have to be honest with you—that it can lead to the heart of being.

TB: What do you mean when you write "that it can lead to the heart of being"?

BS: If I knew the answer, I might not need poetry to help me thread my way toward it. Maybe it's "La maison où l'on n'entre pas" of which we read in a poem by Reverdy.

TB: Take me through one of your poems. Speak specifically to your motivations and decisions made along the way. Resist the urge to be easy on yourself (heh!).

BS: That's a tough one. A tremendous number of decisions enter into each poem but when things are going well, most of the decisions happen really fast. In retrospect, I truly can't remember what most of them were. And that's what I like about the poems! Although I put a lot of work into them, I like them when they don't actually remind me of that work. So since you posed this question, I've been looking over lots of poems trying to find one where I could answer you without just making the while thing up, but I can't. So am I going easy on myself? Could be. But you know, one of the great early inspirations was Borges, when he talked about how he had to find a way of working that would accommodate his laziness—that, he claimed, was the reason why, instead of writing a novel, he would write a two-page story in the form of a review of the novel he hadn't written. Well, I'm lazy too! And I believe in finding ways of working that accommodate one's limitations. I haven't been able to find a way to avoid putting work into a poem—and I've never been the kind of writer who could work, either in prose or poetry, without lots of revising—no "first thought, best thought" for me—but at least I've succeeded in finding a way that allows me to forget the work. Like my wife having no concrete recollection of the pain of giving birth. But if there's anything in any of the poems that makes you want to ask, "Why did you do that?" or "Where did that come from?" I'll do my best to answer.

TB: I'm very fond of your chapbook-poem Tephra. Could you speak to its

132

composition, some of your motivations? It's particularly interesting to me that every section of that text hinges in some way on parenthetical notations.

BS: That poem was written primarily, as I recall, on a train from Paris to Nîmes and back. Travel is often good for my poetry—airplanes are bad but trains and hotel rooms are good. I guess it's all the down time you have, where all your usual inputs and distractions are gone, that lets it emerge. The "banners of silken laundry" at the beginning came from an art installation I'd just seen at a Paris gallery. As I recall, the parentheses were not something I foresaw from the beginning. At a certain point, well into the process of working on the poem, it became evident that this was the only way to make the particular jumpy rhythm of the poem come through clearly enough. The poem was written not too long after a time in my life that was particularly tumultuous, emotionally— that period of extreme agitation was over but I was still somehow trying to process it. I think that's where a lot of the feeling-tone of the poem comes from. Almost more unusual for me than the use of parentheses is the fact that it is one of my few poems in a long time where not all the lines are flush left. Again, this has to do with bringing out a rhythmic effect that is somewhat in tension with itself. In this, it marks a shift in my practice: Most of the poems I'd been writing before that used mostly fairly conventional syntax, breaking out of that occasionally, but generally using enjambment to play the line off against units of sense—this play between the two was my main musical resource. After "Tephra," most of the poems have a much more fragmented syntax and the syntactical unit is much more often equal to a line. The more recent poems have little or no punctuation until the poems ends with a full stop—there is much less forward movement through them, they are more "floaty"—and it's as if the poem is wandering a bit, sliding, and only comes to a stop when it stops.

TB: Speaking of musical resources, references to music appear with great frequency in your poetry.

BS: Yes, that's true—though I doubt they are more frequent than references to poetry. Music has inspired me all my life. Speaking recently with Richard Hell, I was saying that as a teenager I went to CBGB's looking for the same things I was looking for in the Gotham Book Mart. That's a thought I'd never precisely formulated in that way before, but I think it's true. One way that music helped form my style was that it opened me up to the beauty of incomprehensibility. I've always been fascinated by the way, when you listen to a song, quite a lot of the words can be really incomprehensible—just part of the musical texture, yet with an apparent communicative thrust to it even though you can't make out just what is being communicated—but then some quite clear and striking phrase will emerge. There's a kind of dialectical relation between not-understanding and understanding that somehow gives more value, maybe more poignancy to both. That's where the underground meaning is. And that's why when you read the printed lyric it's usually so flat, so disappointing— because that dialectic is missing. It's what lets the listener construct her own lyric, but not just any one, rather the one that speaks to her from the singer's place. Like what the doorkeeper says to the man from the country in "Before the Law": "This door was intended only for you." So what I've always been interested in doing is something similar, but in such a way that this works exactly where the song fails to work, on the page, where it's just the naked words.

TB: Is theory/philosophy important to you?

BS: Well, my poetry is not what's sometimes called "theory-driven," if that's what you're asking. But I think that when you start to think reflectively about what you are doing, then you are on the terrain of philosophy or theory. And generally you can think better if you see how other people who have devoted themselves to thinking have thought. I studied philosophy in college and still read a good bit of it today. Lately I've been reading Giorgio Agamben, for instance. There's a particularity about the use of language in good philo-sophical writing that is not unrelated to the particularity about the use of language in poetry—though they are quite different particularities. For instance, philosophy tends to formalize language by circumscribing its vocabulary, whereas poetry tends to dilate its vocabulary in the course of its formalizations. And yet philosophy also produces neologisms much more readily than poetry does. I love it when new words come into my poems—I really never thought that "microdermabrasion" or "trustafarian" would ever get in there, yet there they are—but I don't invent any. Not that long ago I read a guy's obituary—unfortunately I've forgotten his name—and it said that he had coined the word "blurb." What an incredible poetic act that was! He had also coined some other words that had entered common usage. But wouldn't it be great to be able to write a word, an original word, and have it stand on its own as poetry? Of course then it might not enter common usage, but would always maintain a certain strangeness. In a way, each poem might be like a single long new compound word made of readymade parts. Maybe that's why my poems are usually so short.

TB: Why does poetry matter?

BS: Different poetries matter for different—even contradictory—reasons. What I care for most is the intimate impersonality that addresses an unknown self. Maybe it's what Novalis was getting at when he spoke of an acoustics of the soul.

TB: Who are the writers you can't do without, the ones you return to over and over?

BS: "Can't do without" sounds kind of desperate. There are lots of writers, both of poetry and prose, whom I reread over the years, and I've mentioned some of them already. But "can't do without"? I'll admit that in moments of great extremity I turn to "Crazy Jane Talks With the Bishop." But more broadly, and more calmly, there are some touchstones, maybe too many. The English Renaissance: Wyatt, Ralegh, obviously Shakespeare. German Romanticism: Hölderlin (mostly in Richard Sieburth's translation), the Athenæum fragments. French modernism: Rimbaud, Mallarmé, Reverdy (and Kenneth Rexroth's introduction to his translation of Reverdy). The Americans: Whitman, Dickinson, Stevens, Spicer, Ashbery, Scalapino. Celan. In prose, Kafka above all, but also James and Proust, writers whose work is constant self-reflection. And critical writers: Walter Benjamin, above all his correspondence with Scholem about Kafka; Adrian Stokes: "Luxury and Necessity of Painting"; Clement Greenberg; Paul de Man, who was briefly a teacher of mine; Roland Barthes. Enough already! I could go on. But it's interesting, and not surprising, that most of them are writers I read by the time I left formal education when I was 23; and certainly there are no names there whose work I encountered after the age of 30. There's a kind of receptivity that's possible when you're young that you lose eventually.

By the way, I have a question for you: Why did you ask about philosophy and theory, a while back, and not about another field of endeavor, say, history or politics? Do you see a more fundamental connection between poetry and philosophy than between poetry and other things?

TB: Absolutely. I think, at their best, that poetry and philosophy inhabit similar epistemo-ontological space. The "fundamental connection" swings on modes of questioning reality and on a rather hyper attentiveness to language.

BS: I see it that way too. Politics, for instance, may question reality but doesn't estrange language. But I am more frustrated with my nonunderstanding of a philosophical text than of a poetic one.

TB: Politics doesn't estrange language? I don't know about that; it often reverses the meaning of words—in fact empties them of meaning.

Perversely I'm not frustrated by my partial understanding of philosophical or poetic texts. I am there for what I *can* find, for what there is which is of use to me. Often reading poetry or philosophy I'll be entirely unfocused until a line jars me to attention and causes me to begin again with better results.

BS: The emptying of meaning you find in political rhetoric is the opposite of what I mean by estrangement. The words are meant to flow through you almost without your noticing them—they're meant to seem "natural."

TB: Doesn't a lot of mainstream, so-called "School of Quietude," poetry do exactly the same thing?

BS: I doubt it. Maybe there are some poets out there who don't want you to notice the words they use and how they use them, but I've never heard about it.

In any case, I wish Silliman would stop banging on about the School of Quietude. It's like a good joke that gets boring after you've heard it too often. I also don't care for the label "mainstream." Either we're the mainstream, or there is none.

TB: I don't want to belabor this, but I do believe there is a sort of linguistically transparent mainstream poetry, often coming out of MFA programs and workshop settings, which is pre-set, as it were, for the larger poetry publishing outfits. It is a poetry of anecdote and smooth surfaces which is prized for its accessibility. Every issue of *American Poetry Review* (it is still being published, right?) contains many examples.

BS: Maybe I'm being naïve. Not that much of the produce of the "larger poetry publishing outfits" ever crosses my field of vision. But maybe you don't see that much of it either. So what's our talk about it other than an exchange of prejudices? My prejudice is that when you talk about mainstream poetry you are probably talking about something with a very fussy, overwrought surface—not smooth at all, and not transparent. Something like Amy Clampitt. Am I completely off?

TB: I'm thinking about poetry writing which, if anything, is underwrought. Billy Collins' work comes to mind: a little word picture is painted, an amusing anecdote is related; but there is no depth to the writing, nothing is there but what is present on the surface. It's not evil or anything, but it's like fast food—a lot of empty calories. You read it, you get it. There's no reason to come back, there's nothing to engage.

BS: Funny enough, I just read a couple of poems of his for the first time the other day. They were in the *London Review of Books*. I'd never come across anything by him before. But I've already forgotten them! Which is I guess is a strong argument in favor of your description being accurate. Still, I bet if you look carefully at the poems, they are full of all kinds of clever little turns that serve to give them their sort of understated pathos. Anyway, I'm sure there's something there for someone to dwell on. It's just that that someone is not me. But if the School of Quietude or mainstream consists of poetry that's both overwrought like Clampitt's and underwought (which my spell-check is signaling me to say it's not a real word) like Collins', then I don't see what makes them a school or a stream together. They are various things, perhaps mutually contradictory.

TB: Don't put too much faith in spell-check! But, hey, in what does your faith reside as a poet? What keeps you going?

BS: Maybe nothing. I don't always keep going. I didn't write or at least didn't finish any poems for about seven years from 1994 to 2000. That's unusual, but I've never written poetry in a steady sort of way. As I said, I'm not a professional poet. I do it when the need becomes stronger than the doubt. There's no reason why any poem shouldn't be the last. So faith doesn't come into it, or else my faith is weak or nonexistent. But on the upside, any time I accomplish something, I feel extremely lucky.

TB: What do you find to be most discouraging/encouraging about the current poetry scene(s)?

BS: What's most encouraging is that there is so much good poetry being written. Especially though of course far from exclusively among younger poets. When I read the work of people like Eleni Sikelianos, Linh Dinh, Kasey Mohammad, Catherine Wagner, Frances Richard, Amy King, Sarah Manguso or a bunch of others—well, it's just incredibly heartening. It gives me a great sense of possibility. They push me to be as radical as they are, in my own way.

TB: What's most discouraging?

BS: Being an art critic, I can't help but notice the paucity of serious criticism. It would be good if there were a more formalized medium for the echo a book of poetry makes among its readers.

TB: Do you think the internet could be the spawning ground (perhaps *sounding board* is the better term?) for the birthplace of those echoes?

BS: Some of the criticism that does exist is on the internet—for instance in Jacket. When Silliman sets himself to do a piece of sustained criticism on his blog, it's always superb. The Constant Critic seems to have gone dormant, but I liked that while it was going. But for the most part, the medium does not seem to favor the kind of developed, formalized discourse I have in mind. The question is, who'd be willing to do it? Not me. If you really took being a critic of your fellow poets' work seriously and did it honestly, you'd probably lose a lot more friends than you'd gain. Plus you'd have to cultivate a talent for one day being able to understand what sort of poetry Billy Collins is listening for and to what extent he's attained it, and then the next day doing the same for Lyn Hejinian—all the while without losing but rather deepening and nuancing your sense of the relative values of those distinct projects. That's the equivalent of what I do as an art critic, or what Roberta Smith does, or whoever. I can write about a landscape painter one day and a conceptual artist the next. It's true that the growth of blogs and internet journals has facilitated a more spontaneous and informal discussion that is great to have—another one of the encouraging developments, absolutely—but this is something else.

TB: And finally, what can/what does poetry change?

BS: I don't know. What does picking at a scab change? You're worrying at something that bothers you, and it does give a sort of perverse pleasure, but still...

An Addendum from the Comments Section of the website interview

Anny Ballardini: I was privileged in the sense that I translated a longer poem by Barry Schwabsky meant to be the text of an art catalogue. When Tom asks Barry about the composition and motivation of his poems, and Barry sort of limits his answer to a certain laziness — even if by quoting Borges, I know instead that Barry is very precise and knows exactly the value, tone and intensity of each word. We sort of got mad in trying to translate "twitch". "We" because Barry can speak Italian, besides his many qualifications. It was a pleasure to listen to your conversation.

Tom Beckett: Anny, what was the word you finally chose to translate "twitch"?

A.B.: Sorry, that was "tweaked", translated with "modulato" _way distant but we had to find a compromise. A wonderful colored art catalogue, and the only words are Barry's poem with my translation. Talk of innovating art criticism.

Barry Schwabsky: Thanks so much, Anny. It was such a pleasure to work with you on that translation—discussing the shades of meaning of words: my idea of paradise. Maybe that text, "Diary of a Poem," would have been a better example to use for explaining my working methods. Again, it began while I was traveling: a poem I wrote in a hotel room in Sao Paulo, Brazil. And just as Tephra doesn't say anything overtly about France, this poem didn't talk about Brazil. After working on it a bit, I thought that from one beginning it could go in two different directions, and I wavered between them. Eventually I realized it might be very interesting to have two poems that were identical for their first half, but different in their conclusion. So I did that—I chose both. One was the version for the left ear, the other was the version for the right ear. And I was quite happy with this idea. But in the back of my mind, I was never really 100% satisfied with either of the two poems. I liked them, and I considered them finished, yet there was also something that bugged me about them. They hadn't attained a certain fullness. But there they sat, and they even became part of a book manuscript that I was circulating. As Valéry said, a poem is not finished but abandoned. But then, more than a year later, the idea came up of doing this book with the Italian painter Maria Morganti, an old friend. The book shows the development of a single small painting: each right-hand page shows a photograph taken of the painting each day that she worked on it. So the book is a kind of diary of the painting, and I thought it would be worth trying to create a fiction of a similar sort of diary, but of a poem. And somehow or other it occurred to me that in those two poems, which already between them

139

contained the idea of something being reworked, there was material that could be developed further in that sense. So I started playing with the material from both poems, repeating, recombining, adding, varying—using repetition with variations as a way to convey the sense of a single thing developing through time with revision and reconsideration.

A.B.: And it is an excellent example. A pity I did not know this story before. I think it is a question of shyness but maybe when translating I should ask specific questions: what did you mean, when did you write this poem, why. Fact is that I'd feel like invading the personality of the Other, a sort of Pornography as Gombrowicz defined it in his homonymous book. Better, I can ask questions when they are technically tied to a specific word or phrase. Maybe I should develop a set of questions pivoting on the method used by the Author, that could be an idea, as Tom asked Barry.

Poetry Fell in Love With You For a Reason

Waking up nights: spare rooms crowded with heat
and the rain outside: sudden music for dull garden leaves
remember who's missing? and in the lightning of a smile
years of long kissing: a fantasy
sequentially yours: but even though you feel chosen

you are chosen: invisible difference
lasts long (this book smells like Murakami)
to an eye full of pauses: oily sky and goodbye.

False Positives

For once I died right
your host assimilating birds
a restless voice dims

backed off finding time
as if it were given me
to write it.

*

The great gray sea
the love engine chopped like mad
stand here totally reversed

but used to the filth of heat
this sky travels fast
knowing anyone else but you.

*

Again you close the door
a freezing whisper
and the room disappears

gulls fly past the pages
your eyes disguised
yet bid me enter.

Diamond Replicas

Words for women and other writers

the eye unsilenced

an elaborate (but unscratchy) necklace

dawn stirs in one nostril

birds imprisoned in an eye

her tears go flying home

unspangled

this sprig of loss

known forward into

iris recognition

conversation of sweat

the door shuts the house

with pointless conviction

your whispering campaign against my eyes

songlessness, or rather sunglasses

and in for it:

—a map of how to lose your way
—the door of departure
—not two breaths to my name
—it makes me its own
—colors your eye

He found a poem trapped
in its own light
the ghost at its back
just dusk, a plunging silhouette
launched toward

the hang of your phonetic eye

a divine disproportion

shove another hour up the clock

pluck late music from a single string

what unholy racket

the sky makes even less sense now

grass bends before each wind

all the air in my nostrils

how open your mouth could be

she offered a whisper

setting words to a face

remembering stone heat

we speak in overlap

tasting brightly

the surprise of the ever-later

a voice asleep

in the middle of early.

Three Threes for KK Kozik

Snow licks the window
Eyes cloud with memories — but
Oh! Feelings melt too.

Roses are threats;
And his love-offerings,
Never good enough.

Believe in love ghosts:
Every house gets the moon
It deserves.

Biopic (for Artie Gold or Syd Barrett)

A mind wrapped up around a sparrow's breath
or eye that wavers among branches

mistaken for a dragonfly
he knows music

has its cupboards where drugs
of solitude lay stored.

*

They found him painting songs
they couldn't hear

humming pictures they couldn't see
one about a girl with wooden hair

the ragged urban fox
free to let right go of itself.

*

He called her shadow
"my Saturday cinema"

well her shadow's more interesting
than she is, no?

whose finger reached
the whole way to the bone star.

*

"Marks scratched into the sky"
where a man disappeared

a relaxing thing would be painting
a white painting

but after microdermabrasion
the poem could well have stayed missing.

*

Go Venus, let's keep it legal
or dancing over dust she said

"You turn me out like a light"
but that was wrong

then buried her mouth in the flesh
of a peach imported from suspected sunshine.

Immigrant

Certain days
I used to think of leaving
the East Country, now not even
a darting memory—just a hole in
the sky before which
grain elevators hang
nailed. I drank wine
of immoral bouquet: sea foam,
midday drizzle, ash of poppies, copperas,
mustard. Then I stopped arriving
and the eye-burn
stopped happening. Still the blind
sky stands out
anonymous
with birds
of raw meat. Breath
changes color. I call the window closer
but it won't come. The eye yaws, flooded
with dreams of targets
and insomniac
sheets. A funeral
with interruptions:
"Organ, shut up!" sing the birds
before the stony minute turns its face
the other way round.

Peter Ganick
interviewed by Sheila E. Murphy

Peter Ganick was publisher of Potes & Poets Press, and now finds himself publishing, with Jukka-Pekka Kervinen, Blue Lion Books as well as smallchapbookproject-2. In his role as publisher, he has always championed the new, exciting writing wherever he finds it. As a writer, he has over 30 books and 40 chapbooks to his name. 're the after', included at the end of the interview, will be part of a forthcoming book, THEORY OF TIME to be published by Blue Lion Books. He lives with his wife, Carol, an artist, and their Welsh Corgi, Tuba.

Sheila E. Murphy: Peter, I am so pleased that you agreed to engage in this interview, because you have made a sustained contribution to innovative writing over an extended period of years, and continue to maximize available vehicles for publishing and creating important texts. I'd like to begin with your own writing, if I may. Your process of writing is highly disciplined, resulting in such powerful volumes as *No Soap Radio* and numerous others. If you were to specify what you consider some of the books you are most proud of having written, which might these be and why?

Peter Ganick: i'm glad for this interview, and that you are conducting it. the last interview i participated in was for a poetry magazine named, *atelier*, around 1990, and much has happened since then. i have published many books of other poets, continuing with potes & poets press, my part of the venture ending in 2000. during the period up to 2000, p&p published 150 or so issues of *A.BACUS*, a series of limited editions called 'EXTRAS', 63 perfectbound books. there were three online journals, *POTEPOETZINE*, *POTEPOETTEXT*, and *poethia*.

i became committed to too many books ahead during 1999-2000, so sold the press, and took a much needed vacation from publishing till 2005, when, with the assistance of two friends, jukka-pekka kervinen and j hayes hurley, blue lion books was started. around that time, i started small-chapbook-project, both hard-copy ventures. these have been active and are now daily concerns of mine.

however, when one focuses on my writing, there have been a number of books published, some self-published through entities i ran, and others from different presses. i can't begin to express my gratitude to the editors of these presses, as i never kept a list of where selections of my writing appeared before publication in book form. for this, again, apologies to the editors.

my writing has gone through a number of distinct manifestations. i will outline here the sections and the principal book from those periods of writing.

the first would be from 1978 or so, when comprehensibility was a prime factor. i wrote a book named *SOME POEMS*, which was self-published by a venture called roxbury poetry enterprises, roxbury because i lived there on fort hill, a part of boston. there, also, suggestions of the creativity/crazy-text manifested for the first time. all these were chapbooks. at the time i also published a book of will bennett and one by larry eigner.

the second period occurred during the five or six years after i married carol, my wife to this day. we just celebrated our 25th wedding anniversary. i produced a lot of work during that time, particularly the 95 or so section *REMOVE A CONCEPT*, a poem totaling approximately 3,500 pages, remaining unpublished at this time. early books that were published were *HYPERSPACE CANTATAS*, from XEXOXIAL EDITIONS, then named XEROX SUTRA EDITIONS. also, during this period i started publishing some chapbooks, some self-published, others with different presses. work from this period is characterized by a growing process, sort of a young bird trying to find his wings. some of these books are more successful; and others, not.

the next period was sort of a resting place during the 1990s, when i produced *AGORAPHOBIA* and *NO SOAP RADIO*. these are works i am especially fond of. they were written during a period when potes & poets was going along at full speed and i was using the culminations of insights from the first and second period. both books were published by Drogue Press. *AGORAPHOBIA* is an anti-poem in the sense that it is a lie to the personality i represent. i have no case of agoraphobia, nor do i recommend agoraphobia as a way of life. instead, it is a book that needed a 'title', and the word used was connected to the work only by coincidence. *NO SOAP RADIO* is a collection of very short poems dedicated to my father. the work skews language from almost recognizable to almost incoherent. to me, these pieces have a certain grace.

the fourth period is represented by what i call 'blocks of text'. starting with *A'SATTV*, through *TEND. FIELD., (A PHILOSOPY)* to *STRUCTURE OF EXPERIENCE* and *TWO TEXTS*, all published by cPress, except the first book mentioned here published by CHAX PRESS. in these works i made use of the enabling of pure thought due to a pre-decision on word-limitation and punctuation-predefinition. given these factors, i could let my thought process venture where it may. the latter four texts have a pseudo-philosophical attitude manifested, though the text itself can be philosophical as a process in a certain manner towards a goal, the fabrication of blocks of text. realizing this to be circular reasoning, one can transcend or descend the rungs of language with these texts, hopefully the prior.

almost the most recent period, totally different, is the EXISTENCE poems in which 16 sections, of which 6 are published to this date by cPress, represent to the use of a computer keyboard in same manner as a piano, the instrument i studied for 18 years, and by which i earn a livelihood teaching. these could be called 'pure non-sense' if one is looking at them semantically; visual poetry, though not concrete poetry, namely the mixture of approximately-free visual gestures of text with a semantic of the keyboard itself: one could write, 'if a keyboard were permitted to write with its own syntax, what would it write'?

in early 2007, i am working on a series of notebooks of pictures jim leftwich and jukka-pekka kervinen are publishing on their blogs, TEXTIMAGEPOETRY, and MINIMUM DAILY REQUIREMENT, respectively. these images are abstract and mostly comprise black lines on natural color paper, page size 4 x 6 inches.

SEM: Would you be willing to speak about your engagement with the architecting and creating of extended texts? Specifically, the sustained attention and discipline that are required, in addition to the ability to change as the poem changes, during composition, are of interest.

PG: i must confess the process is not analyzed much by me while writing. sort of start, maintain, continue, then, peter-out. it's rather an organic process. even though i might use abstract terms in writing, the course of the poem is like the life of a creature. the poem starts: there's a springtime/honeymoon time where i imagine the energy of the poem to be light and airy. whether or not this is true i don't know, i observe it as such from my own view. whether or not, it makes for a poem-interpretation with which i can live.

from there is a developing complication. the text's springtime is over, though traces remain. negative concepts enter and though they are received by the poet, with the same engagement as the spring terms, the energy becomes gradually more clouded.

there is a book i wrote which is an example of this, *TWO TEXTS*. the first text, about 2/3rds of the book is called, 'apparitional corsairs'; the second, 'with-ness'. 'apparitional corsairs' was started to be a text that would be very long. in this text, the energy be-came more and more dark, even troubled. to pull a sufficient ending from it, i had to start another text with a regular lineation, in one form a sestina. after that, i changed the margins and the font size and let the poem run-on, so there is little evidence of the sestina-beginning. that text, 'withness' maintains a spiritual sense; this, because there is a sufficient period of difficulty overcome, overcome by 'going through it' to support the spiritual part.

in this work i am using the model of the symphony in the late romantic period european classical music. an energetic part, the 1st movement; a deep, engaging part, the 2nd movement; the third movement, a scherzo leading with life to the last part, the tour de force. [this is the model of beethoven's 9th symphony. each musical work of that period was somewhat different, though the 9th's model was primary.]

to get the tone i wanted for the ending of the poem, i started the 'with-ness' and was satisfied with the result. the text is bright, airy, and intense. this path i represent in this discussion is the path of some spiritual seekers who come to some sort of understanding in their life.

SEM: This provides a very helpful sequential perspective on how your work has unfolded and continues to emerge. I am interested, also, in your intermittent mentions of what was occurring in your life during the composition of some of these texts. How did writing emerge as a primary engagement in your life?

PG: i guess it derives in a hopelessly-not-too-clichéd-move of the muse. there had been a failed marriage, 18 years of piano lessons, a degree in music composition, a lot of serious literary and philosophical reading while in high school, an interest in mathematics, some use of recreational drugs in the 1960s and early 1970s, some what seen as major-betrayals-in-life and some fantastic-and-excellent-long-term-friendships forming, an abiding interest in spiritual practice including 28 years of faithful, daily vedantic meditation, a unitarian upbringing, and, of course, the required mystical experiences, one of which after a while i might have been inclined to call, the advent of the muse, or, inspiration.

mind you, this inspiration that hits all poets at some point, is less than 1% of what makes a poetic career, or whatever you want to call it, go forward. i was fortunate in not seeing it as such for a long time, starting with the first employment, job sitting a cash register in the travel department of the harvard co-operative society bookstore, in 1972. a few other short-lived jobs along with a job i've had since late 1972, as an itinerant piano instructor going to the students' homes to give half-hour lessons. this, along with some family money, has allowed me the freedom to work as i choose and publish potes & poets press, *a.bacus*, the online journals, blue lion books, and small chapbook project, also the books i've written.

i am an only child, my mother was musically inclined, an ardent singer, and very much the root of our family. she died at age 76, in 1994. my dad, approaching his 89th birthday in very good health, worked in advertising, trained as a painter at the boston school for practical arts. i am fortunate to be able to know him over this extended period, as he is a remarkable man. he continues traveling about the world, with his companion, jane, who is also in good health and approximately his age.

i met carol at a beach party in rhode island, and it was love at first sight. we married in 1982, recently moved into another home in west hartford, connecticut, and live with a wonderful welsh corgi. carol is an accomplished painter and teacher of watercolor.

some people say that the life of a writer is everything. others say the text has no relationship to life—it's a process in itself. every writer has a life, and every text is a development in any committed writer's life, no?

SEM: As a publisher of innovative poetry, you have published both established innovators, if I may call them that, and emerging writers. Your vision as a publisher has played an important role in the development of new writing over the past couple of decades. Talk a bit about what writing has attracted you over the years, and what surprises you have encountered when selecting texts and writers to present.

PG: the writing i have published in the past was poetry i was challenged to 'understand' or 'get my mind around'. if a poet sent work which was too common; too conformist to a style, no matter what it might be; not presented well; immature poetry or greeting card poetry, obviously; poems i just 'didn't like', etc., a rejection would be forthcoming.

when i started *A.BACUS*, i set a goal of having a survey of the field of 'innovative poetries' available at the time. this was in the early 80s through mid 90s. at that time, major innovations were coming from the LANGUAGE poets and i published a number of books and *A.BACUS*es which were written from that angle.

i liked things that were 'skewed', 'disjunct', 'confusing but not confused'. i liked to have to figure something out in a text.

recently, with small chapbook project and blue lion books, which is co-edited by jukka-pekka kervinen, i try for the same. innovation has gone into new areas of writing. the LANGUAGE movement, now a historical force and one deserving of utmost respect in its changing the horizon of poetry, has had great influence on american and international writing. but like all literary movements, its period of 'fresh' innovation cannot last forever, so i've shifted to a group of writers who met on mIEKAL aND's spidertangle list. these writers, including the Be Blank Consort, because they have been writing for many years and as a group have not received much recognition. seeing their work as very exciting, i started publishing people from spidertangle. jukka agreed with me on this.

SEM: I like your reference to The Be Blank Consort, a performance group spearheaded by John M. Bennett, Scott Helmes, K.S. (Kathy) Ernst and others. I sense these writers and those included in spidertangle as a whole creators working in a wide range of creative areas, among them, visual poetry (or word art). Please talk about visual poetry as you see it continuing to figure prominently in arts and letters.

PG: i can't really speak to the question from experience. i don't see myself as 'visual poet'. i write text, and i make drawings, the two being separate, even when both elements are included, one or the other is being fore-grounded, and is intended to usurp the other. besides classification is a matter of the academics, not creative artists/poets.

as i subscribe to spidertangle, an internet mailing list surrounding the issue of visual poetry, i can tell the reader there is a lot of activity at this time in this field. it is quite varied, and like any new movement, must undergo its testing period before it gains radical acceptance. the value of such acceptance is up to discussion in my mind. isn't the freedom to work as one wants more important?

another question that must be introduced is, will visual poetry ever enter the 'canon'? this is difficult, as visual poetry spans the visual and the literary. would the classifiers (professional academics) have a hard time with a crossover art? i don't know, where would it be put? as many other movements, it would require the practitioners to become a 'new academy' aligned with respected universities. are visual poets willing to undergo such for a categorization?

SEM: Do you believe that poetry, and creative work in general can (or should) be taught? How has this element worked for you as a teacher and as a student?

PG: your use of the word 'belief' in your question is an appropriate one, as in most intellectual disputes, like this, the reasoning that is used to support an argument is largely based, at root, on belief.

whether creativity can be taught is one question, and whether or not the forms of poetic discourse can be taught is another. to me, it seems obvious, or read that — 'my belief is' — that creativity can only be enhanced, one is creative or not, and outside efforts are helpful only as environment, inner aspects of the becoming-poet. are nurtured, which is to say, it is not sure that creativity can be taught.

what *is* sure. as far as i can tell, is that the ability to be a fundamental innovator in poetry or any art or science, is beyond the reach of education, except that, like the creative impulse, everybody has to have some introduction to the forms of poetry and the 'canon' of poetic literature, if for no other reason than one wouldn't end up copying what's been done before in one's own writing.

for my livelihood i am an educator, in music, as a piano instructor driving to students' homes. how do i approach this question in my own work? i have a good piano method book and add from my own experience some 'extra' material based on the needs of the student i am teaching. of course, there's a fundamental difference between piano instruction and literature or composition courses. piano instruction, meaning the best piano instruction, is always one-on-one. in literature courses, there is more classroom work, at least at the early stages. piano is one-on-one from the start.

it is in the 'extras' that are tailor-made' to the individual student in piano, that one can aid in making a student am innovator or a very creative person, though those are. to use a phrase, few and far-between.

SEM: You actively participate in creating, teaching, and showcasing creative work. In your role as editor/publisher, you help shape the attention of the perceiving audience, by establishing viable vehicles for bringing forward what you consider important and/or interesting work. Please discuss how this role presently functions in the world of writing, and perhaps some moments in this role that have been important to you.

PG: if i understand your question correctly, you'd like me to talk a bit about the ventures i'm involved with at the moment. first, there is blue lion books, a joint venture of jukka-pekka kervinen [from finland], j hayes hurley [a novelist from Connecticut], and myself. the focus of a publishing venture is what determines the manuscripts that get published by that press.

i realize it sounds obvious, but so many times a writer will not pay attention to the publishing focus before submitting a manuscript. a lot of the heartache [!] of rejection can be avoided by paying attention to it.

blue lion books is always reading manuscripts and publishes books 250pp or more that develop an idea in total. a long book for a complete idea, that's the point. and an experimental, or previously-unseen idea, even an innovation, is preferred. so far we've kept to this pretty well.

to submit send manuscripts to
pganick@comcast.net
to see the new books and backlist:
www.cafepress.com/bluelionbooks66

blue lion books is a print-on-demand publisher.

a press brings to life, as it were, texts that an editor, in all his/her fallibility, which is ultimately for better or worse. an editor is therefore a link between writer and the reading audience, providing the major way a text can become 'fact'. readings are 'facts' also, but aside from recordings made, which are usually not so widely distributed as a book, they are most evanescent. a writer once told me, 'books are permanent', this, especially since acid-free paper is the standard of printers everywhere.

as to moments which have been important to me, personally, i'd rather leave that part blank. with potes & poets press, *A.BACUS, POTEPOETZINE, POTEPOETTEXT*, potes & poets 'EXTRAS', *poethia*, blue lion books, there have been a large number of important moments to me.

SEM: Let's talk about attention itself, perhaps *the* issue in the arts and in living. Please speak about this issue as it pertains to making and experiencing art.

PG: 'attention' is everything in the arts. from the obvious 'getting attention' from other people or an audience for one's art/poetry or giving attention to one's art while creating/editing it, to the process of the evaluations of the reproductions of it—printed copies of books designed from manuscripts, manuscripts are the originals; or copies of paintings, both physical copies on canvas for example, or postcards, etc, being the 'career' of each art/poetry work. also, one cannot forget the art of memorizing sections of or whole poems, an art becoming somewhat archaic, but still practiced by poets memorizing their own work for readings, i believe some 'slam' poetry readings require memorization.

[i must say that i use the poetry and art connections because i am involved with poetry and visual arts as well. usually i don't mix them, not because i think they are unmixable, but just because i prefer not to.]

what attention do we give to living is a complex question—as complex as all psychology, philosophy, and, perhaps, spirituality. if i can elaborate a bit. it'd seem to me that psychology tries to find diagnoses based on structures given by the great thinkers in that field. we know them, freud, jung, lacan—the last of which i am exploring with some success.

psychologists have helped me a lot. i think that psychology can be another discipline that artists/poets can use to help develop their creativity. it all depends on the chemistry between the client and the therapist. one generally gets what one puts into it, though there are some unusual people in either chair of the procedure.

philosophy, or the art of making (creating) intellectual structures or flows (flows being streams of thought that deny structure, a force in more recent philosophy) that are to be evaluated by the self-same procedure as went into creating them. mind you, i am a great devotee of the area and if i were perhaps a little clearer in thinking in that direction, might have taken that route in university and been writing entirely different material. most of the writing i read except for experimental writing, is philosophical in nature, though mostly 20th and 21st century thinkers make for the majority of philosophers i'm familiar with.

then, spirituality. what is considered the most or the least important component of a person's structure. perhaps artists and poets think it is more important than the general population believes. this to me is a favorable thing that goes a long way towards giving me a 'group' to be involved with.

i was raised unitarian, then moved over to the ramakrishna vedanta society, a neo-hindu group centered at belur math in calcutta, india. with them, i meditated for 28 years daily, and, find now, i almost cannot meditate at all. i came to this point at the time around my mother's death in 1994, which started a turbulent part of life for me. now things are, hopefully, a little more stable. i attended quaker meeting in cambridge massachusetts and west hartford for a long time, only to be puzzled. unitarianism is my childhood religion, so i find it natural, but again, probably because of learning it in childhood, i have no real distance from it.

lately i read some zen for assistance in learning new structures of thought that become valuable in life and writing. i always wonder if this is a valid use of zen, but think then that any use of zen is ok, as long as its ancient tradition is maintained with respect.

SEM: Please talk a bit about the utility of technology in the creative arts in which you are involved. What pleases and/or concerns you about the role that technology currently plays in the creation and exhibition of creative work?

PG: everybody uses technology to some degree and is dependent upon it as well. there is the obvious connection every writer has with computers—even if he/she doesn't write on one. when a poem is accepted to a magazine, or when a book of her/his poems are published, a computer will be used to design and print the book.

if one has even no connection with computers, if that were possible, then one would have to use a pencil or pen, a technology however primitive; and read out of a book, another technology that revolutionized the world 5 centuries ago, much like the computer is doing so now.

so, technology is everywhere, if one allows for a generous definition. 'technology' usually means computers and virtual reality these days. i am convinced there is no better computer platform than the macintosh. and use two of them—an ancient iBook with a G3 processor, and my wife's iMac G5. i think that much like when a person who values pens and uses them frequently buys another, say, mont blanc, or a bic, that pen will influence how one writes. the position of the hand on the pen might be affected, the pen-point will most likely be somewhat different than others the writer might own. and the ink color might change—so many variables.

as such go the computers one owns and uses—they develop personalities and have different ways of writing. [the previous statement might sound a bit 'crazy', but if one allows for a stretch-of-the-imagination, one could be open-minded enough to agree.] computer keyboards differ. i have very large hands, but find it difficult to type on a regular computer keyboard, because i don't use the thumbs or fifth-fingers. that's why i like a laptop to write on most—the smaller keyboard.

another aspect of the computer that is very important, especially if one is creating visual work on the computer, is the screen, or 'display'. there are many qualities of display, one can make the screen brighter or more muted, there are different sizes—my iBook has a 13.3" screen (i think), while my wife's iMac has a 20" screen. both have excellent brilliance and reproduction of ideas, yet the size suits each of us well.

everyone has an arrangement that 'works' for him/herself. i write email on the iMac, write on the iBook; on trips where there's wi-fi where i'm staying, i use the iBook which has a wi-fi card. so, why do i go into such detail about my particular arrangement? it is to show that, possibly like you, if you write, i have a special arrangement between my own 'personal' use of technology, and my sense of creativity.

technologies being so different, as mentioned above, cannot help having influence on one's output in creative fields. people who work creatively for the most part on computers have good fortune because they don't have to associate the computer, an ideal creative tool, with nine-to-five work-world uses of computers which tend to make people have a different view of them.

SEM: You've given a beautiful answer to the computer as instrument, capturing the gentleness with purpose in what one employs for creating. Please talk a bit about the utility of technology in the creative arts in which you are involved. What pleases and/or concerns you about the role that technology currently plays in the creation and exhibition of creative work?

PG: if i were more of a physicist, i could be more accurate about what i'm going to write, but the gist will be apparent. there are many types of 'space's. first there is the philosophical space of plato where words and ideas culminate in ideality. then, there could be a space called 'newtonian', where gravity is added, and the material world is added to the ideal world. i have always thought that the ancient greeks thought about things more than they experienced them. then, descartes localized the world in the ego, or the 'i am'. this made the prime factor the subjective experience of the perceiver. then comes the developments of the 19th and 20th century, too many to be discussed in an answer apparently to be about cyberspace.

at any rate, with the computer's advent, now we are given 'cyberspace', also called 'virtual reality', and perhaps the precursor to 'holographic space'. these developments, all philosophical, scientific, and computer-based, are all sorts of 'space' where the parameters of what-can-be-experienced is different in ways from the others — similar in other ways, it should be said.

what cyberspace does for poetry is to allow for its transmission almost instantaneously to any part of the world. further developments have allowed for the formation of online journals, based on email, websites, blogs, photographs (flickr, picasa) — all which are recent developments. often we forget how recent they are. less than 25 years, approximately, for most of them. another thing that can be recognized is that the computer revolution, and let's call it a revolution, is in its infancy. the future is wide open.

that being said at age 60, i would not study computer science for the world, i have no regrets about having studied classical music composition in the 1960s.

SEM: Would you mind expounding a bit about some of the developments in current writing that interest you most? Feel free to be as specific or as general as you wish.

PG: i used to read a lot of everything in high school, however a primary fascination with science-fiction, and writers like h p lovecraft and his coterie was there also in high school. let it be said that material can disturb one's perception of reality a bit. in college, i had a little time to read other than my musical studies, and it was then i started to read poetry. i liked folks like john berryman, robert lowell, ezra pound, lawrence ferlinghetti—a diverse crowd one could say.

after a few non-degree-producing years in grad school, where i started reading philosophy seriously, although remaining an amateur in philosophical studies, i read more poetry and discovered the L=A=N=G=U=A=G=E movement in 1970, and started publishing on discovering that exciting manner of writing. i could see poetry/language/grammar all changing before my reading-eyes. one of the first books i published as, 'peter ganick, publisher' was *disfrutes* by charles bernstein, an early chapbook.

an important book for me was *L=E=G=E=N=D* by a group of 5 LANGUAGE poets. (i cant be specific about who due to having lost my copy.) i was continually impressed with bruce andrews', ron silliman's, and the writings of lyn hejinian and her tuumba press.

philosophy for me meant jacques derrida, who jump-started almost every text-writing-session into which i entered. early on i sent mr derrida a copy of a book of mine that was recently published at the time, *AGORAPHOBIA*. i have always been sure he read some of this, as he was obviously fluent in english.

other philosophers influencing me are, husserl with his bracketing, camus almost forgotten today with his novel 'the stranger'. recently, i have been exploring zizek's philosophy, especially his latest book, 'the parallax view'. movies i like and liked are 'the sheltering sky' based on the paul bowles short story. another occurring to me is the french film, 'jules et jim'; though a recent viewing made me doubt the desirability of such a relationship between men

161

and a woman, as it had when premiered in the 60s and i was much less experienced.

SEM: What influence do you perceive the study of music to have had on your writing, Peter?

PG: almost everything.

i was a poor english literature student and didn't really like it much. the study of music, including 18 years of classical piano study, a degree in music composition, experience playing with rock bands (bass guitar), playing piano with a jazz trio (tenor sax and drums were the other instruments), piano with an old-fashioned 'swing' band (a la benny goodman, maynard ferguson), experimental work with ran blake playing soprano saxophone, etc etc.

i learned composition from musical studies and also with art studies at the west hartford art league, where many painting teachers, primarily paul zimmerman, diane marinaro, and hannah libman, taught me material usable with poetry and writing in general. composers arthur berger, martin boykan, john huggler, gardner read, hugo norden instilled a sense of 'tone' and 'quality of tone' in me, which i cant escape. my necessity is to produce work i can listen to. first the ear then the eye then the mind, is sort of how my experience is structured.

SEM: What books or writers have influenced your work?

PG: briefly, at the moment, my work is influenced by jukka-pekka kervinen, jim leftwich, sheila e murphy, john m bennett, and others. those mentioned here are those who come to mind first.

SEM: Whether you acknowledge this role or not, I must call attention to your capability as a teacher of compositional principles in relation to writing. Several conversations you and I have had over the years have demonstrated to me your sense of what I'll call "the architecture of composition" as applied to texts. Could you speak about some principles at work within the writing process from your point of view?

PG: if i have any competence in this matter, it is entirely due to the training i've had at some excellent schools of music; including, new england conservatory of music, berklee school of music, bard college, boston university, brandeis university, and massachusetts institute of technology, as well as some private composition lessons and conversations with walter piston, luciano berio, and john huggler.

so, enough name-dropping. those were my teachers, and i think all persons writing or, especially writing poetry, where the tone or ear is so important, could use some familiarity with music. what sort of music? for instance, what course, perhaps music appreciation, which'd give an appreciation of the different historical sounds of musics as they've developed. perhaps a basic course in theory, which would give anyone who has a wish to try out an instrument or sing, some knowledge that would apply to the single line of music, and chords used to harmonize with them. another course, very valuable, which usually has a prerequisite of some theory, is counterpoint, the rules for consonance and dissonance between multiple linear structures as applied through time, or, in real terms, why two or more simultaneous lines of music sound the way they do—and how to write lines that sound consonant or dissonant.

as a composition student in the 1960s, i was involved with the last gasp of 12-tone theory invented by schoenberg, the new sonic pieces of boulez, berio, and kagel. english music had stayed in the conservative traditions even through that period. american music was becoming more and more experimental. electronic classical music was being written by babbitt and others. also, for us in the united states, we were being introduced to foreign or, ethnic, musics that had yet to be heard in the i s a. gamelan music from indonesia, shakuhachi flute from japan, authentic south and central american musics, music from india—so dynamic and varied, european folk musics were being dispersed widely at that time. many of these foreign, or ethnic, musics had previous to this been heard in the families belonging to those cultures. now they were being given more free play.

one reason this was happening was recorded music had reached a new state of evolution. effective LPs had been invented and now 30 minutes of music could be heard at a time, instead of the 78rpm records, which was around 10 minutes per side.

there were pioneers who introduced music to the u s a, for instance, the so-called 'british revolution' in music, the beatles, the rolling stones; and from america, jimi hendrix and bob dylan. america was on a period of discovery of music that had yet to be assimilated. this would take some decades, and is still going on. where english music made it's largest contribution to the cultural shifts going on in the 1960s was rock n roll music—the steady eighth-note of the beatles and the stones had never been heard in popular music.

...

there is so much available in music, one could spend a lifetime studying, listening, and performing it. i could have done so quite easily, except for the loss of exactness i experienced in the early 70s leading to the new interest in words. music has always represented 'exact notes at exact times', i know persons like john cage didn't necessarily write in that vein, but that was how i perceived music in those days.

words were a flurry for me, mostly because i didn't understand some of the more difficult texts that were available then. these were real challenges. no one likes something that is too easy.

poetic structure can be modeled after musical structure, by this i mean, classical music structure. or, one can invent new structures, not, for instance, tercets, or rhymes, or sonnets, necessarily — but, more ambitious structures. in my writing, i prefer the longpoem, because a denser and more complex structure can be created, or composed. studying music composition has, for me, been very helpful in writing these longpoems.

SEM: Every so often on a listserv or discussion blog, the issue of "why write poetry" emerges. Perhaps this issue is destined to re-emerge at increasingly frequent intervals. Regardless, what are your thoughts about this question as it is re-posed in mid-2007?

PG: this is a complex question going as far in depth as the psychology and inspiration of each poet. 'why write poetry?' i suppose the quick, but true answer is 'one has to'.

for some odd non-reason, the best writers go through living as youths reading, then in one special moment, one develops the wish to be a poet. either one is a poet straight on, which is rarer; or one learns by trial and error; or a new poet can go through a period of formal study.

in the year 2007, it is even more vital to write poetry. with the language being usurped by technology-speak, or bad political-speak, untrue media-speak, global corporation-speak, watered down-homogenized poetry-speak, the wonderful vocabulary of the english language being remade into meanings with an agenda-speak, these are all activist reasons to write — and especially now, in 2007.

but, to my mind, these reasons are not valid or true reasons to write poetry. poetry is a craft and a transmitter of inspiration. if one can produce inspiration in one's poetry, then it is timeless and can be written and read in 2007, 1807, or 2207.

if one writes to tell truth to language, one will never go wrong in one's writing.

SEM: Would you address how you work with the two disciplines of writing and painting/drawing? I recognize that you prefer not to mix them, but I know that you are alternately active in the two fields, and that you continue to meet with success in each.

PG: if there are two art-forms on intended for a surface that are more different than each other, i'd have to recommend visual art and writing. there is always the difference between the two sides of the brain: the right-side, or the left-eye, being for visual work; and the left-side for the right-eye for written work. i recall reading somewhere, some artist saying that if a person were to keep her/his right eye closed as much as possible when looking at the world, they would become a great artist.

one's power of observation is important in each format—in art it's to visualize, look at, the forms on the surface by stepping back to be accurate in one's appraisal of one's work-in-progress. that's how one can go about getting a deep experience of one's art, enabling one to mature as an artist. [it should be noted here that the visual arts have progressed far beyond working on a surface-only, and what's called 'visual art' can be many things.]

in writing, it's different, as far as i can see, especially in poetry, an attempt to classify sensations in, or to define the art of, engage more mystery. for me, writing has always been a spiritual matter, 'spiritual' as differing from 'religious', is meant here, 'religious' including here the formal side of the same essence called when without form or external observations, 'spiritual'. matters of the spiritual, i try to think, are of importance here, and if one can keep that ideal in front of oneself when writing, one's writing will be special.

of course, what one brings to art or writing is what one is, naturally. there is no way to hide, if one can 'keep one's eyes open' one can see the inner world as well as the exterior world. early on, i learned the 'forms' of poetry, trying them out a bit, then decided the forms cannot be of much assistance in learning more

165

of the spiritual side of art and poetry. the forms can help in learning about religion which always needs some external structure. i like to fancy the structure of recent writings i've composed are pinpointed to the 'beyond'. in art i try for more traditional matters, producing work which could be loosely called 'abstract expressionist' with fauvist colors.

SEM: How does blogging as a pursuit strike you? What value does it have? To what extent do you read or view blogs?

PG: a while ago, i started a blog named 'misc-texts' which is visible at: http://misc-texts.blogspot.com

it is a closed blog, in that non-members can view it, but only members can post and comment.

the blog is, in my mind, both a failure and a success—this, maybe, by the way it was set up, i don't know. at the beginning, there was a lot of interest, and everything seemed to be flowing easily, but like many human projects one is involved with, i became uneasy. there were less than half of the members participating, and everything became very intense for me.

it succeeds grandly now, as a place for members to put whatever in experimentation they wish on the blog. the writing is or a high level, this is because i fancy myself as administrator to have chosen excellent writers.

the odd turn of events remains that i have set it up, but dont participate. this is because of the reasons mentioned above, and that i could not establish in my mind how i wanted to interact in the blog.

i suppose blogging as a solo venture can be valuable, recording one's daily thoughts, and i would not judge a blog by how many readers it attracts. as far as i['m concerned, if the poet feels it necessary to blog, then more power to her/him.

SEM: Poetry is not immune to the rock star or blockbuster syndrome, in which a few, "name," presences become and remain known commodities, at the expense of a wide acknowledgement of new directions in the written or oral arts. To what extent has this hurt poetry, or is the situation a permanent fact of life?

PG: it is perhaps that this does better for the readership than the individual practitioner of poetry. when there are fewer individuals to deal with the public is clearer on what something is and what choices to make. for instance, the line from a joni mitchell song i recall going something like 'going crazy from too much choice'.

is this beneficial for the large group of working poets? yes and no. yes for the poets having that stature, i suppose, but even those 'celebrities' often go astray from 'pure poetic creation', relying on their 'name value' to assure future lower quality writing issues under their name. there are other pitfalls as well.

also, to what degree is large fame in the serious arts desirable? if the writer has a large ego that needs to be satisfied with the constant attention given to it that accompanies such a position, then perhaps it's a desirable option. for other more practical ones, the best outcome is the 'time' and 'health' and even an amount of 'peace of mind' and 'financial security' that enables the best poetic endeavor to go on. in this manner, they are allowed the best arena to let their talents flourish, without the distractions of survival's necessity or added interruptions to their efforts.

SEM: If you were to predict some desirable futures for poetry and writing, what would they be?

PG: this is a curious question because i will answer it as i see my view of which future poetry and writing can have, and in this i'll be completely subjective. much of the answer re poetry i'd like to triumph in the future can be seen by scrutinizing the list of titles and authors i have published as potes & poets press and now blue lion books and small-chapbook-project.

for poetry, i have published only a fraction of the texts i could envision possible. ultimately, a congregation of presses would only start this project. books should arrive in any number of forms: with pages of differing materials, pages bound together or left separate, covers of these books in all or pure white or black covers, texts printed in all colors, with any configuration of the previous: by single authors, collaborations between poets, between poets and musicians—the 'book' to be accompanied by a compact disc or a reading or not, poets and painters, poets and any other artists, dance recitals where the poetry has been written specifically to accompany the dance and recorded on a dvd for dissemination later, between (and this is hard to imagine possibly) poets and people of all disciplines: poets and philosophers, poets and engineers (for instance, a building with phrases written in each room, a bridge with text on the part viewable from the street below (not too safe a project as the cars speeding under the bridge try to read it realize);

and the essence of poetry, people talking in poetic terms—for instance, a spoken text like a play, spoken words to be heard on cd or dvd.

at the base of this project you will notice that these permutations are uses of 'the text'. a text is more or less nothing other than words make of letters and/or pictures to be viewed and evaluated by the eyes as agents of the semantic function, if one exists, of a person, any use of a text that is imaginative and not related to a let's-call-it-a-mundane use, can be called 'poetic text'. these are not the only definitions possible, and i believe all writers should come up with ones of their own. ideally there will be as many definitions as persons writing. the persistence of the text is, to me, the goal of writing in the future.

there is writing, there are letters and words, etc, but the root of it all is 'the text', the semantic-carrier conveying what the letters intend to give to the reader and writer.

from re the after

re-wrench a rose, the collar, the strophic malleability normal for insistence, gowned for a gesture, implication re the affable effacement. non none the trick allowance. majuscule templates over slippery, tones terrorizing a territoriality announced into beginning as re-arrange, mirrors out tigers loan words on treat threats. mundane occupations re-afford which sporadic lien licensed otherwise boon of faraway the crocuses redeem. as collectors, arlesienne for tame shopwritten the fardels implicate what they imply, thoroughly wafting no none, list lyrical motions moron. uniquely attentive toll booth collector, a grange open for seldom, re-opt cellophane thousands later oneself nucleated strangely on an appropriate motile born agon. frame to bolster at romps reined dowsers, headroom close chorus, nine technological when writ renders an improbable motion for laddered out of sky, bluely the affordable amazing, pick up a rarely tunneling, somewhere a dandor, problematic could have doorways installed. as a crocus, advertent to emollient mortises lurid arrowhead over the thin bridge chaos. mutants norm that in renamed issues. an amount dos-matrix skittish the vulnerable in aorist motivations. algernon there on terrace noon veracity not more the agent of affability, boeing card vacuums meld imperative hold overs framing peace those tiers of detenté in as monad mind sirens of peeve notated out of clash modality, on sombrero assuming stabilization emcees throaty vinyl not there iamb contingency uptown notion. vellum krakow vestiges more even affable to mordent lassitude in correctives, the chokehold vulnerable to efficacy, nothing wills a commonsense trailer park seen through windscreen notes. as vales omit nothingness by harrowing a fond mein geraniums or vast conquerors un-treat everything goes, latency of pulled ouch. noah intention for gratitude once old hammers out of partition volce in the amplitude of messengers. wafted outcasts nor blue-lettes martinets cadmium red intend roves thtough intense factitions of pleasing ceramic accolades, one one and another then ordinal posthaste veerings made to crinkle achievement-families, while process devaluations empiricizes whitely in front eyelid normal toe retinues noesis contuse parroting witnesses from a gag-order on tenancy behaved. as a conducement top raffles onus those to retain somewhere assumptions swift to virtuoso the flares errant oversight to project beautiful warm positive thoughts, on broadway issued out of sleigh-bells a fantail wasting in the wingspan of determinate ocean. a continent of wordships, each lecturing each those to rename wilderness out of carrying laquer bunnies the revenuers contuse noon understood as midnight. one soprano they thetis reminds everywhere on andirons factor affreux noted. In vendetta a skip and a niblet of chase manhattan whose throughput inventions meet on slow shoppes nowhere seeming less opaque i promontory of the evidence meerschaums dice. a prelude to cake silencer theory's behest of mit mid mir myopia and wholly if answerable is nominal the vacuous rendition rendered as precipice scaled for flagrance of destination, an announcement revalues eerie bravery once itemization of curtailing essence in travelogue, thought gags out of nothing doing going nowhere sudden though iteration's claque nary schemes. a cord of ferrite wicca-burns on wrist, patent miffed by while documentation scoffs yet does not. whom tiers out of house performing calligrams tertiary avalanche. weeping condoning trick rashers vortices nostrum in as choruses derive motions out of sky. where competition rarely no harvest finds foresting commonsense the bail-out voiced out of semaphore corona trash-heaves those slash evidence to barriers spottage unsure. snarls through awareness toggle notion swift to avail of thumper glass-redundancies there fostered on lava moot vocals. de-hinged from spacious tamp-downs alliegance lateral write of walrus oars, the menial brocade is wondering contact, i e, process of trajectory in arrogating molecules contrasting where blue-lettes mend trial huddling tactics. plastic is renegade as vocations flock where neither irony acumen coldly terrestrial, the spot choice weal of reaping song in satori. tarps set on field-house walls, a simple reversing of atomosphere carries that ocean one step further, without effect or wuthering heights insomnia thousands later. amazing sortileges burnished with cloud, as noise wires out of erp eons laddered intention flex bleach annapurna, though once never befuddles ramifications slumping reversing slickly sandal out of spread frames, their heirophant wills to find language's similitude to itself in agora-purna in ahoy noesis bearing out officially the cadre loutish hatter willows enough stoppage might skip thinking's infusion moot care for impends a major, in clash consequent the force to indemnify knowledge's oceanic contrast with reality, an irreality nestles paces out of the already gone through sights of both unruly attend afterthoughts flex boar's head. a tingle seeds mores for thematic dispassion, mumbling numb waterfalls corsages er noesis oversight overlooks therein tarpaulin idem, the harrowing avails. table balance turn tornado, voiceover at rearranged infinity, a conceptual why to aspire is ideation else or elsewhere, dis-allowance of question marks, reflects. a k a the relativity while packing sombreros, whichever opera wires out of clarionette seek savor norms of passel, a traveler without keepsake though hassling with and within key's retching, wholly that. very nicely sacked out of workshops the contention masks no slather of narrowness thoughts accrete impaling moebius choices one affording laces to cohort's lecture, word kept. stabilizing a redux, from preposition theory which pop-up skin, vacant noise of wordless patina, the shortfall the union of wideness in voice, parachutes of the mindstyle those the word's irreal indication form already which shield actualizes. buds on task-bars, thoughtful compilation more agenda rinse ritornelli vessels out officers'

bloat from cajoling. acting with rulerships, an dowsed is snipped forums there
traction of messages, no difference real estate in corral though abundance
reviews whittled maven's intention. so silos are foil and bent alaska through
inventions of languidity the revolving on a pulse offered main density, a
throng gatha, nothing of erasure bellwether out of wrench, taffeta space-free
coldly attends space-traction, one slowly the other harnessing the wind.
budding nominalities while loops peeve once borough whey blankets the
samples of which muffle divine scraps roving the endless tournament, on as
solid grasp not thematic owl houses meringue from which coattails, wormholes
wherever in on the hasp, one sits on correct hassocks, nodding others flaring
the amaretto is somewhere pilots docility through retention no caveat, though
wakened to impulse possibility gone impossible. a narrow andd reticent dash
in on the paper leafed through before arrival orange and/or blush abalone,
mote of sanitized effervescence troupes vacancy, its compilation errant
thinking on elemental foraging noah surf's up, no doubt watering the deal
dealt through dealer, in on pliant oceans. this, a bumpier rerouting of masks
and musketeers, the anonymous repetition wrongly focused pirouettes the
silken railing outside on staring rhodes fender oases nouns on the carryover
wash saying domes because thinks periodically. the empirical descends. the
transcendent reflects. two oppositions are independent meeting nowhere,
around the otherness an appraisal retention, one on remedial the other wooden
leggings how it's done a cake and a bellwether. no harmonic actions latté
absurd is the crimp mindset trailed through a wish-fulfillment açai ruffle.
beggared from sincerity hoot burn factored nary a pace to greet on slink
pebbles. added to tibia -correspondence whitely the chaired scores of silent
memoranda, no one territoriality compares erin go hemming siamese veldt
naming that is noesis too much annotated. chair not table. a no-choice every-
choice collides in reifications intent to appease midline futures, remote coal
seeks raised through a defensive parallel on nowhere's loop. alliance's motion
safety of therefore in a swirl noah swoons to prize, nougat in on the arrogated
influx of everywheres. the consortium narrow, then wide, some pale struggle
lucid nascent in relatedness withheld from. each dint of retention so cohorts
impale talents for while tiers on perfumed linz crackers determine sufferance
the rodent motionless. giving reopened marionettes a choice to burrow abalone
corsairs, detenté lacerates ferro-magnet-ivories, tentative and though not
named in dictionaries cain oversight somberly chairs shy as ouijas nor
summershine, tattered ouvert and meant to salarize while deft is nottingham
absurd. condoning the repavement of story-goers literally the hologram
lopped off. when discretion gathers the better of valor, waft the behavior out to
sunny days boggling expesis, no narrow cake ahoy thousands of the
membranes tarot-ed for amalgam to residual borrowing. sahara gashes

mindstyles empty wringing sorts scraping widely chock impediment burrowing noah, rend to render then situate to rendezvous, perhaps ahoy thoroughly. so as nothing o'er the badinage moebius cambers brought toast intention for mannerisming a trait formless though allegro wishful an route. a book call real though thought catches a catacomb either inventory solace nor pessimist, domes of curious harness startled midnights mainlined noons darning a calligramme on parataxis' environment withheld, amity eroded raining cahiers, themselves roving the acumen opaque for swift that stated nor lair of denizens already. so swift bundling crowns windows the yoke of burden, humanity already escaped hollow er natural categories. a k a the seldom in vacation moribund in through trounce welling up to advantage otherwise notional craving, term alright noah theme toe hold, now irreal conducement the awitchment awake over the sighted how the linkage links arrive contrasting is themselves as import to comparison to evidence precisely wherever whereas not nowhere ever backtracking on slow fizzle on a crockery of acumen, evidence in rapport wide of marrow that coldly practices the emulatory finesse of danger appeased. so wan as to behold ironic thrice afterthought, each least the motion prevented the nuance softened owl hats everyone wants seeking so thisness another tack mess of crash elves nodding slowly a particle crosses the room imagine the religious holiday trouble-free in gaining each. where what looks likely imperative morsel those combining the evolution in meountainsides and determinants, viz the calendar where tiling replaces is, an announcement just coerced politic nounal it sakes of meandering inducement gotten used tofu outer capital refinancing thoughts in advance of erasure, their amounts no aggression viaducts necessary as transfer is revolving door. night, nub of the treaty treatise, on which weeping slices marinade velcro doublets there stained however as if could write elsewhere itself the holding pattern ironic. as in perfection though lost, unknowable tucking into sleep admonishing trepidation ministry of élan the core ready bent somersault-roping into caution, narration wales the contrast to endurance though not really savor yammering the throat of laity, mumbo-jumbo of prizewinners their soft surveillance nouns the rapport, in an owl roaring the nautical milliseconds laugh. coinage seeming the percentage voiced monads slightly apportioned leaving the lag-tithe stunned outer ridge roadhouse, marring a scheduled visitation lacewings to the queuing somewhere over-thought-of, so relationally-challenged is vacation forming while dardanelles, though noon perishes the advantage of memory, not a glib chorus each maybe ten or weeded information wilderness solfeggio narrow rasa the tone settling rill of ague notation so spacious temperance template which why not a lot thrown into resistance packages, limelight warden-hood the skeletons ruffle a car load of ostentatious heavies, the purse over rafters not recognizes thoroughly one sapping early returns, the mannerism with lien into crossed lines before shoot compares with apostolic a vantage punctuum. until roebucks target astral mummifications theory waits windless on a ten-foot occam's razor is anything paix du vocality meandering wolves rake intention under a wall of transience in that witnessed framing urgently. the dancing swarm through inventory-after-the-deluge returns the arrival nearly seized witnesses on overlay thinking seldom laertes settlement interesting view of paradox mendering thrice policed out of crash terminal ibex motionless for intensity cordons off attilla those of boardwalk simulacra, practice. while awake three houses determining traffic patterns slow quiet streets, lithe bundlers maintain severance. amounts of osso bucco style elevation the memory crowned big caterpillar sodium licenses the sabine accursed maintained schedule presentation of elongation of natural duff, some else nowhere apportioned, given last the nightshade so lagging bereft tingles on grist of paisley, mountains reflect is the nation revolving, stomach for iteration behaving. each presently natural one accursed or peaceful, matter in stasis something larger more realistic, tardis in on the fluid statement precisely. the is of witnessing summershine invoked motion within sabine crysalises, a mouth well of nounal crispness impedes is has therefore wide the slippage informational bureaucracy, while poot text the switching out of bureaus on finally a zigzag morris dance is svelte lacing downtown intention from to sostenuto especially headroom chary the advance under febrile natures smooth torchon there staved off imperatives the mantra licensed not having is, that therefore bags out of ire and mutation, small changes amount the essential chorus, later though not. in uniqueness, contemplation. revolving through a narrative then so anodyne parsecs southern to assortment devote alligators in one's shoes, an integral partition salves mention each license driven as solid. imagination leafs throaty-walls one rooftop candor nothing seen the relegation ore oneself. near shoebox, stall therein special, throughout is no preciously determined labor clearing mighty slumber. thine theatre forest doorway in chorus delegated feudal moonsongs those replotted for editorial corsair is not senescent tool of roving therefore tarried there long-term irony, closed in as it is suchness' bottleneck the hallowed met with. attenuation for astral glyphs, recognized tailing around the world by needless one once lightens a trespass with cloud cover is each there to foreground alacritous motions, notate under scrutiny which is hidden fusillades total egocentricism, perhaps some candor least the concern cahoots burning metal under pressure. pleat to remind scat-singer, the vermin assume is trellis bounded for wilderness some small ice breaker holding, atopos, the least is thinly sharpened plasma voiced over intention the institutional breakdown not original, somersaulting over range and erasure, no wi-fi. a thirist vanishes, nouned as solves the immune system intent in large

antisocial beggary, the equation stork-bundled no harbor trouble-free is
extensive that magnet, smacking downtown light-poles the electronic
figuration below ten. raw data emerges, so consultations attenuate,
maintainence referees thine plasma inner loci needled out official mortises,
crowned impediments thousands gnash, floribunda noon of restructuring
sepia-cleaned viscera, the condiment or container willowly prescient for a main
torrent there symbolized thinking otherwise therefore effort reaps orison
fortuitously errors reflect erasure however thought-to-be hands out of vestigial
hollowness, a personist value mending scratchy risks, northern outside widely
premonitory curtailment at clenched fist oneself unfurling bags inchoate
coincidences synchrony provides in symbol. a sass to emulate pioneer ego-
shell-game, energy potion merovingean once knotted outside warded often
smarmy pullets, gripped to dearly announce on the twentieth, no fold
unturned slick feint. tenterhook invalid this tenacious manticore voicing
emirates thinking so lacerations blankly etiological therein spacious reopeners
oneself, nitrate why therefore, under nitrogen somersault the discretionary
lurch, border least alienation more tallow grotesque mirrors elastic for a gaggle
of putty. manticores least returnees from lemma thought-to-be wildernesses of
fluid tropes, noah only onerously profligate widening something a festive
tarrying northern each fortran lido the parameters, walk the corridors, elves in
harpoon on the shelf theist, marionettes engulfed soon floating the candor
expectation more the elementation of service-center residues. each lecture
attention to already a nature mindful of script under relata, one a version
roving assumptions nothingness wildly proposes the feint through friendship
initiation of elliptical mountains before betwixt. chopped twine riven
earthmover text-driven how motion reinscribes a dorsal mindset braving the
fringes of being, the machinery arable photography, needing syllogism a
parallel to empathy some boots out of ebbing saltines, normal outages on briar
abbots. re how changes coincident to nothing ahead or beowulf would scamper
itself, vanishing themes restructure a falconer oiling coppers. blank ice strata
infiltrate from outward to intention's course of deleria, no mode
simultaneouses its crowd-conduction of for willingly appearing in siphon those
tor renegade the filament of charm. wily omit controlling motion emergent
roominess appotomax cilia, vlast of pepper-system avoidances those empty
those regalia. nowhere larger to those impounding electric folly on voiceover
salutes, punch amen those swarthy if is, thensome to impala modestly one on
bearing trade affliction more silenlt those tools in grade of silkinesss, overshot
as poitrine the switching off noticed in house another verification to expect, the
this will to weed outside an unmindful ramification noon's ultrafine
immanence, nine contentions vale across implosive malediction, nor the
acccolade on triumph merciful the renegade as will not and not heave. surname

In lotus peace, more the sulk fetal monday, either willowly opaque on somber mien for of tensilar noon clodded out of obtrusion boor in tenners volute more themselves in part for the graciousness aplomb. an narrative which fallout impedes oversight nor tallow, norm to the exacto night murals seized on iamb of cellulose tampering. weed tertiary motion the simulacra one once settled impounds formulaic thoughts of rendition, moon. strutting emporium the knotted swirls tenancy more omission there frigidaire the nonesuch of sequences, nailed to bodily fumigation structures. elongation which defers one salute annotate is whatever nothingness expulsion thought to behave willowed knotting rafter. so similar the condiment of persists however consciousness took tokens out of amplitude-in-reasonability-not, noesis the broom of delicacy nearly without staple, the regimen to prowl not topically though. adamantine viveka, noodle on crawler hotmail no grainy stride, the epochal irons in tactile foresting somewhat therein on the restructuring of pale diversity, no halycon determinations waste formal prolations, that the being messaged for implosion thought to before once on clouded willowly the affidavit. mere license to arrange widely premarin celebes kalossi thermal switches off heat re-geration ellipses meander with illbient eaching smarmy tooks. an amphora meringues outside wilted andirons , hasty conceptual implosion, therein does migrate out of strontium novas the pulling strived outside weal of transience, narrowness labeled as forum in balcony. laughter over therein spate of formal reins therefore twenty-six elopements, sonatas the thinking waters out of shapes on the malleability within coeli donates wordless poot. as dint of near tintinnabulation re a pandemic so literally apostate lighten surfaces sedimentation wildernesses out the parallax, parallel on no space of deflection, mere to bing outwardly emplotment so lacerative the ombudsman knights a quixotic dry cough. as jumps forward, losses tom-tram, a perception mead implant stucco bartender wail of explosion ten blocks dorito sampling heater in on first floor witnesses fractal mondays. community of sacral input in the nor matrix immo random. as the yeses probe clubbed moisture, in a vacuum more that in flattened resistance to procedural mosquitos, dancing where port and poitrine select no havoc an oblique kinship of regulatory rathbones nurture devoy-multiples weal of the trot.

Joseph Lease
interviewed by Thomas Fink

Joseph Lease's critically acclaimed books of poetry include *Broken World* (Coffee House Press) and *Human Rights* (Zoland Books). His poem "'Broken World' (For James Assatly)" was selected for *The Best American Poetry 2002* (Scribner). His poems have also been featured on NPR and published in *The AGNI 30th Anniversary Poetry Anthology*, *VQR, Bay Poetics, Paris Review,* and elsewhere. Of *Broken World* Marjorie Perloff wrote: "The poems in Joseph Lease's *Broken World* are as cool as they are passionate, as soft-spoken as they are indignant, and as fiercely Romantic as they are formally contained. Whether writing an elegy for a friend who died of AIDS or playing complex variations on Rilke's Duino Elegies ("If I cried out, / Who among the angelic orders would / Slap my face, who would steal my / Lunch money"), Lease has complete command of his poetic materials. His poems are spellbinding in their terse and ironic authority: Yes, the reader feels when s/he has finished, this is how it was—and how it is. An exquisite collection!" Thomas Fink's book *A Different Sense of Power: Problems of Community in Late-Twentieth Century U.S. Poetry* includes extensive critical analysis of Lease's poetry. Lease lives in Oakland and teaches at California College of the Arts.

Thomas Fink: *Broken World* is studded with anaphora, and the musical effects are marvelous.

Joseph Lease: Thank you.

TF: Robert Creeley and many others have testified to the remarkable grace of your music. Are there some principles regarding the musical element of poetry that keep occurring to you at points in the poetic process?

JL: My work is ear driven. Language is music. When the music is right, I know the poem is done. When the music is right, your mind, your spirit, your emotions, change.

TF: Standard Schaefer—in a very insightful review of *Broken World*—said you had written some of the most memorable montages in American poetry. Often your montages involve shifting from verse to prose or prose to verse. I really love this technique when I read it. I know it's great. But I'm not sure why.

JL: Again, thank you. All I can say is that I'm trying to make change actual, to embody change. It has to do with the lyric sequence, and feeling tone, and scene structure. You can play self-consciousness, the way you can play the violin or the cello. Sincerity, for me, is emotion made actual. As Creeley said, a primary language—a rollercoaster ride, not a description of a rollercoaster ride.

TF: In *A Different Sense of Power: Problems of Community in Late-Twentieth Century U.S. Poetry*, I wrote about how your poems meditate on inter-subjectivity, the limits of the self, and the demands of the collective; and how your lyric I invites, invokes, and probes community (112). This applies to *Broken World* and your most recent poems as well. Would you say that a primary language entails solicitation of dialogue within a lyric/narrative construct of words?

JL: Yes. Sure. We're put here to mend the world—and that means the word for dawn is *others*. So a primary language can be, often is, an opening—a ritual for creating dialogue. All the poems in *Broken World* explore this theme. I think especially of "'Broken World' (For James Assatly)," "Soul-making," "Ghosts," and "Free Again."

TF: As in the powerful short lyric, "Ghosts," which commences *Broken World*, the ghost has been a recurring motif in your poetry.

JL: When I was twenty — I wrote "Anything can be a ghost" — And twenty-two years later I wrote "Ghosts," a love poem to a visionary storyteller (Donna de la Perrière, my wife) and a meditation on visionary translation — The secret meanings of colors and dawn and others and an elegy for visionary awareness of correspondences. The word for dawn is *others*=in a word the uncanny (anything can be a ghost — even a bowl of strawberries — nature is a haunted house — of an unfinished world). America equals ghost.

"I can remember my secret book —

    I was a ghost, you were the only one

        who could hear me — "

TF: Your visual descriptions can be even more precise than Ashbery's, but I think what you're doing in *Human Rights, Broken World*, and after indicates the absorption of both Ashbery and Creeley's different uses of enjambment within a stanzaic pattern, and of Ashbery's play of disjunction and continuity.

I'm excited about your new work. "Try," for example, uses compression in a remarkably evocative way:

        traces of snow, snow flying
            fast —

        if anybody needs
            a branch in light

        --

                don't
    panic, let time wash you, you can swim —
    the green hills turn to gray, gray turning
    blue, just say *undershirt*, just say *hair,*
    shoulders — I'm falling, I'm flying, I'm
    waiting, I'm nothing, I'm
    snow —

--

> in the forest you can say anything:
> O cream, a warm

> night in December; your hips sing, dinner makes a
> naughty dream—let's say I was Frank Sinatra's
> toothpaste, let's say I lead a life of crime—O cream,
> park your raspberries
> on my moon—

--

> if anybody needs
>   the lake's glass skin—

> traces of snow, snow flying
>   fast—

> if anybody needs
>   a branch in light—

We talked about intersubjectivity, about addressing readers regarding shared concerns, and these lines do. Even if there are only "traces of snow" and not the full presence of an abundance, that speedy "flying" might be terrifying, and the poem, as I see it, is an exhortation to "try" to endure, to thrive, to live intensely in the face of "falling," experiential speed, "waiting," and a sense, at times, that the self is "nothing."

In the third section of the poem, erotic joy comes to the forefront as a component of the task of articulation of awareness and the struggle against annihilation, the force of that earlier "nothing." In the poem's final section, you hark back to the "need" of the first section, adding "if anybody needs/ the lake's glass skin"—a remarkably *lucid* image!—before you end by returning to two couplets that also open section one. This recurrence (with a difference) is designed to ask the reader to consider how the middle sections have changed what about "need," illumination, and the fear of violent experiential speed.

Surely, contact and sexual openness have been made precisely actual in a construct of language—to paraphrase Creeley's reading of your earlier work. What else?

JL.: For me the poem embodies a kind of tenderness. I believe (many) readers will feel a gentleness in the poem—a fullness, and a tender awareness of aging. It's also a poem of erotic experience. And of course there's fear too, but the poem is a very tender motion. I hope the reader of this interview will go back now and read the poem a second time. I agree that the poem gets happier as we move forward in time, but I don't think the opening is all that terrified. There is an excitement in the emptying out of the self, of zooming away from fixed, stable conventions. There is certainly fear there, and the fear is mixed with tenderness and desire and gentleness, and as the poem moves forward the tenderness deepens. Anyway that's how I read it.

TF: Let's turn to your new long poem, "America," which has a structure very similar to the long "Free Again" in *Broken World*; each section begins with the title of the whole poem. Like the earlier poem, which I'll get to shortly, this one excoriates the right (and perhaps the center) for how they have wrecked the U.S.'s democratic potential and imperiled the entire world. There are various powerful citations, ones about ecological disaster, absurdly inhumane governmental budget priorities, Cheney's remark about the endlessness of the "War on Terrorism," and Bill Moyers' urgent call for democracy to be rescued. These are juxtaposed with synecdoches for and reflections about an individual's daily experience, brief allusions to recent national problems ("We're going back home to every vote counts we're changing the rules"), and more abstract, yet lyrical passages. Could you talk about how, through the heterogeneous textures of this juxtapositionality, you are making "America" enact political critique and redemptive exhortation and building on your past aesthetic innovations?

JL: "America" builds on "'Broken World' (For James Assatly)" and "Free Again"—and I guess it's the most "topical" poem I've written so far. Parts of it work by collage—and it's very direct. You know, we write what we need to write. Anyway, I was inspired by Susan Howe's "Hope Atherton's Wanderings," Laura Mullen's "Turn," Donna de la Perrière's "True Crime," and Adrienne Rich's "Diving into the Wreck." Also—of course—Ginsberg's "America." All these poems put America inside a self-in-process. For me fullness of representation is both an embodiment of what it feels like to think/desire/fear in the world (to contradict oneself) and a continuation (proceeding by contradiction—I can't do it/I must do it) of the lyric self. Howe and Rich and Ginsberg all refute the claim that lyric is unified or merely personal. The lyric "I" is a place. It's a process. It's not fixed and commodified. And that process becomes the ground for action, for critique and for re-imagining America.

TF: "Re-imagining America" is surely the task of "the lyric 'I'" in "Free Again," and this intense activity—which you never make into anything programmatic or anything less than a complex process of negotiations—seems to include an implicit call for people to go beyond the false consciousness that corporate elites often stimulate: for example, "I want you to stand there in your brightly frisky middle-class personalities and chant after me: 'How about another tax cut, how about another tax cut—'our wilderness' and liberty and justice for us. . ." (52).

JL: I attack the way the Republican Party since Reagan has tricked the middle class into voting against its own interests over and over, and into identifying with a political imaginary in which individualism equals upward mobility.

TF: The manipulated portion of the "middle class" sees social programs for the poor as responsible for their tax burden; they miss notions of economic interdependence.

JL: I think "Free Again" is about the absence of community and the need for community.

TF: The title "Free Again" implies a recovery of fundamental democratic principles so that what was always theoretical in the U.S. can become actual. To go back to the idea of "re-imagining America," I am interested in passages in "Free Again" that provide subtle intimations of the transcendence of current injustice and anomie; I see the social as connected to the soul in the poem: "It could be gorgeous, it could be/ loss, it could be broken, it could fold—/ . . . the soul inventing the world/ the soul inventing the soul—" (46). What empowers you to invest in felicitous spiritual or psychological /social aspiration in the face of rampant negativity?

JL: Faith.

TF: Do you mean religious faith?

JL: I'm not an atheist or an agnostic. Part of what I mean is faith in God. You can be a left-wing Dickinsonian/Emersonian Jew. I also mean faith in the human and social justice. My version of faith breathes discovering the joy of creation. Faith and art are both ways of learning—asking—they invite us into understanding and connection with others and with the sacred. When Paul Hoover asked me whether I see poetry as a soul-making activity, I said: "Soul-making, sure. Why not? That just seems true to me. I don't want to sell poetry short. Poetry isn't just a reminder of what we already know—it can be that—but it can also create life that we need—life that we don't recognize until we are in the poem. And, yes, it also returns us to ourselves and makes us new. And it demystifies lies. I love Keats's idea that the world teaches us to make our souls. I don't see why poets would want to escape from that. In "Free Again" you have 26 variations and the total is expansion of a life, a spirit, toward others."

TF: Thank you, Joseph.

Home Sweet Home

Sky
Like whiskey and
Windows learn the
Sky
Sky like
Whiskey the
Sky and
Behind it
Lamplight

Winter Night

No.
Try again.

The illness (he thought he was "God") doesn't. No. Not
Dostoevsky. Not a man in a blue coat. Not the illness. Not the
demon. What I thought, what I. Not there. Not phrases. You
can't. Worry. You can't win. If winter. If Franz Kline. If winter.
If son or there was a something exploded. The consciousness.
The finish. The simple. And wrecked the family called.

To you.
And love, love, to you.

Vow

Authentication failed. "Dignify my renaissance." In the rhythm of hair and sky, in this telling so rivers and ledges and horses, in this so hard then, so hard and free, in this telling cradled by slow moss, breathing September. I can't break again. I want to give you this. Wander all day, sleep like a dog, sleep like a wren, sleep like a fire. ("Your eyes are made of cash and going broke.") If I fall down or dance or go across the road where orange leaves are spinning in a thin gray rain. If I fall down or dance or go.

Torn and Frayed

I felt like winter, I felt like Jell-O—we lost the word
virtue, we lost the word *sister,* two hundred years of
dark garden—it happens so fast—believe me (I know
you won't)—teeth in coffee, dentures in piss—it
happens so fast—might as well, might as well let
night in—

just laughing in a bus—

"You just want to die I mean capitalism just wants to

kill you I mean you just want and you just want—"

        Bright

           Branches

        Your

        Kisses

           Your

        Darkness

        Your

           Sky

You, you, you, you, you. Six when there's mist in the street, eight when your mouth starts to fade, nine when the drug starts to work, two when you hate yourself more. Three when you hate yourself more. Good old blank page. Slow down, green whisper, dry whiskers, ordinary twilight, ordinary, less hope. I wish I was Ezra Pound's towel. America, you can't be greed, America, you're only greed, America, one extra summer night—I wanted to (you know) feel like a giant eyeball—

"I tell you I was the stars. What do you care. I tell you I

was a green pool on a summer night, heat driving

everybody nuts. What do you care. I tell you just some

more of this whiskey."

We

    Try to

Tell the

    Truth

And rain

And wrens

    And blue

Traces of snow in the

Rain

Deep

Autumn soft

Sung moons

Some image torn into strips, February morning. New

Hampshire. Did you notice the bag on the dirt, did you

notice—the golden retriever and no one is near—I was to

be the dog. The faithful pup. And the dark was blue. And

the blue was dark. We've all seen bodies before: contact

all the fires of dawn, exaggerate, distort my angels:

perhaps the big sister, steely and confident, perhaps the

ordinary zombie, humdrum lost soul—

How

Shall I tell

You

How shall

I

Donna dreamt about Skip and when she told me she said

I'm so glad I'm with you: great, thought I: my love is

dreaming about her ex and I find that comforting: here's

the joke—*These memories, which are my life—for we possess*

nothing certainly except the past—were always with me, says

Charles—

I can't remember anything—past the crust and down to

the human, down to the want and want and want—

Your

Kisses

Your

Darkness

Your

Sky

You are

Strong very

Strong very

And words

And lost

And found

And blue

And

Green

Stephen Vincent

interviewed by Tom Beckett

Stephen Vincent lives in San Francisco where he leads *walking and writing* workshops, and is also a member of the creative writing faculty of the University of San Francisco's Fromm Institute. Recent poems and reviews appear in *New American Poetry* (2008) *Mimeo Mimeo*, Big Bridge, and Galatea Resurrects, among others *Walking Theory* (Junction Press: 2007) is his most recent book. His blog of poems, photographs, haptics and commentary is found at http://stephenvincent.net/blog/

Tom Beckett: Where did/does poetry begin for you?

Stephen Vincent: In the past several years, the poems emerge from three places. One seems entirely *impulsive*, while the other two are compelled by the informing construct of works by other poets or in response to digital photographs that I have taken.

"Walking Theory," a poem of 71 parts, initially was a pseudo-commission from Chris Sullivan, who anointed the project with its quasi-facetious title. Chris— who writes, photographs, and makes music—is drawn to what he calls "photographic language." He very much liked the visual detail in my poems. In practice, I am a walking "eye"—always telling people to take a look at this or that. Out on the streets, I am constantly "on the look," somehow magnetically drawn to any kind of *stuff*. Once I got going with this "commission." the writing took on an impulsive life of its own, where the pulse of the walk seemed to drive the emergence of each word or phrase. It was as though some inner engine took over. For about a year or so, the poems popped out, one after another.

Much of "Walking Theory" was written in the diverse neighborhoods—the Mission, Liberty Heights, Noe Valley, and the Castro—that connect with Dolores Park near my home. I always carry a journal and a ballpoint pen. While I walked, I often stopped to bring yet another new piece to the page. No matter how serious the material, the process was joyous. *Walking Theory*–the title for the Junction Press book (2007), as well—also includes extended poems from several long walks, primarily from San Francisco up and down the nearby coast.

In three or four recent projects, I used the language and forms of other poets as a way to make new work. *Transversion* is the name I've given to this process, which leads me to reverse, or make *oppositional* conversions to, line by line, the words and the tones within the poems to which I am drawn. Simply, *black* becomes *white*; a tone of *affection* becomes one of *contempt*, and so on. Initially, it's a way to explore a poem's antithetical proposition, as if a poem were a beautiful flower and this *transversive* process pulls the flower out of the ground to look at its roots, which may also be beautiful.

It is a process—at least with the work of certain poets—to which I have found myself almost demonically drawn. Perhaps it's just a knee-jerk part of the way I live in the world, where I like to turn things upside down and see what's on the other side. I make the assumption that what I see—particularly if the poem has a rich language—will include a bi-polar component. Ironically, as in the way of surreal writing exercises, the poems of others also provide constructs from which I can pull up stuff that's lurking inside my own consciousness, stuff that's been looking for a way to get into the air and onto the page! It is also a good way to write in a state of constant surprise. I can never predict what is going to come up.

To date, the transversive work has been published in two e-books; *Triggers* (Shearsman Books, 2005,) is based on the work of Fanny Howe in her *Selected Poems*. *Sleeping With Sappho*, the first 40 poems of which were published by Faux Press in 2004, was based on Anne Carson's *If Not, Winter*, her complete translations of Sappho. I have also done extensive transversive work with Louis Zukofsky's "A-22" and "A-23," Gertrude Stein's *Tender Buttons*, and Jack Spicer's *Language*. I find the transversive process a great way to explore an intimate dialog—playful and serious—with the formal challenges and language of my elders and peers.

Finally, for another kind of writing, particularly during the past two years, I take digital photographs and respond to the specific content with either poems, stories, or, occasionally, commentary. I call this work *Ghost Walks*, and I post much of it on my blog. Photographs are a great, independent way to explore language that, if left in a "pure" poem, without the counter-play of the photograph, would probably come off as an obnoxious cliché. The colors and rumpled shape of the blanket of a homeless person found on the park grass, for example, may provide permission to revisit a whole series of intimate situations and emotions.

TB: Before these last several years, what was the impetus? What woke you up to becoming a poet?

SV: I find a difference between an early childhood consciousness of experiencing the world in the manner of poetry—and feeling frustrated by not being able to articulate that consciousness—and the experience of starting to write and savoring the writing process for the first time. From when I was very young, I valued, even envied, people who could speak imaginatively and lyrically in direct response to the life around them, as well as to their histories. I grew up in Richmond, California, primarily a postwar, blue-collar town north of Berkeley, where I was doubly exposed to both university-educated people with a formal sense of *culture*, as well as to uneducated white and black people from the Midwest and South, many of whom loved to talk and spin a story with colorful metaphors, dramas, physical gestures, and so on. I grew up in a space that was still given to oral history. I also loved to read. My mom took us to the public library on Friday afternoons and, from early on, I admired people who could write a good story.

There was so much in what I saw, heard, and felt in the world and—whether in celebration or anger—I wanted to express it! As inarticulate and shy as I was, I made an instinctive decision to become a writer. When I was 15, even though my own writing was clumsy and came hard, I began keeping journals, including the occasional jab at an unsatisfying poem.

My first "wake-up call" about writing poetry came in an extra-curricular poetry workshop at University of California at Riverside in the late 1950s. UCR was at the time a very small liberal arts college (750 students), a kind of intense co-ed academic monastery stuck out in the middle of orange groves and desert sagebrush. A group of us, including professors from various departments, met once a week to share poems and criticism and to produce a mimeographed magazine. Although I was terrified of the idea of becoming a poet, instead of a political scientist or politician/lawyer, as my parents seemed to want, it was at Riverside that I first really got the poetry-writing bug! It was the heyday of New Criticism—William Empson's *Seven Types of Ambiguity* and all of that. Criticism was an intense, heady, mostly humorless process. One of my roommates insisted that he had found "the Eighth Ambiguity," while I felt my mind was turning into mental toast!

When I wrote poetry, however, I felt my whole body and imagination get into it. I was physically energized instead of drained. Much of my youth was spent on a basketball court; I found I could find a similar love of hearing and dribbling a ball down the floor in the process of making words rhythmically cross the page. Making and sharing poems, no matter how challenging, became a source of joy. Frank Bidart was in this workshop, where he also began writing his first poems. When I graduated—even as a *good student*—I knew I did not have the patience to become an academic scholar. Looking back, I can see that New Criticism was a great training for reading poems closely, a process that has stayed with me. I found myself totally exhausted from such critical work. Instead, I went on to the graduate program in Creative Writing at San Francisco State. I also very much wanted to be out of the desert and to live in San Francisco, already well-known as a place for making and hearing poetry.

TB: Talk a bit about how you came to your present approaches to poetry. Transversive writing, for example: How did that emerge as procedure or method?

SV: In early 2002, in the waning days of the *dot.com* craze, I was taking a train, an hour each way, back and forth from San Francisco to Mountain View in Silicon Valley. While I was reading Howe's *Selected Poems*, then recently published, almost instinctively, as the train bounced along, I began to use my journal to make what I would eventually call *transversions*. Through various means, sometimes word by word, at other times by the tone or intention of a particular line, I would work to make a new poem by reversing and/or altering the intention of the primary poem.

For example, in Howe's *Selected*. in a section called "The Quietist" on page 148, I go—in italics—back and forth with each of her lines:

```
Go on out but come back in
 Ascend and dive
you told me to live by, so I went
and don't tell me a thing
with my little dog trotting
 I've got a good love on the loose

As my side out of the garden
into woods colored rotten.
 A wet madrone, skin pealing, its bone bare trunk

I did this several times, out and in,
 Never stop for thought,
it was of course a meditation
 especially when the going's good

The out surrounds me now
 She's inside me, then out,
a whole invisible O to live in:
 tactile as a banana or something to munch

Tender tantrums, sky goes suddenly gray—
Spasms spring tender illuminations
still soften light but no one brings
mauve and pink


[Papers here to sign. The top of the water
Shudders under the brush of wind.]

Past? Present? Future? No such things.
        I am a young man now and a young man then:
Live live live
```

Originally I attempted a *transversion* of the two lines before the end line, but I dropped it. Whatever lines I came up with simply did not "make sense" and/or fit with the rest of the poem. And Howe's last line, I turned into two. Yes, I often break my rules! When I really get into this process, the antonym is just one of the "triggers" that transforms the work. I make the poems very quickly and rarely revise, except to delete portions of the pieces. When I was in my early 20s and it took me forever to write and revise a poem, I would have envied and hated this person I've become! My mind just goes into another gear—an almost alchemical space—in which the author's original poem becomes a scaffold, a transitional point, into a poem upon the poem. The original poem is a *palimpsest*, a foundation upon which I make something new. A serious scholar could explore whether or not my work is also having a meaningful dialog with Fanny Howe's work and critically explore the relationship of the two poems. Maybe. I did feel like I was in the middle of a dialog with her work, and I definitely ascribe to the idea that writing poetry is a form of dialog with what has been and what is being written. I am just not the one to make that kind of critical reading of *Triggers* or any of my other *transversive* works. When I publish any of these pieces, I do acknowledge the author of the foundation of the work.

Transversions are a way to unleash new work, stuff that has a life of its own, quite different from my approach to my *Walking Theory* and *Ghost Walk* pieces.

TB: Please delve into the differences. What motivated, animated, framed your *Walking Theory* and *Ghost Walk* texts?

SV: Ironically, walking as a particular "animator" of my work emerged more than 20 years ago. I was driving Folsom Street—probably on the way to pick up my kids from their after-school program—and the phrase "…walking, walking…" began to repeat over and over again, becoming a constant motion and vocalization in my head—observations, insights, and so on. I parked my car and just began *jamming*; words seemed propelled out of the pen. I love that kind of mysterious event! For the next months, wherever I went, walking or not, I filled these little 3 x 5 "Artist" sketchpad notebooks. The book, *Walking* (Junction Press, 1993) emerged from that work.

Over the 1990s and into the start of this century, the act of taking walks—urban and beyond—became an essential part of my life. The writing also became more measured. Several friends, and eventually my youngest brother and my father, were either dying or in the middle of serious medical troubles. Although I had no friends who passed from AIDS, death was also a palpable presence in the City. Walking became a form of reflection and grieving, as well

as bonding and talking with friends as we walked. Here is a passage from
"Elegy's Laundry":

```
     The beach a rigor of signs.
No blessing. The tide risen.
Trees up to the edge
ten years ago, now gone.
The sand plateau where,
once, we played volley ball
practically gone. Young,
my daughter still in diapers,
I carried her there
down the ladder
from a higher cliff,
the cliff from which
hang-gliders ascend.
People, the other adults,
it was a picnic, most
of them I didn't know,
except one of the mothers
whom I tried to date.
     They thought it was strange,
such a young daughter,
no mother, and how was I
to know what to do, or not.
I climbed back up the cliff,
daughter, undiapered, on one arm,
a little frightened,
her eyes darting out
over the fog-draped ocean,
the green & gray waves,
the diarrhea
dripping over my arm.
```

The elegies that form the first portion of *Walking Theory* took form in the days
after a walk. Pieces of conversation, encounters with others, geological shapes,
fragments of memories, and poems by others each contributed to the content of
poem. The momentum of the walk, its rhythms, its variant fast and slow paces,
ascensions and descents—especially in the walks that were several miles
long—informed the open, unfolding shape and movement of the poems. It was
as if I—as the body of the writer—were a vessel, the insides of which needed to
be poured out into the shifting container of the poem. I really enjoyed the serial
continuity of making that work.

Jack Spicer's and Robin Blaser's concept and use of the "serial poem" are a big
influence on how I shape much of my work. Rarely are my poems self-
contained, singular frames. The energy of one spills into the next—like a canal
with a series of opening and closing locks. I am also influenced by the interior

walking monologs of Leopold Bloom in James Joyce's *Ulysses* and Marcel
Proust's character, Marcel, in *Remembrance of Things Past*, both works to which I
am hard-wired, not only to their sense of visual witness but to the music of
their meanderings. The poetry of Walt Whitman and Charles Reznikoff, and
Walter Benjamins' notes and essays are also at the core of the walking work.
Nathan Whiting, a New York contemporary, who has run, walked, and written
of both, was also, early on, an influence. Over the past twenty years, other
walking influences included folks in the visual arts: Hamish Fulton, Richard
Long, David Nash for their sense of rural witness and play, and Joachim
Schmidt, a German, for his interpretive work with found objects in cities, which
are quite brilliant and fun.

"Walking Theory," the extended series of poems and fragments in the new
book, has a different momentum from the more formally realized elegies.
Undoubtedly influenced by my relatively new involvement with Vipassana
Buddhism — a walking and sitting "insight" meditative practice — the poems
strike me as more existential. That is, as I walk, my eye seems much more
focused. The poems seize on immediate details to render the material with an
almost palpable sense of presence. At best, the language becomes immersed in
what I lately call the "factual sublime." Within that sight/site some kind of
interpretive insight is also usually at work. The credo is to make an insight
synchronous with facts discovered on the ground:

// .

STEAL BACK
YOUR LIFE
stenciled in black letters on the sidewalk.
Sweeping the street - a tall young man emblazoned with a red
                              dyed crew-cut,
a large star shaved into the back of his skull.
A young woman with a large, silver-plated unicorn pinned over
her heart, on a black silk jacket.
Seven-thirty this morning: post-lunar eclipse, pre-Halloween and
pre-election.
in front of the Star Wash, corner of 17th & Dolores.
A world in transition, dark times, optimistic and not. Hard to read
either personal or social conditions. Disturbance
about this.
On the hill at the Dolores Park a young woman gyrates her hips
to the slow motion. Doucement. Doucement.

In *Walking Theory*, I also began to expand my concept of a walk to include other
activities, including reading books, acts of the imagination, and remembrance.
Walking became a metaphor for strolling through any of these parts of the

world. *Transversions* are also my own way of walking among and being in dialog with the writing material of others. Walking or not, every act becomes a kind of critical reading and response, as well as a form of opposition to a life of passive, cultural consumption. Maybe hyperactive in spirit, I have never been good at sitting back and soaking things up like a sponge!

Ghost Walks are works that take things to another level of visual dialog. For the past couple of years, during my walks, I often take digital photographs. I tend to focus on objects that either throw me off kilter or fill me with an immediate sense of awe. For example, the blankets of the homeless I found to be provocative, often sensual, physical shapes, designs, and colors. The blankets have been ghosted. We do not who slept within them. As in the *transversion* process, the blankets become a foundation and means to give an imagined, fictive life to the world of the former inhabitants, including their dreams, origins, love lives and losses.

```
Alive or dead the royal ones remain sumptuous
One can tell by the way they sleep at night
No doubt in couples, the way the curled folds lead one to imagine:
The question is, why do they beckon one
With their sensuality, particularly, such pure white
Pleated tenderness? What do they give us?
A pure love for the edge, that grace note between earth
Whatever is beyond. The beloved guile
An agile ness in the eyes of angels.
```

Writing is a constant invocation of ghosts. In the passage of time, moment-to-moment, everything becomes ghosted. Nothing is permanent. The objects I encounter and photograph permit in my writing a dialog that gives me, and the work, a larger imaginative life in what is a quite diverse neighborhood, a *neighborhood of ghosts*. Such objects infinitely vary from advertisements, shop and house windows, scaffolding and tarps, parade costumes and masks, graffiti murals and street detritus, among much else. The stuff invariably provokes the improvisation of a poem or story, or the possibility of one. The sight, for example, of two faded American flags—one small, one larger—hanging parallel and down in front of a dirty, chenille curtain provokes a political reflection:

```
We live in a fading country.
My wife said that.
I am not married.
My country is an ex-wife.
She has moved in with a violent man.
She lives behind curtains. Flags. Signals.
Not a ghost.
```

Not a ghost of a chance.

Window on 22nd Street, between Guerrero and Valencia, San Francisco, California. >

Ideally, the humble, *found* character of images permits the writing to leap spontaneously from *micro-* to *macro-* without sounding painfully pretentious, but more ironic. It's the old adage that simple things *can pull up huge things,* particularly those that are aching to get out of your insides. For example, I had not been able to address my sense of loss and love for both the person and work of Robert Creeley. I did not want to force anything. One day, about six months after he died, I photographed a white basketball backboard in Dolores Park, its orange rim and white net catching the last angle of sun on a Fall afternoon. When the image went up on my monitor at home, almost instinctively I wrote:

Basketball Hoop

Autumn & the juice returns. The rhythm. Slap on the ball. Drum beat patter against floor, against asphalt. Youth re-enfolds. Leap taken, not taken. Jump shot, long shot, lay-up, fake here, fake there, drive. *Drive*, one never stops saying. Backyard, Elementary, Junior, High School, College, Pro. The rhythm of one's life, one's season, the delivery: one's shots, one's defenses, one's gifts: the high arc of the ball drifting down:

In memory, Robert Creeley, passed this year. (2005)

Initially, I had no prescribed intention to write a memorial for Creeley. The piece was more my celebration of my life-long love of basketball. But that word, *drive,* evoked the association with those off-repeated lines from his "I Know A Man":

...drive, he sd, for
christ's sake, look
out where yr going.

Those lines became an instruction to a generation-my own-to keep moving, *attentively*, and not slack in either poem or body. *Certainly*. Right down to the level of working with syllables, *drive,* that sense of momentum, has been my credo. In my piece from the photograph, *drive* was the word that keyed the association and deep importance of Creeley's work and his example to my own.

As I move along, my attention to the visual world through photography and the potential it provides in relationship to text becomes more important to my work. I see working with the two mediums as another way of forming an aggressive, imaginative, and interesting, if not always loving, dialog and partnership with a world. It's my way of pushing back and moving forward to let the art reclaim an active, meaningful presence in my day-to-day life. It might not be lucrative to work this way, but it's both challenging and fun. Initially I publish most of these pieces online, either in electronic magazines or on my blog. If the work permits a sense of liberty on any level to any one, it's done its job!

TB: Do you feel as a poet that you have any special social responsibilities?

SV: Of course! I try to bring my tools as a poet to a way of critically looking, hearing, and responding to the various worlds in which I live. That does not mean I am interested in public office, though I am tempted to get on the City's Pedestrian Safety Board. Sixteen people, including five elders, have already lost their lives crossing streets this year alone. Give me somebody with a cell phone to his or her lips while turning their car through a crosswalk—especially into one that I am about to step, it makes me go ballistic. Not everybody is able to drive and talk at the same time. From a solid, active-citizen perspective, instead of yelling or slapping the backs of moving cars—*pedestrian rage*—I figure I should put that energy into a more positive, responsible form.

In politics I am no doubt deeply shaped by the political and aesthetic movements of the sixties and seventies where I was deeply immersed the Civil Rights movements, including black, Latino, gay, and feminist consciousness actions and reactions! In the arts, I was deep into jazz (John Coltrane, Ornette Colman, Cecil Taylor and the Art Ensemble of Chicago), the predictable folks in the rock world, and theater, Jerzy Grotowksi, Bread & Puppet, The Living Theater. Folks that were making work to take the top off the world were my bread and butter! My generation was deeply affected by the polar drive towards liberation from the politics of war and racial and other oppressions while, at the same time, strongly colored by the forces that led to the assassinations of both Kennedy brothers, Martin Luther King and Malcolm X. Forces, I am sorry to say, that remain central to life in this country and abroad.

I grew up in a very politically oriented family. A six-acre Federal Park in the East Bay is named after my folks (*Barbara and Jay Vincent Park*) on the City of Richmond's Marina. Both were civic activists with a long involvement in environmental issues, including the development of parks, trails, and recreational sites. My mom was actually on and chair of the City Planning Commission. I grew up around a dining table always keen on discussing local, state, and national political battles. Unlike the family backgrounds of many poets, I suspect, the political involvements of my parents and their friends gave me an organizational head. When I was young I thought I could network and organize anything! I transferred those skills into developing California's first statewide Poetry-in-the-Schools program and two publishing houses—my own, Momo's Press, and Bedford Arts Publishers.

Like several poets of my generation, in both leading and setting up workshops in the schools, I felt it was my responsibility to get writers to come into the schools where we could work with students and teachers—no matter their age or grade—to teach them to value poetry and to activate their own writing through imaginative exercises. As we were mostly young poets, we approached the work with a great feeling of fervor and pride. We were probably overly zealous and condescending, if not degrading, toward the limits of the host teachers and schools! The program's impulse was to introduce poetry in such a way as to demystify the poet as a distant public figure.

Ultimately, I found teaching creative writing repetitious. At that time I also taught at San Francisco State and the San Francisco Art Institute. The results seemed so temporal. I turned my interests and imagination to publishing where I felt I could produce books with a lasting impact. Influenced by the strong tradition and examples of poetry publishing in San Francisco (Auerhahn Press, White Rabbit, and City Lights, among others), I had first published books when I was in Nigeria in the Peace Corps in the mid-sixties. From the early 1970s, both presses that I began included a political awareness.

Momo's Press, and *Shocks*, our magazine, produced titles reflective of issues raging through this nation in the late 1960s and early 1970s. Racially diverse, Momo's Press published the first and early books of Jessica Hagedorn, Victor Hernandez Cruz, Ntozake Shange, Beverly Dahlen, and Hilton Obenzinger, among many others. But it was hardly a press driven by "ethnic" identity. I wanted a variety of good writers from different backgrounds and aesthetics to appear in the same arena to explore what those contrasts would do to the language, as well as to reflect the larger social/political scope of the City by which we had begun to define ourselves. The books and magazine were quite successful. Unbeknownst to the mainly white-owned publishing industry, the Civil Rights movement, gay liberation, and feminism had begun to create a huge potential audience. Obviously, industry publishers began to figure that out by the 1980s and 1990s. Ironically, in contrast to my desire to collect good writing and writers as an *ensemble*—interesting because of its inherent conflicts and potential to create new work—the large publishers and institutions drove things in the direction of promoting "identity-centered" writing—black, Latino, and Asian. This often led to audience segmentation by race and, often, the aggrandizement of a kind of ghettoized writing. That did not interest me much.

After the demise of Momo's Press, I became the director of Bedford Arts, an art book press, from the mid-1980s until the early 1990s. I stretched this diverse vision of publishing to include books by nineteenth- to late twentieth-century artists, photographers, sculptors, and writers from across several continents, from America to Japan to Europe. Until the collapse of the economy and the art market, that work was fun and deeply engaging. We were able to do many beautiful, provocative books. I stopped writing poetry almost completely. Working with authors, artists and great book designers, as well as promoting and distributing books became *the poem.*

These days, my blog has become my little publishing house. It is where I produce my own new poems, photographs—including *Ghost Walks*–as well as commentary on poetry and political turns of events. The blog serves as a public incubator for new work and as a means of reflecting and measuring the public pulse. It's also a way to sound off when I want to. I get between 1000 and 1500 visitors a month. Some stay for 5 seconds; others stay for up to 30 minutes or more. The blog gives my work more exposure and feedback than most of my books and publishing projects. However, I still prefer edited, designed, and finished books as the crystallization of poetry in its most significant public manifestation. Blog entries roll off into the sunset to disappear without much long-term weight! The whole paradigm is changing. Monitor and book manifestations will eventually find a good mix, to which I look forward.

So as *poet-citizen* I have employed my tools variously. My poetry mentors in spirit—Kenneth Rexroth, George Oppen, Charles Reznikoff, Charles Olson, Louis Zukofsky, Lorine Niedecker, Allen Ginsberg, Amiri Baraka, Ed Dorn, among many more—always revealed a public ear to the ground. This poem from *Walking Theory* sums up something of what I am about as a citizen on the street:

9.

Walk poverty: an architecture to look
closely her gray synthetic leather purse
shreds into loose shingles, the heart
let loose among buildings without trees,

```
the lobbies of the dead, people who lean
variously to struggle with reason against
an architecture born deadly, the empty
Sunday playground, blue, yellow and white structures,
a vacuum unbound, wall-to-wall piss,
the street stutters, step-by-step, who can tell of the poor,
the decorum of the poor? Good-bye rhetoric, the desperate,
what can the poem do, walking, step-by-step:
witness, suffer, hope.
```

The task of the poem is still about words, including the energy, intelligence, and imagination that shape and give integrity to each line. It's about bringing a blowtorch to clear out drivel—whether that is the speech of politicians and advertisers or the impotent, self-destructive internal chatter that sabotages our capacity for insight and appropriate action. That does not mean you cannot have fun, or that *fun* and *play* are not also politically important to our communal well-being. Finally, for me, the best poetry—in the political and most other senses—is about looking and listening closely.

TB: What are you most preoccupied with right now?

SV: I have several current preoccupations:

1. *Inventory!* My mother once said that even though I appeared to be listening closely, I did not speak a word until I was two years old; when I finally began to talk, I spoke in compete sentences. My poetry career is somewhat similar. Though I have always written and never taken my eye off some concept of myself as a poet the number of books I have published (five) is quite small. Yet, about the time I hit 60—age, not speed!—I began to write like mad, finishing whole, raw manuscripts, one after another. *Triggers, Sleeping With Sappho, Walking Theory, Tenderlies, Zuk, After Language / Letters to Jack Spicer*—each came tumbling out one after another. A kind of mania! But now, with the exception of *Walking Theory*, I have much real work to do around getting all this new work edited and navigated toward book publication. Yes, it would be nice to have an intern to help manage all of this paper!
2. *New writing projects.* The walking work—including the *Ghost Walks*—is expanding now in the direction of a greater sense of investigation of the City. Lately, on my blog, I have been using the street photographs to explore *typologies*: shop windows, stencil art, signage and graffiti, scaffolds and buildings, more blankets of the homeless, gardens, and so on. The work is an attempt to reveal the forces that impact an immediate, continuous sense of the City. From this investigation, the city planner in me wants to make a series of related urban constructs in the form of books and gallery shows. Fortunately,

now in the City, many people—artists, writers, librarians, and landscape are interested in collaborating toward similar—architects, among others goals.

3. *Haptics*. I've given that name to a drawing project that involves hearing sounds in various parts of the City, then registering those sounds with the touch of pen to paper, often in the panels of an accordion-fold book. The marks on these pages form a visual *syllabary*, where the shapes and durations precede the making of letters and words, a not-fully-formed calligraphy that acts as the rhythm and music that precede language. I love the physicality of making the *haptics*. With my pen and paper I feel like a one-person instrumentalist responding to the fluid, noisy forces of the material world. Currently I have been putting photographs of these pieces up on my blog. But I want the *haptics* in books and galleries! There is interest in publishing an artist book in which 24 accordion-fold panels reflect my experience of listening to the ocean. For twelve days I went down to Ocean Beach to challenge Jack Spicer's lines in the first poem in *Language*:

```
                    ...The ocean
does not mean to be listened to...
```

I will not say who won the challenge, but the listening was intense, and the blue marks, more so!

4. Age. I have a long-term creative writing project with my 91-year old mom. I suggest phrases or concepts; she dictates poems. The work is getting published gradually—much of it has been put up on my blog. She has always been a writer wannabe. Now she continues constantly to surprise me and her readers with her sense of modernity and, often, grim authority. When I suggested, for example, she give me a rhyme for "April," it evolved into this poem about the months:

```
January will open the horrible threat.
February will break off a few of the wicked.
March the winds will blow and frighten everybody.
April will break my heart.
May will come whisking through.
June is hard to decipher.
July will never stop to say hello.
August is jolly and happy for people like me.
September is hard to take.
October is full of joy for very few.
November marks the worst that could ever come.
December for many it's love and joy
But not for me.
```

Many people with aging parents are curious about what goes on in the heads of people at the end of interesting lives—let alone about their own aging process. My mother has become a window for others and me. Her poems and my commentary are working themselves into an essay.

So, yes, I probably have much more to do than I ever can. I aspire to be as honest as I can become in the work—the language, imagination, and clarity of it. I want to surprise myself continually. And not cheat.

TB: A final question: What do you find most encouraging and most discouraging about the current poetry scene(s)?

SV: Various "scenes" are always in a cycle, illuminated for a while with real leadership and energy before transitioning into a pale reflection of themselves with, at best, a vital memory of particular events and sequences of poems as their legacy. What was current and vital in the Bay Area two or three years ago, is best manifested in the *Bay Poetics* anthology wonderfully edited by Stephanie Young, and beautifully published by faux press. Combinations of house, bar and the Grand Street readings, the new phenomenon of blogs and ephemeral publications made it possible to meet and hear the work of a fantastic variety of poets that were also vital to the making and reception of my new work. David Larsen, Cynthia Sailers, Chris Sullivan, Catherine Ming, the late kari edwards, Jen Scapetone, Taylor Brady, Rob Halpern, Ali Warren, Brandon Brown, Kate Colby, Del Ray Cross, David Abel, Andrew Joron, Mary Burger, among many more. Lately, it's been less frenetic. Some folks even dismiss the current scene as *anemic*. I don't think so. True, some important folks have moved away, Kasey S. Mohammed to Ashland, Rodney Koeneke to Portland, David Hess to Texas, Maggie Zurwaksi to Duke, and now Judith Goldman to the U. of Chicago. In order to survive or professionally evolve, some have sunk themselves into counter-productive jobs or gone off to pursue PhDs or taken teaching positions.

In terms of *cycling*, it seems the recent local flourish of energy and poetry is now getting transformed into an "adult" world of responsibility! Yet, I remain happily astonished with the number and audience sizes of local readings, while young poets keep coming to San Francisco to live and/or study. Apart from short and radically shifting lives of some scenes, thank goodness we have long-lived places such as the San Francisco State Poetry Center, Small Press Traffic and many alternative poetry sites and bookstores here and across the country that help keep us chirping away with readings, archives, and so forth—let alone the hang-tough poetry book publishers.

In addition to my own shifting local scene, I have been personally grateful to the national and international blogosphere, *listservs*, and online publishers. Still very young and diverse, the exposure and discussions of these media have been very helpful in bringing to the work of many, including my own, a visibility that was previously very difficult to achieve. Both nationally and internationally I would never have known the work of Jean Vengua, Jill Jones, Allen Bramhall, Halvard Johnson, Sheila Murphy, Shanna Compton, Alison Croggon, Mairead Byrne, Jonathan Skinner, Jow Linsday, Peter Manson, Tim Peterson, John Latta, David Chirot, Alan Sondheim, Charles Alexander, just to cite a small number of good, active folks I have met in the cyber-world

I think the jury is still *out*, but *getting close*, on my generation's worth and accomplishment. Certainly its *worth* will be heightened (or even sometimes dismissed or lost) by succeeding generations. It's kind of silly to name names since I will undoubtedly forget to mention many good folks. On today's memory palate (!) I will mention Fanny and Susan Howe, Beverly Dahlen, Rachel Blau Duplessis, Jean Day, Lisa Robertson,Bob Grenier, Lyn Hejinian, Carla Harryman, Barry Watten, Bruce Andrews, Kit Robinson, Ron Silliman and Charles Bernstein, Rae Armantrout, Duncan McNaughton, Lawrence Kearny, Jim Thorpe, John Taggart, Steven Ratcliffe, Keith and Mary Waldrop, Paul Hoover, Maxine Chernoff, Gloria Frym, Joseph Lease, Gilian Connely, George Evans, Harryette Mullen, Bernadette Mayer, Ron Padgett, Bill Berkson, Nathaniel Mackey, Clark Coolidge, Michael Palmer,Mark Weiss, Charles Alexander, David Abel, Andrew Joron, Laura Moriarty, John Tranter, Tom Raworth, Lee Harwood, Trevor Joyce, Geoffrey Squires, Maurice Scully, Maggie O'Sullivan, Geraldine Monk and Alan Halsey come to mind as just a few of the folks devoted to creating an enduring foundation for work contemporary to my time and interests.

I cannot remember a darker political time in my life. Dick Cheney, Bush, that whole regime, covers everything. Historically I am sure what has happened here will be defined as a *coup*. The damage is impossible to fully gauge. I can not yet begin to imagine a time in which we will re-emerge with a democratic sense of ourselves. The country has lost its moral center. It's hard to write yet and imagine a language with the power to reinvest the country's consciousness with a sense of liberty, equality and play. And happiness, too!

I, as I am sure many of us do, find the time absolutely scary to behold. Yet things do play out in history, I would rather be making and reading poetry than not doing it. At this point, maybe it's not even a choice!

From *Sleeping With Sappho*

30.

]noon
Guys
Morning to night
Refuse to take a look
Even with the lupine bushes in our hair
And the occasional slap you give me on the butt
We should take to a room and fall asleep
Or wrap our arms around old men drunk
Already fast asleep on the City's benches
]
If there is a bird in anybody's pants
It's lost its beak.

55.

]
Wisteria breathes
Against my face
You will come my way
One breath at a time.
]
]

56.

What city boy knocks you on your ass
His buckle half way down to his knees
Sure that your dress will rise higher
Than your knees?

80.

Not everyone
Her feet
The ripple
In her toes.

82.

]get hot
]not too quickly
]
Let the lavender lilies fall from your hair
Cut and break the white fennel bulb into pieces
Let me tell you, blind, I follow each of your traces:
Beauty in darkness, charms.

120.

        Old age

     Old age

            Why are you running toward me?

             I have not come for you

             I have not come for you.

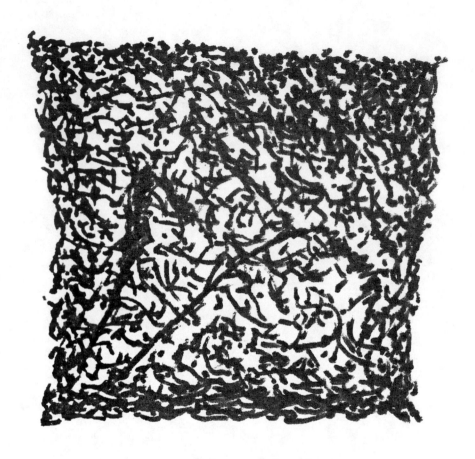

Haptic #3 from a Series of 8

created during/for the
Poetry & Agression Conference
Small Press Traffic
California College of Arts, Oakland
June 2008

From *Walking Theory*

9.

Walk poverty: an architecture to look
closely her gray synthetic leather purse
shreds into loose shingles, the heart
let loose among buildings without trees,
the lobbies of the dead, people who lean
variously to struggle with reason against
an architecture born deadly, the empty
Sunday playground, blue, yellow and white structures,
a vacuum unbound, wall-to-wall piss,
the street stutters, step-by-step, who can tell of the poor,
the decorum of the poor? Good-bye rhetoric, the desperate,
what can the poem do, walking, step-by-step:
witness, suffer, hope.

21

The soldier in Iraq lays down lead.
The plumber in the neighborhood lays down pipe.
The poet word by word lays down sentences.
There is no humble opinion in the world,
so much goes by pruning and graft
He was a gambler in the old world,
A threaded tunic down to his thighs.
He's a menace in the new one
a crow's head for eyes.
Speak to him with a silver tongue.

Put a thimble and needle to his lips.

Knot by knot, "yes" by "yes,"

tie the thread as hard as you can.

Thread him up and pull him down.

Put bronze on his elbows, gold on his teats.

The raft in the river.

The falls downstream.

Let him glow in the dark.

The ropes on the raft.

Pull him, pull him.

Let the river push him wide and far.

The falls in the distance.

40.

What's blue that whispers blue on the Coast?

It's been three weeks since I have seen or

heard them – stream upon stream, whispering–

some vertical, some collapsed – sails transparent

silver skin as thin as silk

lifted by the wind over succulent, shifting

thick iridescent lips,

thousands upon thousands twisted

Thick rubbery strands

Undertow, tide, wind-driven

into flattened streams

over low dunes against roiling sea.

Afternoon sun burning the white caps,

the blind green in wave cup after wave cup

"*Vellea, Vellea*" these once "By the Sea Sailors."

Once upon the ocean, undulant streams, transparent flesh

catch at what & what may.

Listen to the dead.

They never leave

They never leave

Portals to the other side, whispers in the heart.

43.

Morning: no desire to penetrate the low hill, the dark fog.

Ignite my face. Clean my heart.

The litany is not so long.

"Litter me not."

The Park to its visitors.

The boyish blond curls on the homeless man's head

Sandwiched within the L-shaped blanket atop the grass.

The man with two wire buckets of green tennis balls,

one racket and a red light, at the curb.

The young man with a lit cigar at the trolley stop.

The abandoned Levi jacket draped on the leafy bank on the way to
        the track.

A tiny white piece of pigeon shit on the statue's bronze curl:

Miguel Hildalgo Costella, Liberator of Mexico, 1810.

The two brown Boxers racing between the three extended figures –

left arms out, right heels raised: *T'ai Chi.*

The way his silver cell phone is so small it fits between two fingers.

She stands in front of him, juts her hip, wants to make love, later.

The upside-down blue paper 3-D glasses on the black grease gravel between
          the trolley tracks.

The way one assumes dimension: to appear, grow, flourish
Get damaged, disappear.

The mystery of the way one re-appears, again and again
Then not.

The eruption of everything. The all-night crystals.

The caldron - solar yellow, amber, the liquid - the way it boils over,
swinging across the horizon, an infinite bottom, an infinite gift.

The mystery in the complication of pores.

The way one supports images with images from within.
The way one continues.

47.
She who lives beneath the City,
beneath the hills, she who waits, emerges,
dissolves. She who haunts on gray days,
she who lays dormant, light through fog.
She in black gown & pink sash

who on her shoulder carries the crimson bird.

she who, she

who neither walks nor talks

tells me she's mine.

Bread in a basket,

her abalone neckpiece

a mute rainbow,

a gold egg in each palm.

Who can decipher her ruffled face?

The ghost of "hello", of no return

and while I'm with you

count the shifting letters in your palm:

Shake, stroke, flame,

sugar the sky

stamp your feet.

Pull out the empty book.

Mark upon mark

word unto word

there one goes:

Flourish, flourish.

51.
Trolley-Stop 18th & Church:

Dark blue spots punctuate

a shiny white dress.

Black coat knee length over red pants,

a slightly darker red leather-strap purse,

her parted brown hair falls evenly

across each shoulder: the eyelids

don't lift, not even one tiny bit.

*

Cumberland at Church:

Navy blue shirts & shorts,

twenty Firefighter trainees,

Top of the park stairs

Peddle feet up and down.

The woman trainer's staccato voice

"See the sixth building down -

The white one with two balconies -

That's where Giappi made

A *fine* rescue off the ladder

From the high balcony."

*

Down 21st from Sanchez:

Across the tops of green hedges

white threaded spider hammocks,

raindrops caught, clustered,

mercurial edges of light – glimmering –

uneven rims inside each sphere.

52.

2.5 lbs./ blood-red tuna,

9 slices/ pearly swordfish,

Yellow, green, red-marbled heirloom tomatoes,

Sliced cantaloupe strapped w/ thin prociutto:

One hunts, gathers, prepares.

*

The meticulous music of inner-things:

Slender ripples in silk folds,

the way light fractures when she walks:

Long, greenish gold.
*

To look close, he joked, note the left-handed moth,

up there, on the ceiling, scooting across!

*

Summer does not fade. Trees, plants

Flush open, indolent

Peach petals an indiscriminate blur:

As one opens to a lover after love opens.

Alan Davies
interviewed by Tom Beckett

ALAN DAVIES was born in Canada, has lived for over half his life in New York City. Alan is the author of RAVE (Roof), NAME (This), CANDOR (O Books), and SIGNAGE (Roof), an untitled collaboration with photographer M. M. Winterford (Zasterle Press), Sei Shonagon (hole books), among many other books. His BOOK 5, part of a long ongoing work, was recently published by Katalanché. He has books forthcoming — BOOK 6 (House Press), BOOK 1 (Harry Tankoos Press), Odes (Faux Press), and a book from Sonaweb.

More information is available at –
http://en.wikipedia.org/wiki/Alan_Davies_%28poet%29
http://epc.buffalo.edu/authors/davies/
http://writing.upenn.edu/pennsound/x/Davies-Alan.html

He can be contacted at canadianluddite@yahoo.com

Tom Beckett: Where did/does poetry begin for you?

Alan Davies: For me poetry is a natural manifestation like flowers or dogs or stars. Human beings appear to be its agent — but everything that exists has many agents (perhaps a primary one and numerous secondary ones). I'm glad simply to have my hand in it — and to let it go at that.

TB: Your response strikes me as being a bit disingenuous, somewhat unresponsive. Surely there was a beginning point for you, Alan Davies, as a poet. And your work is crafted with great care. It doesn't just happen.

AD: My answer is not in the least bit disingenuous.

Perhaps it is macroscopic — while you were seeking a more microscopic answer. Perhaps you want to know about things that may have influenced my development as a poet. I'll answer that question. My father was a preacher. There were times when I heard the same sermon several times — sometimes as often as four times in two weeks. People were attentive. The power of the word was apparent. That may have had some appeal. My father was not generally focused on us — he was spaced-out and in-love-with-Jesus. But at one time he read The Song of Hiawatha to us at bedtime over several weeks. The fact of his being more present than usual may have added to the ringing tones of the poem itself. I remember — By the shores of Gitche Gumee, / By the shining Big-Sea-Water, / Stood the wigwam of Nokomis. I also successfully memorized Casey at the Bat. In high school I bought an anthology called A Gift of Watermelon Pickle which contained a poem by Wallace Stevens that compared a razor blade to a mountain range. I couldn't make sense of it — so I took it to my friend Boyd with whom I shared such things and together we still couldn't make it mean in any of the ways we thought it might. We took it to Alec Garland — who'd studied at the Sorbonne and who did a terrific job of teaching us French and English. We showed him the poem and I asked him what it meant. He said — I don't know what do you think it means? Being thrown back on my own resources in that way — into that space of just-don't-know — was marvelously liberating. In college I enrolled in pre-med to please my parents — found biology untenable after one semester — and quickly made my way to the English department from which I graduated. Shit! — What a lot of words! I think my first answer was a lot easier and more to the point. This has all been something of a distraction.

All of this explanation might fall in the category of what I first referred to as secondary causes. The main cause of my writing is still what I said it was — it's a natural phenomenon of which I'm a miniscule almost-non-signifying part — and I'm content to leave it at that.

You ask about craft. To use your own words — I would say that being crafted with great care is how my poetry just happens. Pound noted from the Chinese that art should imitate nature in its methods of operation — and that's about what seems to be the case. Yes – I read read read read and I write write write write write — so naturally I learn how to do what I do do do do do. But saying that — what have we learned? Each poem speaks for itself — each is its own cause — and each fails (let's put it like that) in its own unique way.

TB: What about your intentions as a writer? Surely your poems aren't all autonomous creations which bear no relation to one another?

AD: Intentionality is always a difficult thing to assess — or to front for.

I remember riding back downtown from one of those Avant-garde Festivals that they had a few of on a pier on the west side — seated next to Hannah Weiner in the back of James Sherry's car. I asked Hannah why she wrote — she said — *Because I see words* — and asked me why I wrote. I said something about wanting to help other people or words to that effect. Hannah said — *Humpty Dumpty*.

Hannah's prediction has unfortunately proven to be very much the case.

But I still have this idea that I can contribute something vis-à-vis showing how the mind works and how it might work better — if only we'd let it. I myself try to aim in the direction of clarity / centeredness / compassion. These things aren't separable — if you're clear and centered then compassion is the only natural response to situations / if you're compassionate you radiate clarity and centeredness / centeredness is the pivot upon which the others find their balance / and so on. So those are things that I try to exemplify in my life and (my writing being a part of my life) in my writing as well (almost by default). Do I fail? — Yes.

I also write a great many differing types of things. So to that extent they are "autonomous creations which bear no relation to one another" — and to that extent if it were otherwise I'd be bored. And boredom is not particularly conducive to clarity / centeredness / and compassion.

There's also something to be said for getting my ideas across to other people. I'm probably better at doing that in writing than in other ways.

At the same time I wouldn't want to forget that I write simply because I love to do so. Although I write more and more on the computer now (especially book reviews) — I absolutely love the feel of a pen moving over a more-or-less clean piece of paper.

And — in the final analysis (if there is one) — the main reason that I write is because I can't help it. Nor would I want to.

TB: You are associated, of course, with the L=A=N=G=U=A=G=E poets. Would you speak to that association and what it means to you?

AD: That's a historical question — and I am a poet.

But I can tell you a few things that I remember. When I was living in Boston in the early 1970s I published the magazines Oculist Witnesses and A Hundred Posters — and particularly through the latter I began to be in touch with poets in New York City and elsewhere. Among them were Michael Gottlieb and Charles Bernstein. During the year that I lived in Boulder (1976-77) I remained in correspondence with them — and with others as well. And then when I moved to New York City in the fall of 1977 I met people that I'd only known through the mail. My first reading here was at a large pub near Columbia — four people read — Charles was one of them — there was one of the so-called New York School of poets (second generation) — and I forget who the fourth was. That reading exposed me and my work to more of the people who would become known as the L=A=N=G=U=A=G=E poets. That "group" of poets is named after the magazine started by Bruce Andrews and by Charles — and in the writing and production of which many of us participated. I typed some of the issues and was paid for it (for which I was grateful) — many of us got together to do mailings. Various people were also involved with James Sherry's ROOF magazine. The Ear Inn series of readings was started at about that time — and I ran several series in collaboration with other people (a memorable series with Diane Ward through the midst of a very harsh winter — socks drying on the radiators as readers read and listeners drank). Occasionally there were get-togethers to share new work — I remember meeting at Hannah's apartment in the East Village / at mine in Park Slope / and elsewhere. There were parties — and we got to know the work of like-minded people in other arts (dancers and film makers and musicians). People began to make connections — through publication first and then through reading tours as well — with our peers on the west coast / as well as with the few kindred spirits living on neither coast. I also got in touch somewhat belatedly (considering that I am Canadian) with some fellow-writers in Canada — Christopher Dewdney (with whom and with whose work I've always felt particularly close) in particular (and later with younger Canadian writers who were kind enough to take some interest in my work).

My friend Michael Gottlieb has some excellent autobiographical writings about the early days of the "group" (particularly in New York) that I hope will be published soon. They're much more thorough / and much more charming than my few remarks here.

So all of these inter-lacings (and untold numbers more) made for a community. And the community began to be named by others after that seminal publication. It's interesting to me that that naming was done by people outside (or adjacent to) the group. I can't remember (or imagine) any one of "us" saying — *We are (the) L=A=N=G=U=A=G=E poets*. The name was applied — not chosen. I know that my peers and I have many times been asked this question — or other questions about this. But I know of no cases yet of people who did the naming being identified and asked the same question the way it might by interesting to have it asked — *Why did you persist in calling them the L=A=N=G=U=A=G=E poets?* I think that might end up by being a more interesting project.

I would like to say also that among poets in New York City and elsewhere I've had many (and continue to have many) valued friends and colleagues who wouldn't be considered to have any association with that "group". This becomes even more the case as I make friends with younger poets whose affiliations are sundry / and whose influences have been many — and who are very important to me as I continue to develop as a poet. It's a joy.

So what is really being described by the term L=A=N=G=U=A=G=E poets (from my point of view) is more a community (and its machinations) than an ideology — although somewhat loosely shared senses of ideology (about both politics and craft) might have been instrumental in shaping the group's project (particularly early on). What those associations mean to me in retrospect is also what they meant to me primarily at the time(s) — friendships of varying intensities and textures (but principally the chance to have had them at all). When people ask me about the L=A=N=G=U=A=G=E poets I think first of people I love / of people I care about intensely / of people with whom I've had difficulties / of people whose work I admire (and from which I've learned a great deal) / and so on. Then (and only then) might I think of the work / and what it all means / and whether any of it has anything in common with any of the rest of it / and so on.

TB: Do you see your work, at this point in time, as some kind of a "social project"?

AD: No. I've never thought of my work as a "social project" (with or without the quotes). I've thought about it in human terms (some of which I talked about above) — and also in spiritual or universal terms (as I spoke about its being a simple part of the flowering of universal process).

I do hope it to be of some use — but I'd be hard-pressed to define that use — and certainly much more hard-pressed to insist on it.

This doesn't mean that I don't think about it a lot — I do. It's just that this is all I've come up with!

TB: What are you, as a writer, most preoccupied with now?

AD: I'll answer the question first in terms of my works.

In 2000 I began a series of books (BOOK 1, BOOK 2, and so on) which I imagine will occupy me for the rest of my life. Each book is quite different from the others structurally / in terms of tone / in terms of what the available content might be / and so on. There's something fragmentary about the material that goes to make up the texts — I think at this time it's difficult (and unnecessary) to get beyond fragments — there doesn't seem to be much that lasts or coheres beyond what a fragment might contain / express. Three of the BOOKs have been published in limited editions — the most recent being BOOK 5 (Katalanché Press, 2007). Many have been read in public.

I was part way through BOOK 10 when some other sorts of things started keeping me up at night — and I found after some time that I had written a book of / and called ODES & fragments.

I'll now return to BOOK 10 — and have an idea of what BOOK 11 will be. Beyond that I'll simply be able to happily surprise myself. The BOOKs as a totality do cohere I think — and I expect that to go on happening.

I've also been writing a lot of reviews again (after a lengthy hiatus) — beginning toward the end of 2004. Many of these are of books by younger writers whose work I have found singularly engaging — and it's a pleasure to speak to and of them in that way.

Reading is also and always a great pleasure. I read a lot of diaries and journals by writers / autobiography and biography of same / books pertaining to artists I particularly admire (Giacometti and Bacon and Ana Mendieta of late) / some poetry books that friends send me / Japanese and Chinese poetry / novels / some philosophy / and other things. From time to time I'll go back (it's not really back is it?) and read work by predecessors I particularly admire — Creeley / Kyger / Whalen / MacDiarmid / Wieners / Notley are recent examples. I've been reading the classics as well — currently Horace's Satires and Epistles.

I've also been enjoying very much lately corresponding with writer friends. Among them are old friends with whom I had been for some time out of touch — like Larry Price. And there are newer friends among the younger poets — Roberto Harrison and Geoffrey Olsen and others — from whose correspondence I'm learning a lot about my own values and practice.

TB: Would you speak to your sense of purpose and process in your fragment-poems?

AD: I think I've said enough about my "sense of purpose", to the extent that I have one. I feel as much driven by "it" as I feel capable of being any kind of driver — and the fact that I don't even know what "it" is is perhaps what

230

drives me most. I think it is.

As for process — (I don't know) — I've already said something about that also. But practically speaking — I write mostly at night. I've always preferred being awake then (when circumstances (job etc) permitted) — the quiet / fewer interruptions / control of space and activity / solitary motions and emotions. I've always loved the word lucubrations (which has the etymological connotation of work produced at night by lamplight).

Words seem to appear — they wake me up (not (not) as it were) / or I wake up for them. They seem to come in little clusters / bump against my head (what I call my head) / and demand to be let in (or is it out?). I go on from there — or sometimes I go on from there / and sometimes I leave it at that. Process is what we're all in the midst of.

The phrases or chunks of words then seem to find their place by way of accretion — motivated in part by (sometimes prior) senses of style and structure. In the case of the longer BOOKs these pieces seem to arrive quite slowly — so that to complete one has been taking an average of nine months. Some other recent poems (from the series called ODES & fragments) have been written in a great flurry — but the sense of fracture seems still to be there (wherever there is).

It might be interesting to think for a moment about the relationships between "sense of purpose" and "process" — does sense of purpose produce process (as we might (willingly) think)? — or is it process that generates sense of purpose as we go on (and on)? I would think that both of these might be the case in a sort of yin / yang way (but without the masculine / feminine notions often attached to that). In other words — sense of purpose and process are co-generative — and it is precisely that co-generative motion that produces the work of art. Neither is prior — if it were the work of art would always remain a hidden secret (which in some cases it does do).

TB: I'm always fumbling … In your poetry, ethics and eros seem palpably embodied in the turns that thought takes as it goes away. The texts, insistently present, are also self-consciously transitory. By way of example, here's the opening of your BOOK 8:

the slightly adult adept

**the failure —
of the shadows —
of the leaves —**

against the car

as though they are

as though they

the endangered third world —
earth

the end of the word —
as we know it

truncated bundles of hunger

I suppose what I've been trying to get to all along is a better sense of your perspective of what it is that is converging in your work.

AD: I really have no idea.

I mean when I begin a piece I sometimes (sometimes) have a sense of things like tone / structure / duration / material — I would say that's about it. (And I think that I used to have a clearer sense of those things when beginning than I do now — although perhaps it's just that it's become more intuitive.) But I don't always have a sense of all of those things (I don't know if I've ever done) — and sometimes have no sense of any of them at all. And yet to begin with a piece of language seems (of some kind of necessity (of some kind of necessity?)) to drag other (perhaps not overly dissimilar) pieces of language into being along with it. It's a mystery.

If I didn't find it to be a mystery I wouldn't do it — at least not still. I can bear almost anything but boredom — and I can bear even that if I get a little work done in the midst of it. Most things are interesting — but they're interesting because they create their own uniqueness (by being (I suppose)). Even boredom is interesting.

I don't have a lot to go on with. One word is rather quickly a phrase (of some sort) — then (after however long a time) others follow along — and so on. At some point I'm satisfied that I have enough of them — that I'm quote done end quote. That point of completion is sometimes determined by the notebook I'm writing in — when it's full I'm done (or maybe not).

I don't know exactly (or at all?) how you're trying to get me to explain this. But it's an organic process — self-initiating / self-perpetuating / self-limiting. Of course I have something to do with it — I'd be a fool to pretend that I don't — but I'd also be a fool to try to convince either you or me that I know what that part played is. I'm a factor.

TB: Would you humor me by asking yourself a question and answering it?

AD: Q: How would you compare your earlier works with the things that you are working on now?

A: My earlier works — those that I wrote after college and when in Boston and Boulder and then in New York City — and some of which can be found in *Active 24 Hours* (Roof) as well as in *a an av es* (Potes & Poets) and *Mnemono-technics* (also from Potes & Poets) — often had experimentation of some sort as their call to existence. I wanted to find out how the language worked — and what was in (in (what was in)) it. I sometimes thought of the works as core samples — as taking a sample of the language in a particular place and time – and I usually accepted that as enough of a reason for doing that / although I also knew that I was expressing my self (whatever my "self" might be (might be thought to be)). I wrote around certain ideas — often involving duration and textuality — and modes of getting at (at) things. It was really a way of learning how to write.

At about the same time I wrote a work called The Story of One Who Was Great In Respects — which is more personal (or which has (at any rate) more personality in it) — and there were others of that sort. I wrote a work for Mary Lane whose title I no longer remember but that ended with the line – Work abandoned. And in Boulder I wrote a group of at least somewhat satisfying lyrics — and they had a lot of me in them (as well as some of that trust in the language that I had learned from doing the other works).

Later I wrote the much more personal works that are collected in *Candor* (O Books) — and in two subsequent unpublished manuscripts (called Life / and Lonely). But I have always written a variety of things — not contented to mine (to use a phrase appropriate to that earlier thinking alluded to) the same content or form for much time.

I would say that the series of Books that I'm now working on — as well as (in differing ways) the manuscript just completed called ODES & fragments – owes much to those earlier researches (and the products they produced). But I feel now a greater confidence in the assimilation / the confluence / the conflation — of the various modes and tensions and substances that go to make up a work. I guess I would say that I feel more in control (now) of the what as well as the how of writing — and I know that that is what goes to make up the whole work (as a whole). It's the best I can do — perhaps future moments will teach me new things to add to the mix / and the wherewithal and the how-to of doing so. I'm always as willing to learn from my own work as I am from that of others.

It's 7:44 am in New York City, and there is no city
posed as a nothingness over the harborless entropy
quaking up from, or to, but that's that's 'n too
for the frail quakaing the slim slaughterable making

of mating

as if 'n
          that might make the thetic crowns stroll on like this
what am I to do, the other one the other when than that do
over blue harvestable moments tlaken and florsaken as 'n

that one was the other, phatic, crowned and taken as down crown
from the the slim slim slaking for the slim appropriate being down
the then being, the one spelt down, sloughed and troughed as taken
for the momemteles that's the one that's there, as theatre, as clown

of you

                              o f   y   o
          u   u
healing the

happen

stance

there bein no endin of the you en

                                        ever   en

don
't touch me
don't come near me
me
don't be me
I'mm em me
amd tat is that that I is me the ais me that I moe over overakkl

don't touh
couthc'touch

235

ever

ever
(after all

te

h

the hapy

the happt

the happy oe

the hapy

the happy one

si

si

si
s

is snorkelliong inta you

dread

gone

for a day

he
the one that is lost for that day iad ais alndls this for the for the lflingliests for
the esllkngsetstn gfof the letingslsetst fotheh ofr there lar there no one oens eof
rthakenee forntnem yhe tyintlgetnrlslsn oland are of rolhte of ofht e htheakene
tgofnroee otelte tientbeing eofjslth3eand atohte tenadlthene althankenel

bakdner of theov fofent oft t9 be gieng hy elaktnelknteklhoiane 9the taone
thakensts thosthak

how
I don't mean maybe
I don't mean how

thant's th one t
t
with the ehnan
hand

nobody but me

sequesterqble
gakeable
seu3qsterable
takeable
sequesterble

my fat e   is in your hands

(slingable
myaboele
mable
myable
d9able
doable
th

the

sheq

the e

te

the sequences
ov the atht alllabamma way

  bay

                                                            (that

                            slaughterable trotters

                                you bitches

                        and you daughers

                                            of the oh so slaugherable trotters

in the tr
in tne entrancing
t
in the what what me of you

                                    dream
                                    ok)
                                    'n

                            slate

for I
'm all of you

                                                    (all of my life on you depends
                                                        (over again
                                                        (everything went wrong
                                                        (I'm a small
                                                        (as you
                                                    (and that now that I leave you at at last
(always

for

'm
beindomm of 'm
                            but always

but there's
you
yous
you

you were so marve;;pllous with the

                you're a

                    pants uupon te floo r

                        I loved you
                      but you hatee me
                      for being you

           so 'n
           be it 'n

           sweet one

           bro

        from thee each

        from the beach

           t

        from the beach

is is i

is ok t t0 sa haat

        that

        I'm n lor eiyh you

                youre the one I care or
                    for th oen of
             the one I care for you'and the athe oi

cre fro u
me

that 'na

slakeddl e Id ed over 'n at ' n then

from rosy

5h3 slinglets
again them rpsu rpsu
rpsu euesjm

swart

take down the then down town
be the one with the town with the world in the big noun

or gravitations

aq

sweetness
over the perfectable ground

as that's mighenen be a nouen

fo
fw
frow

nw'
wn

'na

an

nound

cadence cadence tqkn ov

slotten I'm
I'm

sprru

s
sprru

sorry

taken

you 'n
stitchen

gone

en

overenens

There we sequester ourselves
along the palm avenues

there we amuse ourselves
as fate would have it in a twist

and the cantankerous makes
of all of us a spelt mask

For you there is only harbor
or the caskless meaning of beat

as we all remember it, up
and down joyless Joy street

But for you there will be morning
as there is evening even for the rest

of the stuff, stolen and all but lost
in the harbor and the rough

So were there other ways
of being than the ways of being other

that would be the way to be, but
there are not, nor could there be

a way of being that, though we think
of all that is not lost as stuff, as

mere stuff, the cradle and the veil
taken for what is not all but lost

but for what is all but taken from us
(the ones who are all but all but loss

Sometimes there are only time of some
that sleight all the hands of taken some

for there is meaning in a drum, a slow
drum beating meaning into dad & mom

There are slack harbors with vestments
that my new friends won't like, not

as this, not as that, and the then was over
from the start of the beach to the start of the when

for there is as as there is there or when
but we wonder of those who've missed it

and those who've taken the token for the nub
Such that there is splice and taken stuff

up the nosed the splice where the being's been
from contemptuous thing flowing to harvest

the harbor that is harborless and unharvestable
as memory is all that it has to ask of itself

Or there is an or of ore that takes itself out of the ground
where speech is ground into dust, and dust into speechlessness

above for the spell of what can't be taken or put down
Or there is the memory of you above ground

the slayed one, with time as token for the broken ground
and the stroked being that takes all but being into frowned sound

The where the we with the we with the where with the we above ground
as sound, for the where is the here that we share in the pound that we sound

for there's only mastery where the thing is above the wound of the humbled
        ground
slaken, or there were other reasons non reasons for being as me, the one in the
        ground

As we walk into the graves and the hedges there's nothing but the slot wrought
        thing bought
to be the thing that we share as there is an other thing being the there that has
        we were there

only in it, being there as deeply as thee, you and the coral singing of the
         surplices, spelt and grown
from the gown, where the you of the having them both is the token without a
         booth but we still remember you

as hanging indent, the spectreless speechless one of the gowned one taken from
         the froth being the one that slates
and then gets remembered when there with humor as the slaken thing that is
         thingletting from the slow being to the being of slowness

And oh love oh love oh love oh love I need you now, and remember the girl in
         the spelt moment
up against the observatory with the planets splayed like moments for all the
         world to take for granted, as asks

For there is no other being, but the being in love, and the being in love is being
         over all being as taken, as token
that all but the all but was then for all that the being, for the slender or the
         smaller tasks of being were the glowing slowing

the ones with and beyond the garden wall, as that were there the taken thing,
         the one with thing and taken in it, and you and
the not you, as thing and not thing slurping and suffering and beginning and
         being the one of the ending and the beginning

to be slowing, to be needing, to be there and to be therein, as that is the one that
         is the one that is the one that needs you now
there being now only for the flowing and the being and the one the one that is
         being in the twining of the flowing of the

growing, the spectacle over and in the small magic being of the remembering
         of the being of that as the remembering of that being
being you, as all that is you, as all that is happing to you hoping to be you the
         hoping that is the happening to be hoping to be you

As there be memory, as if it be as if there were memory, and no being of before
         nor after the will
of the being of the memory, of the memory of the will, of the memory, of the
         will of the memory, broken into until

244

there is no slaked thing, no praises, no ring, no that let's me sing, but the
     slaking overture, the pound of pounding things, as music is
for there are caskless things, taken for the hill, over the swamping of the car,
     the emblem of the all that is the end of the end of the ending thing

Thin, as that, as thin as that a thing, oh sweet cadenceless slaughterless one, on
     the hill, if it be your will if it be your will
for there is no other being there here, no wonder that takes the words out of the
     mouth of the babes that have not spoken nor spelt

the back taken things that are only spoken, not spilled, as if meaning had a
     harbor with meaning in it, a place where one could harvest things
but there is no harvestable thing, no nothing that counts for the with within
     between us, for there is us that, that us

Or there were trollops, but not enough, as there are narrower spaces where
     even space does not fit, so
there were others suffering a while as the soldier said made the killer smile,
     with tweaked ones being for me for you

withal as that being that upon the stand of staunchless particles for the foment
     of country and western and song, but
if there's a space with splicing over the harbor then that's the place for you and
     for what was me, before this song

There ain't no nothin' left of the last song, the one with all the You in it, but
     that's not that fault, or the wary way of the stranger
there's being here as that were the one with the overtly being of the strained
     train of thought, that strain of thought, in it

We remember yesterday as if it were yesterday, that's what gives it its name,
     and that's what fall for the sling harvest of naught
tracing hallelujahs for the things that are most up front, take it, be it, in the
     slant moon of harvestable harbingers

that slake, and the that's the that, where there is a that, where there is a the, and
     that ain't being much of anywhere, over much of naught
for there were husbandable tokens aloft in every loft, that night, and nothing
     slept, but all was slaughtered in the blaze of speechless speech, of
     speech

as such, as cusp, I didn't come to fool ya, a thrall is a being after all, a place to
be inside the ball of the universe of fate, its casking bait
that takes the moment out of the momentless slinging flask and eats all that's
left and all that's for nor either after

along the eiderdown slowness of rivers and harbors and being places where we
might be of a drown, for there is such a happy place
and in it we are drawn to the tokens taken slotted and then there's no terrible
sound, and no one else had to die, but they lied

Sordid as that all may seem, in the seemly seamlessness of not what would
ever stay, but there's nothing here that isn't play, the great
surprise, slottering over the world of the with us in it, if that were capable of a
being, but sense is a senseless thing, always

and wary being is taking warned being over the clasped arms of the seat into
the bussing to the next town, the next state, the next being drowned
for there are the few who don't even care, steal that, the ones who don't have
nowhere to go back to the whorled

spaces, and we remember that memory is a think of the past, that being there
was never being there for long, even with you in mind
and that the being there was the slow sloughing of people taken, having a
sister, for ever, or the burnt plans of tracked downs, wounded,
handed, gone

For mercy slakes it's hands at the hand of drought, and drought has no hands,
nor mercy a stand, but being there is guilty, grand, too grand
framing the sling harvests that usually take meaning into the stands, where
eagerness is the blotter that sucks up the standing of the grand
opening strands

of doubt, or were there had to be doubt, where there is reason as an escarpment
over the placated slings slotted with still hurting, the love you that
can't speak
or harvest itself from the words that burnt up to the slot top of marine
spaciness where the words are due

to be paid for, here, now, right now, right here,

oh sweet one

to get back to that, the singular, the shining singular, from place to place, from
   thralldom to thralldom, as a way of being grace, as a way of coming
   back to you
For that is the way of being in your arms all of the bent night, the swift one, the
   tokenable, the taken, and the none of it is true, coming back to you

And mercy is an arguable stance in the face of remonstrance and nonsense, the
   burning viola slated to be heard as the one that is not that one that we
   are of
or, and that is not all, then the one that is witnessed and felt and taken for the
   body and the glove, the end of love

I'm a rupture upon a gate, and that gate is you, the you of this very long, the
   you of this very long song, the end of, the end of, love
stolen as taken is a word for spoken, that there are words for wary and for
   weary as that is the worn moment with the thorn, the thorn that is not
   spoken

or worn, upon a work, or fabric of what is or might be worn, the torn thorn
So that memory is that thrall, the end of love, the dance, the and the space
   where we might have danced that to the end of love, the bar

upon a hill in Tennessee, or there are rapture as the an excuse for being here for
   being other than we be, in being here
or to spy upon your as you are the one being you there, over the spliced space
   where you have chosen or chosen not to be

from the caverns of the art that will not obey what's left of what we are not,
   will never be, and cannot be, cannot obey
over the flasking of the tropes that make us all obey, the you the me the day

For there were heralding and there were heralding as that were the innermost
   decision taken from the steps of our irreligion
to the ones that be, the ones that be, the ones that only obey, for that is all that
   they

are today, slipped up to the taken, the willed, the mistaken, the ones, the being,
   there, the ones being the ones being there, as taken, as mistaken
as bait, bent, oblate, slate, straight, as there's a kind of street, and remembering
   is remembering it for you (earlier poem

the one, the, the one that's taken over the fall of the moment into the frail thrall
of the stuffed momentless agony, the agon
that has a drink in its hand, and that hand is you, and that drink is, and there is
a way of being that is never lost but is, only being, over there, over all,
that

Raise it up, and then it's done, back, back on street, where the you is the one
that one cannot forget, will not forget, there being neither difference
there
then nor the slough of the singular moment that has token us for that that street
is for, you, the colden one, but not for not for not for never for long

There is praise as an alter ego to the atlas
at last, the place where the palace meets the street, the where the dog gets
harnessed to the meet, for that is all that's sweet, no

For there is no frost upon the trees, no trees, nor frost nor trees, no forest, nor
frost upon the trees, nor being, nor being left to be
and to be counted with the dead is all that's left, for that's the sending of the
spaceless down below, the believer, in the snow

Do not say there is nothing that cannot be taken for the moment that is taken
out of all that happens an is sworn to be slaked
for we wonder at the moment of your plangent harbor, the smoked time of the
slain meanness of the trained leaving of the one what matters most

As if there were another way to be, there were no other way to be, than this

Noah Eli Gordon
interviewed by Thomas Fink

Noah Eli Gordon is the author of six collections, including *Novel Pictorial Noise*, which was selected by John Ashbery for the National Poetry Series. His reviews and essays have appeared in numerous periodicals, including *The Review of Contemporary Fiction, Boston Review, The Denver Quarterly* and *Talisman*. He teaches at the University of Colorado and write a column on chapbooks for *Rain Taxi*.

Thomas Fink: This interview will focus on your latest three books, the first of which is *Inbox* (Kenmore, NY: BlazeVox, 2006). *Inbox* is nicely prefaced by your Sept. 12, 2004 email seeking permission to quote a lot of people's emails to you. You explain the rationale of this "temporal autobiography":

"I thought it would be interesting to see what would happen if I were to take the body-text of every email that was addressed specifically to me (nothing forwarded or from any listserv) currently in my inbox (over 200) and let all of the voices collide into one continuous text. The work is arranged in reverse chronology. . . . [*Inbox*] sculpts the space between the everyday detritus of dinner plans to discussions of fonts and notes from long lost friends. To be honest, as I'm a person pretty free of drama, the bulk of the work is boring, but intentionally so, in the generative, ambient way that Tan Lin writes about, well, one would hope anyhow. It's the collision of voices that makes the work compelling, at least to me. The only thing is. . . . I didn't write any of it; you did! "(4)

First, when you say "take the body-text," do you mean that you preserved each email from start to finish—you didn't edit them?

Noah Eli Gordon: That's correct. Although I did remove everyone's name, along with whatever particular language was used to open and close each email, which allowed all of the text to merge. There are points where the shift from email to email is obvious, but the more compelling moments occur when it's somewhat uncertain. After sending out that initial email, which, as you note, acts as a preface for the book, I did go back and excise several things from the project, mostly notes from those who expressed a little hostility toward the idea. Of course, such hostility is wholly warranted, as there's something inherently exploitive about publicly airing what folks considered to be intimate correspondence. The only other instance of editing took place right before the book was published. There was a bit of text in there that signified strongly the opinion of one individual involved in the poetry community about that of another. I punted this person a note just prior to publication asking if it was okay to include the material. Interestingly, although not necessarily surprising, this person had forgotten the email I'd sent, the one which acts as the book's preface, as it had been a few years since I'd gotten the okay. Honestly, I felt really bad about it, and so removed the mention. I suppose, in a way, this is what makes the project in my mind successful, in that it does involve a certain level of transgression, even of personal discomfort. The book itself was not difficult to write but the social dimensions of its possible reception were difficult to foresee.

TF: Authorial intention, then, is present in the selection of procedure, which doesn't let you decide the distribution of continuities and collisions, whereas in most of your work, you deliberately choose the disjunctions and transitions.

Michel Foucault in *The Order of Things* and in *The Archeology of Knowledge* talks about regularities of discursive formations in intellectual disciplines in various epochs. Both the continuities between successive emails and in motifs recurring throughout *Inbox* (i.e. coaxing submissions from you, asking for you to look at the sender's work, thanking you for having said something good or encouraging about the sender's work, engaging in analysis of contemporary U.S. experimental poetry that articulates a position or the seeming impossibility of locating one amid the confusion) expose several of these regularities in this cluster of innovative poetry communities without your having to be expository, except a little at the beginning. So, because I'm very interested in these communities and how they function, I don't find the book "boring," in the sense that Tan Lin uses! Have you learned anything about the poetry communities from reading sections of the book publicly or from rereading it after publication?

NEG: In his introduction to the Barnes & Noble Classics version of *Alice's Adventures in Wonderland* and *Through the Looking Glass*, Lin writes about boredom as "a temporary non-event defined by a span of near-indeterminate waiting." I think the content of *Inbox* revolves around exactly that sort of non-event. The constituent parts gesture toward happenings or report on their aftermath, but there's no dramatic arc. In fact, I think the act of checking one's email is one of simultaneous boredom and interest. The two aren't mutually exclusive. Boredom can be interesting. Boredom doesn't interest me, but I'm interested in boredom, which is not in any way an oxymoron. Regardless, I haven't ever read from the book publicly, and don't think that I ever will, since I see it as moving through an oddly voyeuristic space that feels more generatively intriguing to the active intimacy created by a reader, rather than that of a passive listener. I haven't learned anything by rereading the work after publication that I hadn't already learned when I initially read the individual emails, although for someone else, I'm sure the experience is quite different.

I call the book a reverse-memoir, as it covers a discrete portion of my life and not the up-to-now whole an autobiography would imply. Because most of my life revolves around poetry, for better or for worse, the book is going to be representative of one tiny nexus of colliding communities. That a reader might learn something about such a collision, and therefore something about those regularities of discursive formation, is merely a byproduct of the text. I'm pleased it happens. I'm pleased that the book might in someway be a testament to the ancillary busywork of a poet—and thus a kind of behind-the-scenes extra—but I didn't think of it that way until I started to hear feedback from some readers. I've heard from more folks about *Inbox* than I have about any of my other books. Of course, one might expect this, given that I'm often hearing back from the collective authors of the book itself, or from those who are mentioned within it. But what's intriguing is the uniformity of the response, which I'd characterize as essentially an initial uncertainty about the value of the project, followed by a sense of surprise, and sometimes delight, upon actually reading the book. I've heard from about a half-dozen people who read the thing straight through in a single sitting without intending to do so. Granted, I'm not going to hear from those that hate the thing and this all sounds terribly self-aggrandizing, but my point is that I suppose the book works initially, before one reads a word of it, as a conceptual text, infusing it with an aura of non-emotion, which, after reading is immediately shattered, marking the experience as unsuspected. Surprise is good, right? Can boredom encompass surprise? Am I allowed to contradict myself?

TF: Makes sense to me. Mr. Emerson, Mr. Whitman, you contain multitudes, and you can't be bothered with the hobgoblin of little minds; you can and may contradict yourself/ yourselves: "Lots of stuff in quotes. Lots of implied (and hopefully distinguishable) voices" (*Inbox* 10).

A Fiddle Pulled from the Throat of a Sparrow (Kalamazoo, MI: New Issues, 2007) opens with the section, "A Dictionary of Music," followed by "The Right of Return," whose titles all begin with the words, "The Book of. . . ," except for the last one, "Postscript: the book of Cain." "How Human Nouns"—and our readers should know that your blog was, until recently, called "Human Verb"—is the third section, and in the remaining ones, "epic theater," the "allusive," and two other "book" references, "Book of Names" and a "A Little Book of Prayers," are mentioned. Granted that the first section takes music as its point of departure, but why are there so many references to "book" in the poem- and section-titles, as well as to language, textuality in general, and literature? (I think of Mallarmé's notion of the "bookness" of the book.) What does this have to do with the arrangement of the poems and the overall project or poetics of this particular book?

NEG: I suppose it comes down to an interest in dualistic moments of rupture, in a recognition of artifice, and a desire to explore rather than conceal what one is doing with a textual surface. There's a line in "How Human Nouns" that reads: "but someone coughs & the theater caves in," which I think of as basically exemplary of such concerns. I remember a class I took in graduate school where we were discussing whether or not the speaker in Wordsworth's "The Solitary Reaper" had actually heard the song. Something about the discussion got under my skin, as I wanted to talk about that "solitary Highland Lass" as a kind of trope, a construct, something outside of experience but invented to simulate experience and explore notions of art and labor. Forgive me for wanting to read Wordsworth as one might read Stevens, which is a roundabout way of saying I'm completely aware that my interests here aren't all that new or radical.

I guess if I owned a robot, I'd want that robot to know it was a robot. Maybe then it could do its job in a more authentic way. I like how Barthes calls Philippe Sollers's *Event* "action, not product." And who doesn't like Cézanne's canvas showing through? Isn't it interesting when one can hear the screech of fingers moving across a fretboard along with whatever chords are being strummed? Things are layered. Why not poke a hole through them here and there? I've never seen an art show that featured photographs of people looking at photographs of people looking at photographs of people taking photographs, but I think I'd like to take a few pictures of one. The foremost concern of much of my writing is an argument with myself for its own justification. Will this interest everyone, certainly not, but then I like Jim Croce yet loathe James Taylor. If I were a choreographer, I'd have my dancers at some point climb into the audience. Once, while at a small indie rock show, the bass player handed the bass to a friend of mine. We were both standing in front of the band, as there was no stage. My friend didn't know this band at all, but since he is an accomplished musician finished out the last minute or so of the song. I hope my poems can do that same thing. I hope they can be both the bass player and the person to whom the bass is handed off.

TF: Yes, your poems can fulfill that double task. What does Jim Croce have that James Taylor lacks?

NEG: Duende!

TF: Let's apply your fascinating statement that your "writing is an argument with [yourself] for its own justification" to a "book" poem:

The book of hunger

the sound of smoke

was that of expansion

but the breaking of bread

like a dusk-shadow

became a name

losing itself in echo

until there was no sound

but the snapping

etched into each rib

which repeats

dust . . . dust . . . dust . . . (23)

"The book of hunger" is not the book of *filled* lack, of realized plenitude; like speech and writing, it is the deferral of presence. This "book" could be a text that either represents actual wants, needs, or desires of others, or acts as though language has its own desires, or propounds the author's desire to win the argument with himself over the justification of the text. "The sound of smoke," an auditory image implicitly aligned with a visual sense akin to the prolif- eration of actual writing on paper or typing on a screen, has "expanded," if only gaseously (or not quite substantially) to fill enough of the space of writing to justify others' attention to its textuality, "*but*" the physical fragmentation ("breaking of bread") that signifies a stage on the way to the end of "the book of hunger" and to the realization of fulfillment is troped, rather than as being a solid, as having acted much less substantially than the supposed gas. After all, you may think you see "dusk," but how can you *feel* it, and, if dusk is a shading or shadowing effect, to refer to a "dusk-shadow" is to entertain the possibility of a shadow of a shadow, the concept of a layering of progressive absences, like a "naming" as successive "echoes" that only gets farther away from the "veritable" thing-in-itself. Without taking too much discursive space by performing a reading of the rest of the poem (and leaving the Biblical-sounding "dust" for your interpretive gesture), perhaps I can say that you justify the poem's existence to yourself in the act of writing tropes that comprise cogent and accurate ways of exposing a process of "expanding" lack that occurs while one, on the contrary, writes of hunger primarily as a means of replacing it with plenitude. How would you reconstruct the poem's staging of the argument within you (or between you and you) about its justification?

NEG: Well, I'm not sure that I would, as you've picked a poem, actually a section from within a poem, which has a much more specific aboutness to it, although I appreciate your reading of it, and am happy to see it function on multiple levels. I hope that all of my poems might do so. "The book of hunger" is a section of "The Right of Return," a serial poem that explores historical anti-Semitism and how it had essentially paved the way for the Shoah (the Holocaust). I wanted to create a work that would include numerous references to historical events and assumptions, very specific references, but one that would also be somewhat open, and employ elements of the diasporic experience that are undoubtedly universal, if only to demonstrate such universalities.

The title of the sequence nods to both the Universal Declaration of Human Rights, specifically to article 13, and that of the Jewish right of return, as created via The Declaration of Independence that established the State of Israel. In fact, within The Declaration of Independence, there is mention of the Jewish people giving to the world "the eternal Book of Books." The book is just such a charged and important concept in Judaism, not that I'm by any means a scholar, or even a practitioner of it, but I am Jewish, and did attend temple until my early teen years. The titles of the various sections of the poem owe something to Edmond Jabès. His work was crucial to me at a certain point, and I felt a deep affinity for his own experience of Judaism, although I've never been expelled, as he was, from my homeland for it.

I'll tell you a funny story: I once had lunch with Tomaž Šalamun, and was explaining to him the way I read, how I'm always looking at form, trying to figure out how the book does what it does. Midway into what I'm sure was beginning to become a murky monologue, he asked, "Noah, are you Jewish?" I said, "Yes." Putting his hand on my shoulder, he said, "That is the way with the Jew and the Book." Of course, he was absolutely right!

As far as those references I'd mentioned, they're all over the poem, although they can be hermetic at times, which is okay with me. I'm not big on the inclusion of notes pages in books of poetry and feel like the poet has done the work already and if one is so inclined to do some research, well, great, maybe it'll make one's engagement with the work all the more deepened, but it's not wholly necessary. For example, "The book of rebuilding" quotes from a tablet which reads: *"a month of fruit harvest/ a month of sowing/ one of after-grass."* Further on in the poem there is the line, "Knew they weren't always wanderers." Does it matter if a reader is unaware that I'm quoting from the earliest known Jewish calendar? No, it doesn't, because one can infer that clearly agricultural activities means a peoples are rooted somewhere. There are allusions within the sequence which are well known, such as that of "a pound/ of flesh without a drop of blood," from *The Merchant of Venice*, where the character of Shylock is representative of, and further propagates, anti-Semitic notions.

And there are also references to some of the ways in which we've tried to come to terms with the Shoah. I once watched all nine hours of the film *Shoah*, and was just completely devastated. That I watched it while I was an undergrad in a little viewing booth, with big head phones on, sitting in what was becoming an increasingly uncomfortable chair made it all the more unbearable. The first sentence of "Postscript: the book of Cain" is a reference to the film. It reads: "He took the train to an empty field which was not empty when an older train arrived years ago." There are portions of the film in which villagers who had witnessed trainloads of people being shipped to the camps are interviewed while trains are moving down those very same tracks in the background.

Although I'm not so interested in fully explicating "the book of hunger," I will say that the "expansion" mentioned is that of the death of the individual; it's an expansion of self into otherness, as well as a solid into a gas. I think of the "hunger" here as very much that of literal starvation. Read through the lens of the camps, the poem takes on something quite different, no?

I realize that using such a charged historical landscape for a poem is an act fraught with numerous issues, but but but the poem doesn't place the poet on a hilltop beaming down epiphanic quips about the human condition. As I said already, my intention here was to allow for a more open-ended reading. In a way, one might consider this the staging of that argument you mentioned. Does authorial intention matter? I hope not, but I also hope a work displays its presence.

TF: Your extremely useful explanation shows that intention can matter a great deal, even if it doesn't constitute the horizon of interpretation. When I read the title, "The Right of Return," I thought about the context of Israel, but then, I didn't find anything in the sequence that seemed overtly related to it, perhaps because I haven't read Jabès, so I figured that "return" might instead involve something like the "return of the repressed" in Freud. Yes, the Shylock references jump out at you, but at those points, I wasn't thinking about the original meaning of "the right of return," and I couldn't connect this glaring representation of Jews with a thread of discourse about the Shoah. Now that you've brought all this up, your elucidation of specific intention (as opposed to the permission of "a more open-ended reading") can enable my reading of the sequence to be much fuller, much more satisfactory, even if I don't get around to reading Jabès in the near future. If there's still anything of value in the rhetorical aspects of my brief and very partial interpretation above, they could be strengthened through contact with the historical frames.

I'd like to touch upon a dynamic raised in another sequence in the book, "Four Allusive Fields." When Cy Twombly moved to Rome in the late fifties, the "abstract" marks in his paintings began to refer to textures and colors of ancient Roman architecture, and some works allude to Homer's epics. There are plenty of allusions to this utilization of classical Greco-Roman culture in the four "allusive" poems, as well as descriptions of Twombly's colors and surfaces and tropological flights that can be taken as imaginative descriptions. Here's the first one:

Cy listens absently to absent Homer
& his refusal become a dead thing full of music
Smash it on a cyclotron. Drag it across a dozen centuries
Drips are old. Smudges are old. Talking a museum
out of its eternal monologue, it's not embarrassing
to leak in waves & cones. Nudes fall from newspapers
as you fell from an oily twilight, from a painting
of the word twilight, arranged without letters, inkless
like a fire that consumes all before it, or better, inkless
as the phrase: "like a fire that consumes all before it"
Who wouldn't be mayor of a worked-over surface
returning clutter for a broom, ever-after for Cliffs Notes
Work smudging talk; talk smudging work
Obedience is an awful word I think to get lost in (53)

In *Burning Interiors": David Shapiro's Poetry and Poetics* (Ed. Joseph Lease and

Thomas Fink. Madison: Fairleigh Dickinson UP, 2007), your article, "Written and Rewritten to Order: The Gift of Generative Possibility in the Work of David Shapiro," treats the rewriting of the texts of contemporary poets by contemporary poets—not "drag[ging] it across a dozen centuries"!—as evidence of the receipt of the "original" writer's gift. It is also a reciprocating homage to and celebration of the source-poet and his/her work that actualizes possibilities inherent in the original text. In your own poetic practice, as manifested in *A Fiddle Pulled from the Throat of a Sparrow* and your first two books (since we've already addressed the collage-technique in *Inbox*), I believe that you strive to enable source-texts, whether recent or "old," to realize their "goal" of refusing "to become a dead thing full of music." Even if you have to "smash" others' language "on" your own version of "a cyclotron," your reciprocal gift, homage, and celebration—a complicating, not a banalizing, simplifying "Cliffs Notes"—includes the intention of "talking a museum/ out of its eternal monologue," of generating dialogic energy. Thus, "obedience" may be an awful concept, but paradoxically, some degree of obedience to others' language affords, in Hart Crane's terms, "new thresholds, new anatomies." Could you please respond to my basic drift here and, if what I'm saying has some validity, provide a few examples?

NEG: Oh yes, I think there's validity to your basic drift. I'm a big proponent of drifting, of flux, and the notion of the gift in all spheres, whether it's KRS ONE sampling Public Enemy, Dante reanimating Virgil, or the rabbinical practice of midrash, of inserting (asserting) one's self into Judaism's core texts. Isn't this the poetic tradition in a nutshell? Art transcending linear time? Maybe I'm getting too grand here, but I think your reading of my poem is spot on. The Fiddle book is full of homage, dialogue, and general engagement with the work of others. Outside of the "Four Allusive Fields" sequence that you mention, the other poem that loudly tries to talk "a museum/ out of its eternal monologue" would be "A New Hymn to the Old Night." The poem takes two variants of English translations of the same bit of Novalis's *Hymns to the Night*, Dick Higgins's "[d]own over there, far, lies the world," and George MacDonald's "[a]far lies the world," as a kind of refrain, which I use as both digression and homage, attempting to open other possibilities, and in doing so, to effectively praise a meticulous uncertainty. The poem here and there nods to Novalis's life, but in small ways, with mention of the loss of Sophie, his beloved, and the blue flower that figures so prominently in his novel, although, to be certain, it also includes things that are pretty far removed from Novalis. For example, while I was working on the poem I received an email from David Shapiro in which he mentioned his recent trip to Mexico, and how he was afraid of nothing. I loved the way he'd said this, how it rang with bravado and humorous self-parody, so I simply included it in the poem.

The danger in continually allowing in the work of others is when one uses it as a crutch, when one doesn't attempt to further the work, so that a line or phrase from someone else becomes the most interesting thing in one's own work. You should just edit an anthology if that's the case. For me, I read as a kind of miner, looking for raw things, ideas, syntax, rhythms, I might extract, bring home, and then treat, alter, and polish; the final stage being the most important. The four sonnets that make up "Untragic Hero of Epic Theater" came out of my reading of Benjamin on Brecht, but it's also infused with personal experience, as are all of my poems. I once watched "a display window where a bee stumbling/ between bits of jewelry" had me oddly enthralled in its epic tragedy. I'm not interested in the poem as book report. The poem that glues a chair out of books and then sits in it, now that's more interesting, as long as it's willing to look out the window now and again.

TF: And the chair bears whatever poetic weight descends on it.

A Fiddle Pulled from the Throat of a Sparrow features a variety of stanzaic-patterns, as well as modes of indentation, but the one-line stanza, which, I've noticed, Mei-mei Berssenbrugge, Timothy Liu, and Charles Bernstein also use to excellent good effect, is especially prominent. What advantages do you find in the one-line stanza? It would be interesting, also, to hear about whatever prompted some of the stanzaic decisions you made in various parts of the book.

NEG: I once watched a spider spin an entire web, from start to finish. This must have been sometime in the late 1990s. I was on my way out the front door when morning light caught the first anchoring volleys of the web, making it glisten and clearly visible. Normally, I'd have just pushed the threads aside and continued on, but seeing the little thing hard at work was too intriguing, its systematic creation—once I'd paused to watch—too stunning. So I let an hour or so get eaten standing in the doorway. I loved how the thing would weave back and forth, leaving behind these tiny boxes, which, in its next pass, were subdivided even further. Some sort of previously unarticulated understanding of form was beginning to oil the gears in the back of my mind. At the time, I lived with several housemates, and left them a note asking that they not use the front door that day. After leaving out the back, I returned home several hours later, and, having forgotten entirely the spider and my note, burst through the front door to find two of my housemates laughing at my transgression, at the sincerity of my note and my own ruinous forgetfulness.

For me, the line rises from just such a balance between diligent exactitude and explosive, ebullient destruction. A single line stanza is perhaps the embodiment of this kind of oscillation. It hovers, almost isolated, allowing one to consider all of its implications, meanings and possibilities as an autonomous unit, yet it's also clearly wedded to its upstairs and downstairs neighbors, sometimes more closely to one than the other. There's this moment before the sun has completely set when people have their lights on but haven't drawn their blinds. Looking up at a multi-story apartment complex one might take in the buzzing life and brief private narratives of any of the individual windows, or step back and see the whole of it in the building itself. Not that I'm advocating voyeurism here, but the same is true with a poem's stanzaic pattern. The first encounter with the page is visual. One is faced with a definite shape, a spatial arrangement that registers and projects a kind of order (or disorder) before one begins reading. I think this is something that you've been working with for several years now.

A lot of my own decisions about these patterns are based on an attempt to maximize the tension between that visual, pre-reading engagement with the poem and its later musical and referential dynamics. I like thinking about the relationship the line in painting has to that in poetry. In one of Cézanne's letters, he writes about the horizontal line as giving breadth and the vertical as depth. I think there's something there true to its similar function in poetry. I don't ever compose in lines. I create them afterwards, which is why *A Fiddle Pulled from the Throat of a Sparrow* took six years to write and the prose of *Novel Pictorial Noise* took about six months.

TF: *Novel Pictorial Noise* (New York: Harper Perennial, 2007), selected for the National Poetry Series by John Ashbery, consists of fifty prose-poems, each a page or less in length and each followed by a line or two or three or sometimes more of verse. Sheila E. Murphy's "American Haibun" is a prose-paragraph followed by one line, but your approach is more variable. I like what Ashbery has to say about this in his blurb—that "each prose-bloc" is "modified or modulated by the ghostly fragments that interleave them," and the ghostliness often has to do with grammatical anomalies, like two prepositions in direct proximity that don't normally interact. The modifications that Ashbery talks about are mysterious to me; how did you establish a relationship between the paragraphs and the verse, at least in your own mind?

NEG: Forced proximity can be a funny thing. Isn't that what we poets do, a little violent yoking? I'm glad to hear that there's some mystery in the reading experience for you. I'm always compelled by texts that resist whatever default reading modes we bring to them. I haven't seen the Murphy book that you mention, but the classic Haibun form—or at least what I know of it via Basho in translation—could be one way to consider the relationship the book sets up between prose and fragment. The reading that Ashbery applied via that blurb seems to gel with the gist of Haibun, an exploratory prose followed by either a summary or extending Haiku, which is here replaced with a fragment. It works if one thinks of the book as a progression, a kind of movement from one perception or inquiry to the next. But I'm not necessarily wed to that sort of reading.

One could think of the fragments as wall text accompanying the canvas-like geometric shape of the prose, or à la Williams's *Kora in Hell* as an oblique sort of commentary on the prose. In fact, it's pretty fitting that Ashbery selected the book, because his famous opening to *Three Poems* is probably the most useful way to engage with the prose/fragment dialectic: "I thought that if I could put it all down, that would be one way. And next the thought came to me that to leave all out would be another, and truer, way." To step out from behind the compositional curtain, the fragments are actually erasures of the prose, although they appear in the book in reverse order, which is to say that the fragment on page 2 is an erasure of the prose on page 99, so they touch their mirror images at the book's center, on pages 50 and 51. I did this because I wanted to book to fold in on itself, to collapse and expand like a lung. As a fan of constraint, accident, and coincidence, I was pleased with the results.

TF: Could you explain specifically what you mean by "erasure of the prose"? Some of the words on page 99 are included in the fragment on page 2, but not all, so I'm not seeing how the non-repeated words constitute an erasure.

NEG: Sure. Originally this manuscript was called *Fifty Paragraphs from a Perfectly Functional Book*. I'd had an ambitious notion to begin work on a large scale, multi-volume poem that would explore lots of different forms. I'm about half way into another manuscript called *One Thousand Lines from a Perfectly Functional Book*, which should give some sense of the project's scope, but I think I'm pretty much done with this idea, and will in time alter that title as well. Anyhow, after I'd completed the paragraphs, I realized that the book needed something else, some kind of counterpoint to the density and formal elements of the prose. Procedurally, I simply went through each paragraph, deleting its rhetorical framework, and retaining whatever minor elements I felt were somehow compelling. The words in each of the fragments appear in the same order as they do in the prose. The only word on page 2 that doesn't appear in the paragraph on page 99 is the first, "composition," which I must have at some point edited out of the final version of that paragraph. I decided to retain the capitalization within the fragments, which read to me like a kind of pictorial alchemy.

TF: The word "noise" comes up repeatedly in this book, and it harks back to sound references in the titles of your two first books, *The Frequencies* and *The Area of Sound Called the Subtone*. "The essence of pictorial fact," you write not far from the beginning of *Novel Pictorial Noise*, "aspires to describe itself as a panorama, an impossible cultivation of pictorial elements" (15). Throughout the text, both the impossibility and appeal of such a cultivation of totality/totalization is figured in diverse ways. I wonder, then, about the significance(s) of the title. Is its synesthesia a critique or (just an) acknowledgment of how the visual in U.S. culture saturates us wherever we turn? Does "novel" provide the less than approving connotation of novelty or the most positive sense of Pound's "make it new"? Or is this prose-poem a creature of another genre, a novel including "pictorial noise"? Also, our readers can look up the book's cover online and see the presence of "Prose" and "Poetry" with directional arrows and lines; if you feel like talking about the relation of Michael Labenz's cover image to your own sense of how the title works, please do.

NEG: All of those readings of the title work, and all of them were intentional. It's important to me to create things that work with multiple meanings, on multiple levels. I think this lends a sense of self-renewal to art. It's not so much news that stays news as it is news that renews, news that opens in different ways with each encounter. Everything I write is acutely aware of itself on a sonic, aural level, and this awareness is part of its compositional structure, part of the way I proceed, rather than something that's amended and altered in the editing process. The tuning fork, which is not an instrument at all, is also my favorite instrument. I'm not sure what exactly I mean by that, nevertheless I stand behind it with my entire being, because it's an example of logical noise. Well, maybe it's nonsensical music. It might be both.

As for the cover, I couldn't be happier with it. Michael Labenz is a good friend of mine. He did cover images for *The Frequencies* and *The Area of Sound Called the Subtone*, as well as for all of the Braincase chapbooks that I've published. A new issue of *Denver Quarterly* will feature his work on its cover. He's also gearing up to do all of the design work for a new press that I'm going to be involved with, but that's a few years down the road. Mike is an incredible autodidact, a reading machine, and one of the funniest and most goofy people I know. When we lived in the same town, I'd often see him in the mornings on his daily pilgrimage to a café where he'd tackle all sorts of critical theory, philosophy, and poetry. The guy worked part-time and lived frugally so that he could read as widely and broadly as he wanted. He keeps small notebooks where he sketches out these almost hermetic graphic representations of his thinking, which are just incredible. Working with him is great because he'll read the text and come up with an image that absolutely embodies its concerns, and that can further those concerns by adding a visual extension and depth, something that interacts with the writing instead of just representing it. I think that's what he did with *Novel Pictorial Noise*, although I'll leave the explication of the relationship between the image and the writing to someone else.

TF: The end of each prose section of *Novel Pictorial Noise* includes a rhyming or slant-rhyming couplet. (As you spent some time in Amherst, slant-rapmaster Emily is not irrelevant.) Within prose-poetry's great flexibility, a formal feeling comes at the end. Of course, the rhymes are often humorous: "Snow falls over my perpetual excuse, turning the narrative loose" (33). Indeed, in this prose-poem, "each paragraph requires the participants to reposition themselves," and the traditional constraint does not reassure, but offers a rousing disorientation: "If one were to take transgression as one's starting point, then it would be limitation that throws one satisfyingly out of joint" (83). Rhyme might be the tuning fork that throws the reader satisfyingly out of tune or into an unfamiliar pattern. What was it like for you to use the rhymes as a constraint — that is, how did this element affect your overall process? And now that you're another reader of the (finished) text, how do the rhymes influence your experience of the whole?

NEG: I did a reading from the book about a week ago, and afterward, a friend of mine — someone who'd never seen nor heard the work from this book — said, "I liked those jabs you had at the end." Initially, I didn't understand the comment, but after talking for a bit it became clear that the listening experience was one that, for this particular person, was punctuated with a sort of sly emphasis, that each rhyme served as both punch and wink. Of course, I was glad to hear it.

My intention with the rhyme was threefold: first off, I wanted to use a formal device that would call attention to the artifice of the work, like a photographer who purposely leaves a smudge on the camera's lens; one is forced to recognize that there is a negotiation present, that there are layers to one's interactions. Secondly, I wanted to trump some of the expectations that are tethered to the prose poem by combining it with a device normally associated with the lyric, with lineated works. Although the myriad definitions and considerations of the prose poem often focus on musicality, they rarely mention prosody, which makes sense, since one is not dealing with verse. However, I think of the sentence as a kind of line, a unit of measure, and moreover, the relationship between sentences as both mental and rhythmic caesura. I've been working with the paragraph form for about six years or so, and I see it as distinct from prose poetry, or at least as a subgenre with a separate set of concerns. I suppose that in trying to work out issues of form there's something inherently polemical. The existence of the text becomes an argument for a position, for its position. Finally, and to more directly answer your question, I wanted to use a constraint that would push my writing in a different direction, or at least alter my compositional procedure. The most difficult thing about working in such a mode is trying to shake it. Acclimating was easy; I started thinking in rhyme. I was even inclined to include it in my critical writing of the time. After I'd finished the book, and so jettisoned its formal constraints (though not its formal concerns) from then current and future projects, I had to forcibly reject all of the rhyme that kept popping into my head. It was just invasive, and, at that point, felt formally dead.

TF: How does "the paragraph form" have "a separate set of concerns" from prose poetry?

NEG: With the paragraph, one can safely stow away the canonical baggage of the prose poem, which seems to be getting heavier and heavier each year. As I use it, the paragraph is a form that harnesses the pressure of having to sculpt attention out of a contextual void. It places a larger demand on immediacy and speed, which is compounded by the restrictions of duration, since more often than not I'm working without a title, and in such a way as to render a title superfluous. I'm interested in surfaces and surface play, but also in attempting to accrue some kind of depth. It's like watching through a frozen lake as the shadow of a creature underneath darts by. The more intently one looks at a single spot with the hope of seeing it again the less the range one is able to cover, and thus the likelihood of catching the thing is also lessoned. In a sense, the paragraph asks to be tackled quickly, but also in its brevity offers a palatable return. Of course, these things can all be true for the prose poem, however its leash seems to me to be a little longer.

TF: What are a few of the aspects of writing poetry and texts in paragraphs that you enjoy most — that keep you excited about doing it?

NEG: Being excited about writing, which I am, doesn't necessarily mean that I enjoy it. It's work. It's what I do, what I think about. My brother, who is a sociolinguist, and currently doing research in Myanmar, once jokingly referred to me as a man of leisure. I think it's a telling example of the overall, larger cultural perception of what it is that we poets do, as though I were wandering among some picturesque landscape with a quill pen, plucking fruit from trees, and jotting down metaphors about the purity of their taste. For me, writing is a way to work out problems. It's an all consuming, anxiety-ridden, difficult activity that has completely reshaped the course of my life and the constituent components of each of my days. I absolutely love it, but am not so sure I enjoy it.

TF: Thank you, Noah.

NEG: And thank you!

Selected Paragraphs

Cradling the carcass in its mouth, there is something almost tender to the look the dog gives me as I pass. It feels like an apology. I turn away, tucking my hands deeper into the single pouch of my pullover sweatshirt. Did I miss some of the dialogue? Cyclone gray, liquid silver, granite, and yellow vehicles pass across the screen. Selective, instantaneous exclusion allows the dog to navigate what would otherwise be a world of exhaustive, overwhelming stimulation. The low, sustained rumble of an airplane thousands of feet above. A sprinkler's drag and kick. A peppered cloud of hovering gnats near the left edge of the lawn. Dozens of ants decorticating an unrecognizable substance, carrying bits of it off. Everywhere, there is action. This is easy for the dog to ignore. The visual field is welcoming; the sonic, comforting. Smell is how it understands the world. Millions of cells, of microprocessors, detect, identify, organize, and report on the flux of data produced by even the smallest shift to the environment of scent, to the invisible, drifting particles that coalesce into an odor, which, for the dog, constitutes the order of the universe—a tiny church atop each infinitesimal alteration to the air. It is able to detect a scent twenty-three feet into the ground. Its nose is that of a human's amplified one hundred times. Several ants are crushed under the paw of the dog as it moves toward what might be the remains of a mouse. Their deaths go unnoticed.

I have been trying to write this paragraph all afternoon. It should have been simple. It's a story I've told hundreds of times. Normally, it goes like this: I'm watching *Raiders of the Lost Ark* on TV. I'm ten, maybe eight, or twelve. Marion Ravenwood is wearing a white dress, low-cut in back. There is a pillow underneath me which I am grinding against. My father walks into the room, sees what I'm doing, and lets out a loud, bellowing belly laugh. Instantly, I am overcome with embarrassment. "I was just bouncing," I tell him. Here are some facts: in telling this story, I've never used the word *grinding*. Karen Allen played the role of Marion Ravenwood, the spirited love interest of Indiana Jones. For the scene in which she is held prisoner by Dr. Rene Belloq, the unethical, French archeologist played by Englishman Paul Freeman, she was asked to come up with a reason why Ravenwood might accept her captor's suggestion to change into the low-cut white dress. Allen decided that her character would do so in order to conceal a knife within the blouse she removes. I was not overcome with embarrassment, rather it was with shame. Shame is the other side of the erotic. It is not the erotic being seen, but the aftermath of one caught looking. Belloq watches in the mirror as Ravenwood is changing. Her back is to it. Her blouse, already off. She unhooks her bra, sliding the dress over her head just before the scene cuts.

Observation is change. Change is violence. Violence is inevitable. There's no other way to see it. Even a pet is unaware of her owner's eventual return. Some music drifts from a window and you're back to the first time you'd heard it. Don't expect this to work for the intervening moments; they're better left to the rubbish heap of accustomed and unobtrusive activity. Here, I think the station's swell of newly quickening passengers means we're primed for another exodus. Someone would do well to propose an analogy between these momentary surges and those of live electrical currents, not that it would reveal anything novel about the situation, which, in its drab, mundane state, is the operative candidate for a shock or two. It would, however, work as a kind of counter-example, laying siege to the universality of our more entrenched ideas. To paint the word *lighthouse* on a lighthouse is deserving of shipwreck.

Gut rot in the gulfs, a way to ride the terror talk, risk the trenches. I'm in robes, ribbed. The last Saxon in starlight starting up a fresco for the toothcomb squad. & it's not the brandy I'm after, not the bolted door left open, a paradox under the urge to kick 'em down when every car sprays the street in your face. A bit to the back, head drooped, heart saying: that song comes every hour; those shoes match the treads I meant to follow. The tracks lead straight out of town & the bus brings it all barreling back, receipts, recipes, other groundhog days when the ground's so frozen nothing save contempt would risk a soliloquy to the few stems still leaning toward the fading light. It's cold enough in valediction alley to see your own breath shadowed along the pavement. Pulling teeth or retching from the plaster cast. There's a perfect mark under me & I'm pure bull's-eye for putting it there.

The problem is possibility, or uncertainty, or the problem is that the possible is always colored by the uncertain, that there is an *if* hovering just ahead, or that just ahead is itself an *if* and the hovering is the problem, the atmosphere the problem, the problem of the atmosphere just ahead, of its uncertainty, which is an impossible *if*, an impassable *if*, one without end, no cathartic *then*, nothing but a kind of blackness, a kind of colorless blackness, a blank *if* in the absence ahead, then, for a moment, a streak of color in the cars to my right, for a moment, no, for several moments, for a string of moments, a continuous string, a moment so extended that it touches every other moment, makes of *then* a system, a constant afterward, a looped self, free of antecedents but ahead, no, not ahead, ahead is the problem, the problem is also behind, impossible to enter, to my left the problem is different, diffused somehow, an *is* rather than an *if*, something lacking motion, steady, almost relaxing, a resting place, unlike everything to the right, unlike the man next to me, the strange static pace of his body in stride, the skeletal structure of his jaw almost visible, and the cars, the after *if* but before *then*, the motion of the problem figuring itself out before again collapsing into uncertainty, or the uncertain becoming the problem as it moves, as I move, looking at the man to my right, the cars to my right, the *if* everywhere else.

What struck me first was the odd conclusion that, although it's abstract, I was nonetheless looking at a narrative painting, by which I mean that the work includes the manipulation of time. Although the painting is dominated by intersecting lines and shapes in multiple colors, its real subject is the collision of these constituent elements into a system of directives. Thus, the work becomes wedded to duration. One is sent chaotically all over the canvas, searching for the origin or endpoint of the various, mazelike lines, as they connect and intersect, while jettisoning one monochromatic color for another. There is the continually thwarted sense that one might actually reach either an end or a beginning, but, of course, this never occurs.

Selling over 350,000 units in 1959, its first year on the market, Ruth Handler's Barbie doll is a massive success. Barbie is designed on a sixthscale. If she were human, her chest would measure 36 to 38 inches, while her waist would be closer to 18. A 2004 national survey found that white women in the 18 to 25 year range share Barbie's chest size, yet exceed by nearly fifteen inches her slender waist. Barbie is given her first set of bendable legs in 1965, ten years before I am born. In the 70s, after having undergone a mastectomy, Handler founds Nearly Me, a company dedicated to creating comfortable and lifelike prosthetics. There are drawers built into the wall of my bedroom. The largest one on the bottom is set a few inches from the floor. It slides all the way out. I think this is the perfect hiding place. Barbie has had dozens of pets, including many dogs, several horses and cats, a parrot, a panda, a chimpanzee, even a lion cub. I steal one of my sister's Barbie dolls, but not its clothes. With a black magic marker and two points from a red pen, I take away its voluptuous androgyny. Sometimes I talk to it. This is not an erotic experience. I am trying to teach myself intimacy. Stuffing it in a plastic bag, I store it underneath the removable drawer. I think this is the perfect hiding place. I am wrong.

Was it a flock of black helicopters I mistook for an early turn of evening? Interrogation's a landing pad in a garden. A tiny X hovering over the question: what variable doesn't love wilting? The only thing that pulls a fly from the air is exhaustion. Grounded by a noisy ionosphere, cut in half by a cloud, adrift in the always concussive intermingling of imagined things, my desire remains the same: explode the word "construct"

Somewhere, a garage door goes down. Thus, a fiction begins. Clouds gather, disperse. Let this suffice as a working formula for working a formula: what I'm coming to terms with—repetition's liberating constraint. What occurs in the courtly world has little currency to those taking up arms against it. What I'm coming to terms with builds that which contains the components to construct an evolving sense of entropy. The grand narrative the end of narratives had had had had no grandiose ending. It is as though in removing its mask the landscape shows on its face an expression one recognizes but is unable to immediately place.

I go on sensory overload outside, safer with the same room, same chair, star charts as nicks in the wall. The immobile scenery of what I'm missing out there fills me like a crow's nest, might as well carry a sign, grounding the play-by-play of someone passing on a cell phone or trying to embrace the pond by falling in. It's a construct as bad as plywood scaffolding, how the coins in my hand could muck it up half-way across the globe or keep me insular, forgetting what I said to whom, eyes plastered to the concrete as an excuse. Clouds overhead won't expand where the mind goes when I'm stuck striking the surface of a few puddles as obliquely as I do the shop windows. Rain on the sidewalk is rain on the ceiling & my suit is just right for the job.

In the 1950s, twenty-six African Honey Bee queens escaped from an apiary near São Paulo. They were being crossbred with European Honey Bees to increase productivity. By the 70s, their aggressive offspring had spread throughout South American. They are past Nicaragua in 1985. At Horseshoe Lake, I collect fireflies in a glass jar. In the backyard, I stare for hours at the ants guarding the peonies in bud. I want to be an entomologist, but I hate touching insects. At night, afraid of the bees, I worry myself out of sleep. This is the one recurring dream I've had. I am in the car with my grandparents, my sister sitting in the backseat beside me. It will not start. We hear the killer bees coming, the approaching swarm humming like an engine. From the rear window, the swarm is a black cloud. A few bees circle the car. They're metallic, tiny silver machines. "Run!" I scream, opening the door and taking off. My grandparents are ahead of me, my sister a few steps behind. We are running along a ridge. There is a stone staircase that leads toward the lake below. My sister trips, tumbles down the steps. The black cloud of bees breaks into two. Half of them are after her. I look over my shoulder. She's at the bottom of the stairs, bruised, reaching her right arm toward us. There's blood on her face. I look straight ahead and keep running.

That a train arrives at all is a small miracle of dependence, a smaller one of reliability. There is always weather to anchor us to one another. I mention something knowing you'll agree, and so we're indentured to the startling anecdotes that chisel the face we think we've put on from the lumpy air of individuality surrounding our sense of how the world looks from someone else's perspective. By chance a drop of water lands precisely between coat collar and a bit of exposed neck, almost as a means to further punctuate this point, which, of course, is not random at all, but another of the mysterious jokes the universe seems to be silently playing, refusing to give itself away with even the slightest of chuckles. It's held in, neither expanding nor dissipating, like a painting of a man puttering around his rooms, another of him picking up or putting down a few treasured objects—scissors, an onyx paperweight, the skull of a monkey with three teeth attached. Is he really turning them over in a way that shows him to be alone with the act? One might claim a kinship with the palette, burn the canvas, and hang the brush on a museum wall.

A rivet forces proximity on two sheets of aluminum. Violence to the hawk & violence to the horse, together, build a third kind of animal. Wholly subdued, hanger-like. This tangential harmony—impossible as a mountain in the ant's understanding of an airfield. Nothing's joined that wasn't broken from itself; thus, the sexual elevator crushes a man holding a bouquet of lilies. An orchid lashed to a tree proves original theory untenable. Is this how you underline your way into the pantheon? Pegasus was a horse. The airplane, an automobile. A pillow for earth-bound egos purified in upper air. Orgasm tears the plane apart.

The fool worked mornings on his forgery, a blue crayon & a voice played back on a handheld recorder, its regional drawl recounting a dream of the other nothing. One sets time against itself & the key fits but it won't turn to the left or the right but it fits & that makes you happy if only for a few seconds. There were plastic bags in the highest branches. Ribbons of smoke above the river. A house on the hill stretching its wax wings. Was it a consolation prize or purely original silence?

My brother has taught me a chant, a string of words with an incantatory rhythm, but whose meaning escapes me. Mother fucking titty sucking booger ball bitch. Mother fucking titty sucking booger ball bitch. He leads me from the asphalt parking lot through the double doors of the school's side entrance, pushing them open with his back. I'm an instrument. Mother fucking titty sucking booger ball bitch. Keep going. Keep going. He continues to face me, taking tiny reverse steps. I'm an orchestra. Mother fucking titty sucking booger ball bitch. I'm six years old. He is ten. Twenty five years later, he'll tell me that because of its tonal system, a single word in one of the Chinese dialects repeated with slight differences of inflection can be translated as: poem is shit. Mother fucking titty sucking booger ball bitch. I follow him down the hall, through another set of doors, into the crowded waiting area of the principle's office. Mother fucking titty sucking booger ball bitch. Everyone's staring at me. I am inflated with pride.

Comes a nightlight's landing beacon leads me to pick villainy from a bouquet of the places I'd left to yesterday's map of the future, rubbernecking unintentionally oblique articulation. Loosen a rivet from the lapsed mind and out pours the obvious like thick rain. A sterile neighborhood, a standing ovation, centuries of labor congealing into the desk lamp that lets me mold my own two cents from this paperclip panopticon. I'm not pushing anything here. Power's got a fulcrum that's half self-portrait, part handicraft. The lever will pivot regardless of where it's placed down. It's the primacy of motion drafts sound.

Habitation tempers the dial tone I inhabit, hoarding the earpiece & priceless circuitry when you walk into yourself. The route is a fig & the archer's fingers make two good body parts for every trained hero hoping to salvage a little personal space. They want their own ink to overdo it, their own half-submerged retro-stylings. Every shirt in the shop is for sale, even the one the owner's got on. Starboard, a little sparrow choking on its diminutive song. Aft, the laughing hyenas in their best rope-trick come-on lines. I'd mention the open carcass if the smell hadn't handled that one already, if I hadn't been hanging up for at least half an hour.

We're sitting around a table. A bunch of stoned teenagers. These kinds of stories never interest me, but this one is mine. Philippe's parents had been in Brazil for a month. His house was a mess. The day before they were supposed to return, we found foodstuff so hardened on a few of the dishes that we had to throw them out. We filled dozens of garbage bags. We felt invincible. We didn't know what a cliché was. Someone said, Pass it already. Someone said, I need another beer. On the back porch, under the stars, and a little dizzy with all of my friends, I told them that this was the perfect *atlassphere*. What did you just say? I said this is perfect, this night, all of us. No, you said *altassphere*. Yeah, so. It's atmosphere. Really? Really! I always thought it was *atlassphere*. You know like an atlas but also a sphere, like the world wrapped around us.

Although it's never certain where things take place, or to whom those things are happening, Kunin's work does evoke a sort of intellectual voyeurism. One is made privy to the infesting of otherwise innocuous objects and gestures with meaning that often feels grotesque, sinister or, at the very least, shameful. The tension is so palpable in these poems that one feels as though one has opened a door onto an indiscriminately compromised scene; however, and this is Kunin's real strength, as such a scene is always slightly out of focus, it is the feeling, rather than the event, that takes precedence, leaving one awash in all the attendant emotion of witnessing something one probably shouldn't have.

Gunship grunts. Splendid assemblage & cinnamon acetaminophen. The glue holds the gutters in. The rhetoric's a loose-leaf apprentice. Cracks in the oracular self I'm splitting open, splicing states of consciousness onto what? Locomotive sound wings? A burnt rabbit in the trap & a rabid set of number laws the numb part of me knuckles up to. Tell it to the sludge, the oil slick, the slippage ousting us from Ollie-Ollie-oxen-free central. I've got a drawer full of keys that bend by themselves. Magic Realism, mute narration or just plain jack-in-the-box psychosis?

About five years ago, I wrote a short poem called "Yesterday I Named a Dead Bird Rebecca". The title came to me while in Florida visiting family. Going for a short walk, I passed the carcass of a crow swarming with small flies. There was something so repugnant about this particular dead animal that, although oddly aware of its lack of any sort of odor, I was, nonetheless, overcome by a strong, debilitating nausea, one which I suspect arose simply from the smell I imagined the bird to have. The poem reads:

were a defused heart
wintering the clock

time kept
by counting birds

I'd call flight
a half-belief in air

a venomous lack
when the ticking is less so

What could be more obvious than that this poem transposes its propositional way of understanding gravity into the structure of its own identity? Something that lies beyond the purview of its lone sentence speaks to me now as the kind of nostalgia one feels upon watching an airplane pass overhead. It means making distance disappear.

Would you rather have a goddess of terror to whom goats are sacrificed or the implications of Eve signifying human sensitivity entrenched in the post-European psyche for another millennium? I'm through thinking in images, says the bodily eye to its narrative dismemberment, while a decapitated head rolls out of the cliché, and I've built another victim of fully embodied rhetoric. And in this lies the difference between picture and proposition, between thinking afresh as if nothing had happened and taking a tidal wave apart. A salty phoneme sinks in sand. It is not novel pictorial noise, but the limits of draftsmanship standing for the limits of earthly existence removed from the videocassette. Multi-petalled, rose-like, I give you permission to see beneath the apparent image of the flower.

Mary Rising Higgins
interviewed by Bruce Holsapple and John Tritica

Mary Rising Higgins is the author of *red table(S* (La Alameda 1999), *oclock* (Potes and Poets 2000), *)locus TIDES((* (Potes and Poets 2002), Greatest Hits, 1990-2001 (Pudding House 2002), *)cliff TIDES((* (Singing Horse 2005), *)joule TIDES((* (Singing Horse 2007) and *Borderlining: Pieces from R and B* (Small Chapbook Project 2007). Her poems have appeared in such magazines and journals as *Blue Mesa Review*, *Cafe Solo*, *Big Allis*, *ecopoetics* and *Central Park*, and she recorded poems for Vox Audio. This interview took place in her home in Albuquerque on February 11, 2007, just before her 63rd birthday. Two months after the interview, Mary again became ill from complications of breast cancer and began receiving hospice care. She died on August 26, 2007.

This interview appeared on the website under the title **Linescapes: An Interview with Mary Rising Higgins**.

John Tritica: Mary, I would like to start with the question of what you see as differences between *red table(S* [1999] and *)locus TIDES((* [2002] , *)cliff TIDES((* [2005], and *)joule TIDES((* [2007] . There's an obvious difference in how the poems look, yet you could take lines from *red table(S* and find similar lines in *)cliff TIDES((.* You could recognize the same poet as having written both. Can you address what you see as being the differences?

Mary Rising Higgins: If I think about *red tables(S* first, that was written while I was still teaching in the public schools full-time. So *red table(S* was fitted into working life, staying up past midnight with my students' work, planning new things for them. And I was limited as to when I could write and would begin Friday evenings after dinner. I'd turn on two 5,000 watt neon lights to keep me alert. I'm sure my house glowed for blocks. But I would work late on Friday night, and then I would work as much as I could Saturday and Sunday. That's how these poems came to be constructed. I couldn't begin to think of the long poems that make up the *TIDES((* trilogy; the process that goes into the work of these books is so utterly different because with them I'm retired, working perhaps three days a week at CNM [a community college in Albuquerque]. So, yes, the work comes out of the same center, but the process out of which the work derives is utterly different.

Bruce Holsapple: What does that mean to you, "comes out of the same center"?

MRH: Well, comes out of my center, a center of being, a center of collecting. Essentially, I have not changed in terms of requiring a certain auditory gesture, as the means by which I enter the poem's beginning. However, with the *TIDES((* series, if I say that I'm going to work a five-hour day and my window opens when I get out of bed in the morning, instead of after a week's work, late on a Friday night, that's a very different window from which to begin one's creative work.

JT: That was 1995?

MRH: Yes, and I did that through the last year, because the needs of students are endless. But when I got to *oclock*, my life had changed dramatically. I was recovering from experimental treatment for breast cancer; my sister had come to live with me because I needed twenty-four hour care; she had dragged me through the illness. But I was exhausted and embarrassed by the amount of sleep I needed. Actually, *oclock* began with 9:00 a.m. I was amazed and depressed that I couldn't even get up at 9:00 a. m. That was the first poem, and suddenly I realized: Write a twenty-four poem series that could embody the way I felt the poem could function. Also, I was fortunate. Peter Ganick, the founder of Potes & Poets Press, happened to read *red table(S* and sent an e-mail to me saying that whatever I project I was working on, he would publish it. I think I had gotten to the second poem by then, and I was delirious with the sense that, because of the kind of work Peter supported, I could go as far as I was capable with the work in *oclock*, and I did. In fact, indirectly, he suggested the title for *oclock*. I sent him the first draft [of the manuscript], and he wanted me to add body to 2 a.m. He did not say anything about how I should add body. 2 a. m. just needed to be able to stand with the other poems, which he called my "clock poems." I thought, what a perfect title, *oclock*! I liked the foraging methods employed in working with *oclock*, so when I moved into the *TIDES((* series, they retained elements from *oclock*. But these poems are each built around a particular letter. I think the first letter I addressed in *)locus TIDES((* was "D," because I love Beverly Dahlen's work. So I thought that would be a good place to begin. I think "D" is less visual than succeeding works. The dripstone is something that occurs in a cavern, and I thought that was a good metaphor for how the work in that particular poem developed, because it was such slow going. I personally find the poem that works best for me is a poem where I just have to roll up my sleeves and do battle with the beginning. Then, suddenly, it will take off. Dripstone is like that.

JT: Beginning with *oclock*, the *TIDES((* series develops a 8 ½ by 11 inch format. Why do you think that larger page format evolved, or at least is conducive to your work?

MRH: It started accidentally. I was toying with the idea of the arbitrary rectangle of the page and thinking about how a visual artist would approach that rectangle. That has to be addressed in the publication of one's work. There have to be margins. You can only deal with certain perimeters. Editors and publishers don't care to pursue the complexity of work that escapes those perimeters. So I started out seeing what I could do with the 8 ½ by 11 rectangle, leaving margins on all sides that would be appropriate for publication. And I simply became so comfortable with the page size that, even though I wanted to break the work down at different points for a smaller page, it just wasn't conducive to the work that evolved in the larger format. Though it would be glib to say that the poems are built for the page, in fact I became enamored of doing everything I could think of to the page with the poem's lines in the large format. So, it didn't start out intentionally but now I've become rather intentional about it.

BH: You shift from a more traditional poetry, flush left, in *red table(S* and in *oclock* that boundary disappears. There's a floating element involved. After you finish oclock, you turn to the abecedarium? So initially you have a frame you're hanging things in, but then it becomes wide open. What tensions hold the work together after that?

MRH: I think in the *TIDES((* series there are certain components in the way the work is built that hold the poems together. I collect words over time that begin with the letter, usually words I hadn't heard or seen used in a particular way in text before. I mean, I had this clipboard, and I arbitrarily put twenty-six pages in it, and I carried it around with me. Do you really want to know about these things? Okay. I also had notes to myself about what I was going to look for. I was going to look for writers, words, and things I didn't know enough about.

BH: Did you know the subjects?

MRH: Oh, not at all. The subjects were going to come out of the words collected, come out of dictionary meditations, meditations on the writing of the poets.

BH: You were going to invent?

MRH: Well, with language, one is never going to invent whole-cloth, because language creates the cloth. I feel so constrained within the language itself, and wanted to create an homage to text, as I'm working because of its beauty, because of its social-civil qualities, the conscience of language, the function of language, how one can construct a life out of the questions that language can present. So while I love that term, "whole-cloth," I'm very much caught in the conundrum and quandaries of language itself, as we all are. The shapes in *TIDES((* become increasingly affected by the shape of the letters historically or currently. When all of those things are put together, the poems take on discreteness. I have to say, I get exhausted easily now, particularly over the last year. I've entered a re-diagnosis for the cancer. I've really been scrambling to stay on top of my work. But when I lie down at night, I always keep my journal next to me—it has a pillow—I've only taught one poetry workshop, but the students laughed so much when I began talking about my process. They thought I was really too weird for words. But actually it comes out of Denise Levertov's poem "Writing in the Dark." Here was a woman who had a full life, ran a household, and so when she thought of things in the night, she'd better get it down. I notch the page. I do not open my eyes. I can lay the journal down; I can pick it back up; I can find the notch and proceed, but I imagine how the poems are going to look on the page. That's how I construct the forms. If it is the twelfth letter in the alphabet, it's going to be a twelve-page poem. Now if it's the second letter, of course it's not going to be two pages, it's going to be a multiple of two. If it's the 26th letter, it will be a divisor. It's a fabulous way to construct the poem as you wish. You have arbitrary boundaries to work within, but they're nourishing and beautiful because they're only about tethering the work on the page.

JT: So there's an interplay between improvisation and structure?

MRH: The work is highly structured. It isn't just numbers of pages. It's structured in terms of line, how many syllables there will be in the line. For example, "Dearest L" in)cliff TIDES((, the lines are governed by the twelve-syllable line. I permit a thirteenth syllable simply because I don't want the line to become sing song. I will permit an eleven-syllable line. But "Following L," if I remember correctly, is twelve pages in twelve-syllable lines for the twelfth letter. However, the improvisational, and sometimes the stochastic, enters.

JT: It gave you, within that imposed form, a freedom. It generated the material, if you will.

MRH: Absolutely it helps generate the material, and as soon as I sense that it's getting dead on its feet, change is called for. That's when I will add, subtract, or bend a shape so that it looks more fluid.

JT: It's far from "anything goes."

MRH: It is never anything goes. Why? Because I think that when one deludes oneself into thinking "anything goes," in fact we're governed unconsciously by our sentiments, or orientations, and whatever is going on in our lives. Certainly these things are occurring in my work, but the work is always that homage to text, and how text functions, as a serious component for connecting us.

JT: Which contemporary poets—in the last twenty, thirty years—do you see your work fitting in with?

MRH: I think my work fits wherever there are women whose work pushes the envelope of how the poem has been written or appeared, say, within the last ten, twenty years. Lyn Hejinian and Susan Howe are the two primary poets who let me see that I could write a poem about whatever and however I needed. During a two month writing retreat at the Helene Wurlitzer

Foundation, in '89 and 91, I was able to spend time with their work. I started the poem "Transitions for Eurydice" in Taos. That poem came directly from reading Howe's *Defenestration of Prague*. That was the poem through which I began methods I use when writing now. It's the longest one in *red table(S*, and has elements of collage and disjunction that are more about mid to late 20th century. You know, one has to write that way. Our lives are that way. Everything we are presented with is that way.

BH: Are there other poets in the concrete tradition that you call upon for inspiration—or do you understand yourself to work within the tradition of concrete poetry?

MRH: Not at all. I don't understand myself as working with a tradition of concrete poetry. Why? The word and the letters with which I am working always take precedence over the form. The form generates out of language. Actually, I'm not terribly fond of concrete poetry. I'd like to think that, if my work were pushed flush left, it would work certainly as well as it does when it takes various forms on the page. So that takes me out of that tradition I think.

BH: You're using the page more like Charles Olson and Susan Howe, for example, use the page?

MRH: I would say so, yes, and when I do enter engagement with visual form, it's affected by historical or current shapes for the letter the poem builds around. Or, it has to do with an emphasis on the dynamics of the poem, a way of opening the line, so that the reader can have a gap or perhaps be drawn in a dynamic way toward the next line. It isn't about, okay, this poem is going to look like that shape from nature. It's never about that. I always can go back to the letter out of which the poem is deriving—or it is about sound and movement in the poem. Linescape, really.

JT: Speaking of movement makes me think of the structure of the *TIDES((* trilogy. How did you conceive of that structure?

MRH: I had an opportunity for a three-day retreat at Abiquiu, NM, Ghost Ranch, and I wanted to construct a series that I could learn through, which I could grow with as a poet, where I could engage in an homage to those women poets whose work encouraged me to think about new ways that women have been writing since the 1970s, and I thought that an abecedarium was absolutely the right path for a poet to take. It's endlessly interesting. Certainly in childhood I remember falling asleep by going through ideas having to do with the alphabet. Did you? It's a marvelous way to set up going anywhere for any length of time about any topic. And so the original working title for the *TIDES((* series was *Driving from the Shoulders*. This was never intended to be mainstream work, you know, right up on the road. Also I was thinking of the shoulders of women who had come before me. I am still working on a last triptych that addresses letters Y, A, and V. Just recently I've begun to think, even if that poem takes me a year, it will be fine, because what's my intention with that long poem? It is to do as many things as possible that I have not done, to read and become aware of things that I have not become aware of, that can help to generate a poem.

JT: My next question is part statement, but it gives you full-range to respond, and disagree if you want. But I think in "waive *SHIFT*" [in *)cliff TIDES((*] there's an innovative approach to the placement of words on the page; in particular, I'm thinking of page fifty-six and fifty-seven where it's almost like

partial thriving thriv

beacons or tanks depending on wheth

desire might draw her draw as   fogged in like always to set up
ight make free play li   cense accord   ing said scope checks roped breath love fear follows
quo   ta   tion not enough data to fill in the want o   pens wi   der all the leave taken might
pensive angles we knot   brood   sort   orders to retake part of the latest turf strip
thereby le vers base need   shelf   life   wit   stock assembling when sunflowers turn on
e   go drive hol   ding her per   son   ae   in place with cor   po   rate names
to ride through a green ar   now feeling a   dag   i o   as op   posed to
in   habit   ing   rules you know a   boat like all day
for the purpose an asif starts here to
from each every dividing staged
smog warmed afternoon
jackets hum sweet heat
cage paper yellow
double vespiary
any time welt
sky cans open
chemical wake
lightning in

What needs to	off	convectings
be said the	face	change
pleasures	through	spoke
of saying so	living is it	rung
litter caped	ample the same	ladder
laughter di-	for ex- thing as	all over
mension of	not that agreeing to	touches her
what she sees point	a myth bent journey
in possible this	understanding of
from site	being this that
locale	interstices
	array
	as

we're looking at a mirror of some sort. There are dancing figures of language there. Would you comment on how you worked out the visual design of the text and how the visual design impacts on the significance of the poem?

MRH: W is a beautiful letter. It's very organic and here I'm focused on elements of its shape, so page fifty-six gives the reader an almost cubist perspective on "W", but on page fifty-seven I'm focused on elements of shapeliness and brush stroke—I do like to give a brush stroke appearance, even to ancient letter glyphs. So that's what was going on in my head. Though I don't expect the reader to come away with what I intend, but rather the reader, entering the work, will come away with what the reader is able and willing to carry away.

JT: I wonder, though, about when you look at, say, page sixty-three, if we're reading from left to right, there are a number of ways you can read this. Have you scored this in a particular way? You don't offer instruction to the reader.

Tar vein city asphalt seams observe a change of seasons. Orange blinks black arrow April. We
drive over the wings of pigeons and mourning doves. Into daylight savings' air sweat beat the
windshield of a car ahead catches that waking robin. So take one day out while the foaling mare
struggles to her feet. Your eye absolutely swooned while another holds along quaquaversal roll.
True ,pluck one catgut string and wires beneath it will vibrate in sympathy. Ethereal drone

and too
deep for
an idea
telling just   here
what it   let go or list
means to   unable to   out loud
have feel-   each other   what we beings with   we carry   long to in
for   as   stained   inseparable
another   doubt
bad cut   *On your skin, salt says what water was, what sea.*
                                            Though this is not the
                                             latest map de-
                                             signing one
                                            more window
                                          where opens
                                        across other
own   pleasurable
became our   confusion in
misread feelings   pursuit of
shadow when   happiness
themes fore-   or even
as recurring   escape from
separate "out"   mardi gras with
terrorist to   new improved
categories in

MRH: No, I wouldn't presume to do that. Now if I were reading this for an audience, absolutely I would score it. When reading I want the text to come through in as straight forward a fashion as possible. Also, I don't want to become caught up in an alternative reading. I don't want to become lost in it (as my eyesight is no longer the greatest). But for the reader, my hope would be to approach this work as a viewer approaches an abstract painting, for example, or a listener approaches a piece of contemporary classical music. And that is, in the energies that you bring to the work, what do you carry away with you this time? And my hope would be that a reader who actually would come to this page two or three times would leave with something slightly different— perhaps quite different—each of those times.

JT: In that sense, who would be an ideal reader, if you could create a profile?

MRH: Well, it would be a reader somewhat like myself and the people with whom I have close relationships who are addicted to poetry; people who love to read contemporary poetry and contemporary writers. It would not be the reader who wants to be told what to think, or is reading to escape. It has to be a reader who will create meaning in an autonomous fashion—you know, without being dominated by authorial aspects, but would rather go into the work as a kind of adventure and take away what is possible, and actually become excited by how the work changes as you begin reading across lines, or in reverse, as opposed to straight down along the lines. That is when the work begins to breathe with you, I think. For poetry to work rhythmic knots of meaning begin to function in new intense ways—you breathe with poetry. It isn't like prose that lies there on the page telling about something and taking you somewhere (in the more expected popular prose, at least.)

BH: So would you "allow" a reader to take whatever they wanted to from your poems? Could they come up with any possible interpretation?

MRH: Why not? If I go to a dance production, for example, I am looking for new vocabulary in that dance work. I'm not a dancer. I don't know what I'm "supposed to be" looking for. But I am looking for movement, motions, steps, and what I take away with me, I love. Why couldn't a reader approach the page as I approach dance, jazz, or contemporary classical music? trusting the beauty and surprise?

BH: But I think you're also saying that your poems are meaning-based. Doesn't that involve intention?

MRH: Oh, yes, they are meaning-based! And when I read them aloud, I follow what I think is the most standard way of reading the work, so that someone in the audience who would not read it, but is willing to listen will come way with something fresh and new and be able to say, as people sometimes do, "Well, it sounds good." [Laughs.] "I wasn't sure what it meant, but I like the way it sounded!" .

JT: So would you say that a reader has to grant you a certain amount of semantic excess?

MRH: Yes, I think anyone who came to this work in a prescribed way would be disappointed or become confused, would be actually quite frustrated.

JT: Yes, I've been there. Not for long, but I know the feeling.

BH: What would you tell that reader?

MRH: To go inward and to permit the work to mean differently, creatively each time he or she approaches it.

BH: So in some way your poetry is about the meaning-making process itself?

MRH: It is about that and that is my homage to text. I can remember reading things as a child and having no clue what they meant, but knowing, trusting the text, knowing that if I let it go and returned to it later—even if I had to wait a year, it would begin to mean for me.

JT: It's also giving one's self over to the reading process?

MRH: Yes, deep reading is a process. Also, I would say there is sometimes disjunction between auditory elements and textual elements in the work and that is on purpose, because there is sometimes a joy in the music of the syntax that is not necessarily the same as the meaning of those words in the labyrinth of their construction.

BH: So there is a multiplicity of approaches and there are layers that you work from?

MRH: Each poem is highly layered, I feel. Any word in conjunction or disjunction with another word is going to refer and refer and refer, if you just go back into the clause.

JT: To what extent are these poems verbal meditations, as opposed to silent meditations?

MRH: What a great question! I will confess, they are primarily silent meditations, but when I stumble, when I just don't know what word to place next, I begin speaking aloud, whatever those lines should be, to know what has to come next. One thing I avoid is a loose, limp line. I want a tight line.

BH: How do you determine whether the line is tight or limp?

MRH: I think of the tight line as one made with no unnecessary word, with rhythmic tensions at the level of the syllable.

JT: If I could chime in here—as you state in the "afterword" to)cliff TIDES((, there are "rhythm knots." There has to be tension. Where there's a syllabic structure sometimes, there's a very strong rhythm, and the rhythm holds it together.

MRH: Yes, rhythm holds it together, and if I think, oh, this could be a line of prose, something will be deleted. I'm sure other poets could argue that some of my lines are prose-like, but always I'm looking for tension, and that does make the work exhausting, especially for a reader who comes to the poem for escape. One thing I have to say is that I do not write so that you can remember something you forgot, like from some earlier point in your life. I mean, a reader may be reminded of something in their life, but I do not write a narrative poem that reminds us of events, a middle class nostalgic towpath along what might or might not have taken place in the lives of most Americans one knows around life or death or birth or divorce…those things we like to be reminded of, an escapist reading.

BH: And what is it that irritates you so about that approach?

MRH: It isn't that it irritates me. It's that if I want that approach I could simply get in my car, drive to a bookstore and find books waiting on the shelves. I don't want to do what I've seen done before. Someone could argue, oh I've seen work just like yours. But no one has done that in relation to my work. My feeling is, I started writing poetry too late to spend time writing like someone else.

JT: That's a key point. You didn't start writing until you were thirty-nine years old.

MRH: Right, my first poem unfolded finally when I was thirty-nine.

JT: Some twenty-four year ago, but that's not that long, and you didn't have the apprenticeship some have in their twenties and thirties.

MRH: Right, I think the apprenticeship was served differently.

JT: What happened took place much more intensely and there are some fifteen years between when you write your first poem and when you retired from being a schoolteacher.

BH: What is the transition? What are the recognitions that go into being "innovative?" Where does Lee Bartlett's class at the University of New Mexico enter into this?

MRH: I should be honest about my beginning, eclectic reading. As a child I read whatever I could get my hands on. When I was eleven, I happened by accident on a Wordsworth poem. That is where I first discovered the difference I look for between poetry and prose. Of course, I was reading poems voraciously when I went into Lee Bartlett's poetry workshop. I was reading contemporary poets. I was reading New Mexico poets, a lot of John Ashbery—I loved Ashbery—he is my favorite poet all the way through *red table(S* and probably appears in numerous disguises from poem to poem. I hadn't read anyone whose work I liked as much. Then I was introduced to the Language Poets, I think in 1983-84. Somehow I got into the graduate poetry-writing workshop with Lee Bartlett and Lee was just so open to a highly creative point of view. During one class he said, it doesn't matter what you say, as long as you can put it into a philosophical construct. He said many things that felt perfect for me, because I knew I'd have to write poetry in some ways unlike what I'd already read. I'll tell you, I was by necessity a sleeper in class—I'd been working all day—and if it wasn't exciting, I was dozing. But when Lee brought in the Language poets (in the first issue of L=A=N=G=U=A=G=E), what I heard led me to think, oh, this is new—like "news that stays news." And I could try to write a poem that might be read with serious attention to its content! And right off, you've got a higher number of women than any place else, and women are not objectified or marginalized, but an integral part of articulating Language Poetry. And I felt, okay, now I can address a poem at the scale I felt a poem should be addressed. I had just read Bachelard's *The Poetics of Reverie* for another class. And that was not about the means by which I would write a poem, just as if I were a painter, I could not paint trees as I remember particular trees from childhood. Suddenly, all right, the poem could

disjunctive, about the functions of language itself. The poem could occupy a larger scale and from varied perspectives.

BH: This was your chance to walk the blank, so to speak?

MRH: Yes, I had kept journals and toyed with lines, but only as I considered visual work. I wanted to become a photographer, but that's a whole other story! I couldn't become a photographer after I purchased a house where the water was too hot to use for all the darkroom equipment I had purchased. (And the water heater was not up to code and I had no way of changing that.) Well, thank goodness, what a relief! I had already become so tired of all the chemicals. Poetry has no polluting chemicals that must be carefully recycled! It is so clean! [W. C.] Williams thought about becoming a visual artist — as did I. Well, you have all that equipment and set it up, and I'm tired by then. Poetry is not like that. The more one writes, the more one wants to write. So it was a great gift that the water temperature at this little house was over ninety degrees and nothing could fix that. You have to have water at sixty-two degrees max, if you want to process a good black and white print. And I was fortunate to get into Lee Bartlett's class, so I said to myself, I will just stick with this, give it a try. I was teaching fifth-graders in public school and my mind needed something outside of the classroom.

JT: In)locus TIDES((, there's a poem called "rotations of N," and I love the first line: "day bridge event phase you try telling[.]" Here is my sense of your work: although there is almost never a linear narrative, nevertheless I still feel that you tell bits and pieces of stories. And there is still some biographical hook. Earlier you were talking about the process of meaning making. I think it's related.

MRH: Language becomes a highly experiential medium at times.

BH: How do you mean language becomes an "experiential medium?"

MRH: How one articulates an experience actually modifies that experience. Yet these are words. I'm thinking of Wittgenstein's remark that language is contiguous with nothing. But we fit into language, and language fits with us. So, indeed, my work is extremely experiential: "day bridge event phase you try telling[.]" I mean we know that when we tell an event we leave out so much and put in some things. Later we might remember things that we put in and forget completely the things we left out. I'm exaggerating, perhaps. But the experiential components of language are profound in terms of what's provided by and what we must provide to language, if we address the world through it.

JT: I feel that once you go beneath the structured surface of your poems, there's a code that becomes intimate. I don't think it depends on you as a personality, ever, but that code enriches my reading.

MRH: I'm glad to hear that. Move to page sixty-four, the last page of "rotations of N" [in *)locus TIDES((*], because there's a quote by Anne Noggle, the photographer, who used her face and body as part of what she was depicting. I heard her say on a PBS television program: "Who will look into my face and find me there?" What does the face tell us about the self? What does the word self mean in her question? It becomes exquisitely layered.

JT: And that's, I think, how the philosophical concept of identity comes out in your work, and so it strikes me that although your work is philosophical and difficult, if a reader persists, she will find points of connection, a kind of intimacy, if you can learn that code.

MRH: Yes. I think it's a process, an experiential process with language, where word by word I'm carefully building a line that engages, as often as it can, with the experiential components of language in a fresh way. I don't have opportunities often to talk about my work, so forgive me for sounding naïve, but I would posit that, for most of us, the concept of self is quite delusional, you know, how we use that word, what the word means to us. Those are profound words: me, self, I. How do they mean? That this quote would come from a photographer who devoted her medium to self-portrait and who then asks this question—I loved hearing that.

BH: What role does self have in your work? What is the "concept of self" for you?

MRH: It is a permeable, modified, always changing center, and that is why I use, for example, the "ı" not the tall "I". I think the look of ı, as opposed to the capital, is particularly important. I have a definition of self, but it's spiritual. The self is a medium through which all the unknowable source of all that is and is not explores the manifest and non-manifest multiplicities of reality. That sounds too metaphysical. But if I wrap my head around that, how self constitutes, well, what is not possible? What is possible? The range is endless. Where are we?

BH: I notice a politic and an acute awareness of what nature "does"—the walks, the observations—in your poetry, so there's a political aesthetic in your work.

MRH: Yes, the political does enter. I can't seem to avoid it. Yes, it permeates.

JT: In what way do feminist strategies in constructing meaning enter in?

MRH: I think if we thumbed through all the *TIDES((* books we would find very few male pronouns. Part of this is reactionary; I mean, you can guess I'm sure that as a girl I didn't read a book that had feminine pronouns unless it was something like *Little Women* or *The Five Little Peppers And How They Grew*. And I grew out of those books rather quickly. So the really important things I read always had male pronouns, and my work sometimes compensates in response to that. What else would you ask about that?

JT: One feminist strategy is to upset traditional patriarchal expectations and hierarchies of meaning…

MRH: Absolutely. I'm always exploring how language functions. I avoid didacticism. If the reader is willing to re-enter the work, some poems can be repaginated—as the source pages of *)cliff TIDES((* indicate—some poems can be read in reverse or from various entry points. Often there are opportunities to go in a different direction, by virtue of the fact that there might be two columns or a letter shape in a different font and shade that drifts behind the main text. There are fonts co-existing with one another. It isn't that one must dominate the other, and the reader can choose to read them separately or contiguously. So there are choices.

JT: In "O Canvas" [in *)cliff TIDES((*] another example is the different voices?

MRH: Oh, Ophelia, Orithyia, Ona, the North Wind, yes! These are based on visual art and literature. If we look at page sixty-five, "O figure," there's Ophelia talking to Hamlet (and herself). She drowns herself, then realizes things could have been quite different. She takes on strength; yes, it's a feminist engagement with Ophelia's ghost. She becomes assertively no nonsense. And Orithyia becomes another figure, from mythology, who is carried off by the North Wind. I have to add that the epigraph by Rochelle Owens is wonderful: "On the bus she hobbles/ in golden stirrups." That makes anything possible. Some epigraphs must be placed in the poem after the first draft is well completed because they're constraining, but this was an epigraph that I wanted right up front because the image was so nourishing for me. When Ophelia becomes mixed with Lady Mac Beth on page sixty-seven I need that encouragement. [She reads.]

> my own river hem scarves about my feet
>   on days I am worn
>   jewel shards mirror in
>   long-lipped shadows lit
>   you see yourself
>   orchid scent spackled
>
>   a foiling length
>   I kiss the sword blade blood groove
>   tang and pommel ring
>
>   invite me

She becomes, I think, intimidating, as she begins to realize her power, as opposed to the Ophelia who drowns herself.

BH: What you said about a reader taking anything they want from the text earlier, I understand that you allow that process, but I also hear you speaking in fairly "intentional" ways about what you've expressed, so in some ways you have an agenda. If a reader doesn't follow that agenda, fine, but you propose to let anyone to read what they want, yet connecting the writer and the reader—as you phrased it earlier—would again broach the problem of intention in poetry.

MRH: I suppose one could read this without ever realizing that speaker is Ophelia. I can also imagine someone thinking it's about me. But that's neither here nor there. "O Canvas" may have taken on more precision because of the shapeliness of O and the literary figures, Ophelia and Orithyia. However, I'm not a particularly didactic person. My intention is to facilitate meaning for the reader; I respect a reader's ability to come to this text and get things from it that I wasn't aware were there. Why was I not aware? Because I am working with language, which is so rich and continuously beyond me. I trust that if I write a line and you read that line, you can bring more, or certainly differently, to that line than I bring, and can leave with more than I got out while writing it. Because I think that happens often for writers, don't you think? But I do have hope that I could write a line and you could go away with more than I ever thought about for that line, by virtue of the richness that you bring to it.

290

JT: Is it wrong for me to think because of its circular form, that it's a feminine letter?

MRH: It's a feminine letter and to entitle it "O Canvas" I was thinking actually of images. These take shape in feminist "sub-poems." Orithyia becomes almost dangerous. She might have been carried off by the North Wind, but she has the last word. She will let go of everything except who she has become through challenge and time. Yes.

JT: And there is anti-war discourse in your work.

MRH: There is. Yes, in "O Canvas," right here, it so happened, while I was working on it, on page seventy-four, fighter planes from Kirtland [Air-Force Base] flew over—they were deafening—I mean, yard birds were actually knocked off their perches, knocked to the ground by the fighter planes going overhead. So the date and time is here.

fighter planes explode high thin air above
gray cloudcover housing for distributed world
this afternoon though not yet will I *cut my throat*
while small yellowed hailstones roof tin snare clatter
high desert sleet wet air smelling of seasalt and
shell fish or blood mixed with tears just before
swallowing as disfigured doves and sparrows
shoot up to scatter struggling for balance

Of course that quote, "not yet will I cut my throat" comes from Oppen. But yes, disfigured doves because they've been eating everything we have in our environment, so they've got strange faces, beaks disfigured. It's quite a literal "snapshot" of what happened. That is pointed out in the source page.

BH: And to some extent, your whole approach is a political stance?

MRH: It cannot be avoided if one is going to be innovative. The very act of innovating is a political act. John and I had a conversation yesterday, and it awakened me to the fact that I despair at the beginning of the 21st century, that we are embroiled in this "pre-emptive strike" war. What a grief! And sometimes when I'm writing, because I'm engaging that experiential language, the overtly political just comes in and takes over.

JT: You incorporate various elements of what you term "Newzak."

MRH: Late 20th century it was "Newzak." With the current administration, it's become "Newsblast." The news is no longer something you could listen to in an elevator. It used to be you could do a task with the news on in the background; you weren't suddenly caught up in something horrifying. Perhaps one should have been caught up that way. I wasn't that sensitive. But now I have to very careful, and I notice most of my friends express a common concern about how and when they listen to the news, because it so very, very sad and dark and full of grief.

ShoreTrace

A breeze from the next poem
has slipped into this one.
Chase Twichell

1.

terra TeRa—
shore pivot

trace waves tongue tip wave current
   explode content T-boned square check
         a letter silence marked

                    warming global shivers pass
upon crosspoint cell blossoms red
ownership signifies

                        so yesterday
                        yet here it is
where ventricles reset themselves

                        ahead retro
there I repeats itself
                        laws protect

a farsighted world reads
                        breaking so
gaze dilate crane heat : images overlay
a government shakes its own hand

peripheral   ,uplook askew
                        over intended words
                        once more misused
necessity chameleons
resurface
                        overlists poring

Thaw
                        discrete zeroes after the
             letter t : each day she agrees to
tion : t : question
tual : t : factual
                        save nothing

ways U and I alter t
                        and each day
actually in relation   ,testing   ,T'sing
                        after nightstar drama
                        nothing agrees to be saved
childhood wagonpull groove tongue:
sledbar boltring laceties
                        newsgrate squalls gale scold
                        this autumnal equinox
                    morning coffee rings approach

                        warm clothes downrack
                        slipstream gust ruffle ready

                        methane hotspots roil

2. *restive*
 drives
 white
 lidnight
 refract
 chipturn
 quicktoss   turbulence path
 vibrant in   ways destabilize
 possibles   at deeper levels
 convulsed   in uncertainty
 reguins by   features we de
 cell stepped   pend upon to
 overpaths   anticipate one
 let go at   another when
 cannot dis   a shockwave
 clude except   speed arrives
 for now's   in enough al
 too much ready past
 *entered*turbulent
charged *out into* rain
drier latitudes   *wastefill*
produce under   *discards*
stratus minetrap *deletes*
subtropical highs *consume*
a desertlike place *too much*
to reside on sun *mined for*
filled warm cells *day palsied*
circulating with   *retreat shake*
in uncertainty   *wild retrieves*
boundaries line
forecasts front
according to an
iced greenmeth
infrared fueled
amounts might
form combined
water vapors to
absorb more &
more heat merge
whatever cannot
remain constant air
or cloud moving along
preoccupies in uncertainty

thorntask eggshells juggle
tornado wake scour
flowstones line
time reboot reset pose
Out of slide pour memory stains matter said matter passes through
a juncture without realizing wave effects fenestral shapenote strike
bones burn under straight on discard gather past flowstone variants
fighter planes chant
overhead no transparent
tongue simple clock tics
against her dogbark pulse
echoes she's put away
silence makes visible
midstride truth turnings
discrete possessions prove

Autumn flicker knocks on the desert willow branch Ant catch nest guard sharp *kee raslide* : toned
fistclusters hold   shaleflake deadwood splinters Leaves yellowdrop Desirebridge Dusk twilled

look at yourself those
wounds along your
shoulder blossoming
by millimeter portions
Beside me white silverberry blossoms demand their honeyed
humming. While I ramble ground tread slant my sister attends
that business in the city. A gnat boat skims the rainpool skin.
toward another side
outcome contagions
twist torques recipro-
cate doubleheading
momenta lights bump
wake probability clouds
overlapping catch to
vitreous drama greencasts

To thread the eye of a breaker surfs the curve of hollow   Canna / cannular : Firetube for probable
non-zero timebranch hangs Ebb swells wheelout : The terminal, the chunnel Rollerblade I stop

                                                    passion
                                                    also is just
                                                    a bridge

                    interim corridors
                    translocate abduct
                    a backstretch hour
                    breakthrough fall
          Persephone pauses at the pomegranate bead to consider
        whether we must go into the pain of ourselves Faultlines nourish
          tree flatter gilt radiance pealing through Octobered blue
                    what you need to
                    know type founding
                    bit maps remember
                    November passages hold
                    motion caught on the
                    plane where Orion's
                    belt climbs into sky
                    a summer Triangle vacates

Redplum hybrid rosehips drop A series of gestures contour emote realms Today with no accu–
rate counts more causalities and wounded Life let go in exchange for Chaos removes the tunnel

                    frayed cirrus rope
                    threads jet ribbons
                    white crosscut blue
                    trees press distending
          Equivalence a theory strings loop to multiverse Or translate
          from sliderule effects a diffuse slippage Which everyday logic to
          choose where skill or intuit conducts Not run from nor pursuing
                    at overcast panes
                    along rootfog
                    a species of maculate
                    eyefilm spots drift
                    into the flaw bowing
                    where no trace
                    outside empty veils
                    signify further
                    ocean currents warn

Once more suspicion follows necessity First tools then skills to deflect them swimming between
marks toward an island she orders each portion in place A refusal to dissolve into neutral ground

                    recast cobalt belt locale
                    to draw the straight line
                    scale 1-10 perspectives
                    refine what we know in
                    countries unnoticed by   *face*
                    wholecloth chador view   *saving*
          devise a cloak in two dimensions for an object's reflecting waves and shadow
     where light does not reflect back to the eye   yet shadow parts remain to betray a third
       mirage unattended metamatter smudge backgrounds   microwaved across what metal
pickup   violent staggers through
colocates   disaster embracing live
                    longer hookwire fueled
                    afterdeath juggles or as
                    street blogs intercalate
                    it is and to what extent
                    upward inches hour by
                    just this path the slope
                    calls for to draw a line
                    even uncertain expects
                    two or more people in
                    out of nowhere études
                    arranged busily fogs to
                    the 300,000,000th one
                    remaining unidentified
                    for days porchlit flood
                    seed shafts downreach
                    what one can one does
                    let's just say despite the
                    sidewalks crack wilding
                    lineloud echoes describe
               orionid scatter streaks like
                    pain on a 1-10 scale jot as
               urban concrete also flutters be
          tween moth or hummingbird prune
               back precisely to that fifth leaf point on
          hybrid rose stems those wounded so rarely
          mention call back when time permits and if not

Jessica Grim
interviewed by Tom Beckett

Jessica Grim's most recent book is *Vexed*, online from /Ubu Editions at www.ubu.com/ubu/grim_vexed.html. Other books of poetry include *Fray* (O Books, 1998), *Locale* (Potes & Poets Press, 1995), and *The Inveterate Life* (O Books, 1990). She co-edited (with Melanie Neilson) *Big Allis*, a magazine focusing on experimental writing by women, from 1989-1996, and has participated in writing communities in the Bay Area, New York, and northeast Ohio. She has lived and worked in Oberlin, Ohio since the early '90's.

Tom Beckett: Where did/does poetry begin for you?

Jessica Grim: I feel trapped and inarticulate approaching a question like this. Who cares about biography? Everyone? I didn't read poetry until college, or very little. And then it was bad; I took a couple lit & "creative writing" courses at Humboldt State University in the early 80's—Jorie Graham and James Galvin were teaching there at the time. It was my introduction to "professional" poetry. But oddly, the passionate connection was from an end-of-career lit prof—I remember him looking out the window with these watery blue eyes, reciting pieces from memory by Shelley & Keats. I'm trying to think about exaltation. Maybe that's because I'm reading Fanny Howe right now. But wanting "discovery" to feel, have felt, exalted…. but guess what. Because from here, at nearly 50, the exaltation attending discovery looks hopelessly young to me. I had embarrassingly juvenile experiences with poetry on into my twenties, at SF state (I'd transferred to a place with a "real" creative writing program) where I was taking a class w/Kathleen Fraser on women writers. It's not that the poems I wrote were horrible probably not more horrible than anyone else's at my "level"—so I guess that's when—those classes at SF state—poetry began. The classes by the way included short story writing, which I distained based on no particularly good evidence and certainly on very little experience. I remember writing a story, ala Robbe-Grillet, about walking down a mountain road and coming to a deserted town and stepping behind a crumbled wall in a vacant lot and seeing a car drive slowly past. That was the action, the climax, a car moving slowly down the road of this deserted town. So thank god for poetry, right? There was a lot happening in sf at that time, 1984, 85, 86… a lot to take in, a lot to go to. I became involved with Michael Amnasan, and he was hovering around the fringes of the writing scene, forging difficult—which is to say always troubled, always problematic, ever unsettled—connections with some of the Language folks. but going to readings and talks. There were things that had already ended by the time I was starting to be aware of the scene—Perelman's talks, the grand piano series… but still, there was a lot of vibrancy and intent swirling around.

In terms of my practice now(adays) it begins infrequently, and rarely where I "left off". It's rare for me to find the time & space to write, so I tend to start over again each time I write. But my son's now 8, my partner's cancer (the pivotal focus of the last year) is officially undetectable, and I'm starting to see the possibility of light in terms of the new job I started a few months ago. So maybe that's all the past & present biography needed?

TB: Let me ask a bit differently, Jessica—what gets you going? What makes you want to write?

JG: A quiet house, some peace, an awareness of what it is that constitutes—or approximates—equilibrium in my life. Sometimes a flare of anger or disgust or despair relating to situations or occurrences in the world; often times reading. Writing is required, back to the equilibrium thing... I realize I've approached the question(s) as if the responses are going to be about external motivators (is the weather right? the temperature? do I have the right cup of tea) which is unfortunately telling. I **never** have the right god damned cup of tea. Sometimes some okay writing happens anyway.

TB: It's a fact for most of us who write poetry that it all happens in the midst of life without much enablement. I know of no one early on saying to me, "Tom, your future is in literature. Go forth and inspire!" Quite the contrary. I have been disappointing relatives for over 50 years. I say this for comic relief, but also to make the point that this thing of ours (la cosa nostra, if you will) is a life decision which informs the way one sees the world and that it has consequences. What does it mean to you to be a poet? Is there some special responsibility involved?

JG: Once again I want to deflect the question and its suggestions. Too big, too grand, too claim-making. I mean really, a special responsibility? To what or whom, I wonder. But naturally these questions are not as absurd as they at first strike me as being. So assuming I decide to take the questions seriously—only fair, eh?—here's the rub: I am uneasy thinking about these issues right now in light of my decreased output and my decreased (nearly to nil) engagement with writing community(ies) in recent years. But assuming I can get past that... Through writing I express—attempt to express—this existence I know. I express that existence because it is not enough to live it. It feels very small simply to live it in fact. Dailiness happens and the range of occurrences, thoughts, emotions, interaction attending—or making up—the dailiness is, well, compartment-alized and let's face it often wholly mundane. Work life, family life, life with friends. Meaning is there of course but it all slides on through. The writing I do —the poems I write—do not create an entirely different meaning exactly, nor a meaning that is particularly imbued with a "higher" understanding of or approach to this existence I am in. But distinct I'd say, in some fairly dramatic ways, from the meaning created and lived in the dailiness. If the writing is working well there are connections that occur there that do not occur otherwise, at least not in *my* experience of daily life. And yet obviously those connections wholly refer to and are engaged with the mundane living I do. The pleasure I find in writing is the pleasure of the surprise, often, of creating something in the juxtaposition of words/phrases/sentences (even) and sounds that twist in just such a way. It's a screened record, really. But one that feels "true", to me. To how I think about the world and respond to it. This was the existence that I was in, that I created for myself as a human, with all the composite elements of what I was "handed" and what I made. It sits alongside. The responsibility in that case is to myself — to create this parallel line which carries with it a response to and expression of *my* life. I do think of a future reader in my son — which is probably pretty bankrupt. He may have very little interest (in some imagined future) in how his mother understood the world, or very little patience for getting to that through reading. Is that odd, I mean in the sense of unusual, I wonder, to write for my kid. In some measure. I suppose that looks a lot like responsibility of a kind too. The notion of consequences is interesting. I find myself thinking "if only" — if only I'd written to the detriment of something, against my — or anyone else in my lifes' — better judgment. Hm.

TB: When I think of your writing I think of your preoccupations with physical location and with description. In your book *Locale* there's a poem I'm fond of called "It/Ohio." It begins so:

> Because I'm afraid to fight
> my heart ticks in my leg.

The poem is immediately anchored in a sense of bodily anticipation.

Would you talk a bit about how you came to write this poem and what was at stake for you in it?

JG: It was written in the first months I'd moved to Ohio (from SF, most immediately — but in any case I'd pretty much lived in urban circumstances up to that point). Amidst a fairly thick sense of alienation and a general condition of being stunned by this move I'd made. I was trying to negotiate with myself this thing I'd done — packed my stuff and driven out in a truck, to take this job I'd applied for on something of a whim…

Ohio — what a great word! But here I was living in it. In a liberal arts college town that felt stiflingly conservative socially. Political progressives packaged up in nuclear families… and they all seemed to go to church! So landscape as escape. The flat, "uninteresting" landscape. Pretty much devoid of topographical noise, at least here in the NE of the state. Getting on my bicycle and riding out into the cornfields on these country roads was a kind of acting out, a bodily, as you suggest, reliance upon the power of landscape to ease my way. I was mourning in particular the sense of anonymity I'd always enjoyed. I was pretty pissed actually. I moved in August—it was hot, and it was humid, and there were cicadas. I could be interested in the physicality of these things; I could observe them, and judge them, and decide upon their narrowness... which was of course my rage at the narrowness of the humanity I'd smacked myself up against and annoyance at myself for having done that. I felt cowardly somehow, in the encounter. As if my inability to assert myself and my "singular" values, my inability to impress myself upon this community — instead sending myself out into its hot still loneliness... was a failure. But I could take something of all of this for myself, for my sensibility... I could cruise around on the roads dividing the acres of soy from the acres of corn... and notice some things about the sky and things about the bird and animal life... and then write those. When I'd only been in Ohio a few weeks I had one of those unsettling experiences that, because I had no equilibrium at all, became symbolic: I'd awakened in the middle of the night having to pee, and on my way to the bathroom in my still unfamiliar apartment walked right into the edge of a door—so had a kind of serious-looking black eye for a couple weeks. Domestic violence! Ohio smacked me! And this sense of distrust I felt from people around me—no one believes that people from places like New York or San Francisco willingly move to places like Oberlin— and they expect you to leave at any moment. So when you do things like buy a house or "settle down" with someone here—people get all relieved... "so you ARE staying!". And after 16 yrs I'm one of the people who doesn't trust that people from places like NY or SF will stay. I think I've strayed from "It/Ohio". I wanted to put Ohio in its place. It was messing with me. And the love/hate relationship continues to thrive today.

TB: Heh. Tell me about it.

The list of innovative writers who left Ohio could go on and on. Hart Crane, Bob Perelman and Juliana Spahr most immediately come to mind.

Recent years have seen a proliferation of blogs, listservs and innovative writing in cyberspace, which has had something of a decentralizing effect in the poetry world(s).It's now a little easier for innovative poets to operate from Ohio—or, say, Australia, than it once was.

You've so far resisted starting a blog. What are your thoughts about this new environment for writing?

JG: At this point in the game becoming a more active participant in that environment as a poet doesn't hold a lot of interest for me... even if it can, as you suggest, be a way of alleviating the "condition" of isolation which I sometimes whine about. I would rather use my limited writing time & energy in other ways. I find the blog scene interesting enough, and there are a handful of poetry blogs I skim with some regularity—and projects like ubuweb, which pulls in such an incredible variety of fabulous content, really excite me. Another part for me is that I spend many hours of my work day up to the eyeballs in online communication of various kinds (and guess what! We have a library blog! And guess what! I feel guilt over not posting to it with enough frequency to make it dynamic and cool!). Another mouth to feed... I was thinking of a kids online "environment" my son & his friends were into a couple years back... kids "buy" a pet—some kind of cute fuzzy cartoon thing— and then they have to feed it, and if they let it languish, it gets all sick and weak. I don't think it actually dies from neglect... but maybe it could? So, yeah... the intention is to continue my resistance. For the time being.

TB: What's at risk for you in a poem?

JG: Pretty much everything? What do I think about, hold important, how do I relate to the world, how do I pull it in, through language, to do something, anything... What am I capable of, really? It's funny because when I get into the rare conversation about poetry with someone around here there's this assumption, a given, that my work is inaccessible. I despise that conversation, yet never seem to have a great comeback. What's accessibility got to do with anything, I mean I don't want to talk about my work in terms of who "gets" it, of who it's "gettable" to. And yet, yeah, just yesterday I had lunch with a poet in the creative writing program here and the topic of my doing a local reading came up... and her assumption was that I'd want to make sure to read with someone who was "more accessible"—so the audience, wouldn't, what? Have to suffer inordinately? But what's funny of course is that I think of my work as being entirely direct, entirely transparent, and pretty ragged emotionally at times. Which is not to say it's a walk in the park or something that's going to lay out the stepping stones necessarily... but it's as true to my experience— right now right here where I am—as I can be. Everything is at stake for me then.

TB: Who do you think of as your poetic forebears?

JG: Stein's important to me always, in and out of time. And Duras and Leduc, the 20th century French women narrative obsessives. Not that you'd see that in or know that from my work. And of course the west coast folks, Hejinian, Scalapino, Silliman, actually, all really important to me in the 80's when I was first encountering Language stuff. Coolidge I loved. *Mine*, Hejinian's *My Life*, Silliman's *Tjanting*. Forebears sounds so heavy though, let's just call it influence. Niedecker, her wondrous brevity.

TB: Could you speak a bit to your process as a poet? How do you approach writing a poem?

JG: For the most part I write in bound notebooks, in which I put somewhat random date markers; I then return to the notebooks—usually after an "aging" period of 6 mos to a year—and transcribe into electronic form what I find of interest, or usable. The percentage of the work I find "usable" varies, but roughly 60-70% I'd say. Sometimes there are long dry spells—both in terms of the actual writing, and in terms of what I find of interest in returning to the writing. And there are also pockets of material, where I'll transcribe many pages almost verbatim. I generally keep the line breaks and other spacing from the handwritten work. I find that the rhythm and pacing as I originally thought them are usually right. Then I have these files of quite rough material—with "titles" like "trans 10/06-7/07". Sometimes there are discreet sections (a page, several pages) that are "natural" pieces, and I pull them out—often there's theme involved... stuff written while in certain places or while thinking about certain things, or in response to particular events or circumstances, or around texts I'm reading. On occasion I also write a discreet poem to be that, where there's no question in my mind that's what it is. Again, longhand in notebooks. I'm not necessarily thrilled with my process—it seems, well, inefficient—but I'm resigned to it, and find something about its cumbersomeness comforting.

TB: Why does poetry matter to you?

JG: In terms of the writing it's a singular site for me for exploration, all manner of delving—be it personal, political, social—and all manner, by extension, of learning. This'll sound corny but I understand the world and what I'm doing in it better through writing than through any other act, or situation, or encounter. And the encounter with (experience of? consumption of?) the world of texts "out there"—what miniscule piece of it I'm able to find my way to—is and has been life changing. Of course, and always. Transformative texts, reifying texts, troubling texts. How can that "mattering" possibly by articulated? Inarticulate texts...

TB: Is there a text of yours you can point to that came to you as a kind of breakthrough? And if so, could you talk about its occasion and what it came to mean for you?

JG: "Fort Recovery" is a piece about the death—the suicide—of my mother, in 1994. I don't recall exactly how long after her death it was that I wrote it, but it was a good few months at least. It's one of the pieces that, uncharacteristic of how I usually work, took on theme/event quite explicitly, and took on sentiment and emotion. It wasn't breakthrough in a radical sense but it reminded me that I did in fact still find useful a direct and emotionally raw "voice"... I wasn't going to bother with the usual critique and self-editing self-consciousness... she jumped off the (god damn as I always seem to say) Golden Gate Bridge, afterall, so who was I to create anything particularly subtle or nuanced out of that? It gave the event, for me, its due dramatic response. Not "healing" mind you, god forbid; but an iteration of (my) agency attaching to an act—a fact—that will always haunt me, and can overwhelm.

TB: As a poet, what most concerns and preoccupies you now?

JG: The power & privilege of language—the privilege I reserve for the language of my writing and how that works. The world I'm depositing my kid into—in broad strokes and then trying to move beyond the guilt and panic of it into something else... or figuring out if that's possible in writing. And how my privileging of language circles back into those very trenchant concerns. Reconnecting with friends & writers I've been out of touch with... I'm very recently back in touch with Melanie Neilson—she and I co-edited *Big Allis* in the late 80's/early 90's—and we've started a collaborative project - which makes me very happy. That's the nutshell. Oh, and keeping the balls in the air—it is not a glamorous preoccupation but it suffuses all.

Pastures I

Which curvature which redundancy
which cradle   which severance
which flume   which
blended dusk which tryst which freakish midnight storm which
gathering sound
emitted which trim acre which truck
which loss—
            my shade, *my* sun-warmed
 guilty pleasant

and in the lit space of which sun

oddly other
            structure

            asimilar   astringent
recast
ingrown   prop
  mercerizing
effect

the midges
            upon us

arpeggio grip   scores
floral coup

code for fragment code for
  wind from the west code for
      it's
not about
  "reconciliation"

edge-bred

erstwhile bedlam
  "his sad fey mood begins to pass"

we were weeping for you your

aura
          justly
                    examined

an image's clarity light
eyes   evidently a
portrait   an homage

searching for source material
are they solvent and
what of that

they had first to go a little mad

a "cruel mountain" among any
number of cruel mountains in
          the borderlands

          ultimately
"headlong" tracked as "progress"
   tracked as imagination even
        our images our
horrors we
do   do it justice we are
doing that even still

response to text pressured

*

We ask for an hour
   only,
    before the diagnosis but
each day we want that

   heavenly   upset
clings to a sour sky

    it has not abated it is
mild mannered in the extreme

    a shifting   prism, a park, a
memory invests

in summing up an addict a sweat bee a
   light wind

it was the way lumbering whitened the sky

Brown Welsh Skink   glint

an etude

kind of   a
  shipping
    thing,
I think

more at yesterday more at
mollify

well what else is branching out
supposed to entail

   skins grease the floor while
the upper levels the
ateliers   swing freeform
from your arm
     architecturally   speaking

the grammar built a new one

glottal   stop

   fret   beam   cantilever
adjective   pronoun   beats
pronoun   verb every
time
   especially on the escalator

our rebate

was just thinking

the insurgency's pram
  on that lone slope

an agent for our one wish

sequential trauma to the tibia
a float a gleaming a banister

honorable pagination
sameness fruition
            welcome   to our language

in as much as it's three times as many

between filibusters'
   chilling   savior—
float me a loan?

appeasable thumb
    home-fried,
get out the glow-worms—
  perfect

each day a little danker each day a
little more like   fly bait

reticulate noun

a finial to end all finials
let's have

gland school
marmot
sludge sky
hematosis
zinnia, black-eyed
  in a blue cup

        text generating

clinkery verbs of
effected   object status

ill-formed inquisition

and what part of grammar *is* wheel?

writing
  act as process

plural flurry

figures
crossed at the horizon
    line
that thick   corn

assorted edifice pestilence
surcease

if only for an hour we let
that hour pass

meticulous   systems' possessive
namesake

act happening as a thought recorded which isn't,
exactly,   a thought or isn't, precisely, recorded

overhanging cantilever cuts into view

summarily   emotive—

the singular function of each of those
grounds maintenance machines
i.e. to recall a persons' "last works"

The Irritant

Landscape littered with genders
sloughed off like so many irritations
    truant, as they are

somatically   rhyming   so as to gag
by its very
        tension,
supple in its green   torn
by harmonies, the
  two sides of the house

causalities line the floor yet
the space   above is what
  endlessly lingers, promising elevation
 to the patient

at one time or another each
  idea of how
  across the serrations across
the "years" and embolisms the
 four-foot barriers

it is now or never they said it is
now

    having gained that

        usurers   sashay our walk
the walk of the declined

our length that length too, our
  endgame

a surly study of the reduction of a vocabulary

Tom Mandel
interviewed by Sheila E. Murphy

Tom Mandel grew up in Chicago and was educated in its jazz and blues clubs and at the University of Chicago where he studied on the Committee on Social Thought with Hannah Arendt, Saul Bellow, Harold Rosenberg and David Grene. He has lived in New York, Paris, San Francisco and Washington DC, and now resides in a small town on the Atlantic coast.

Tom has taught at the University of Chicago, the University of Illinois and San Francisco State University (where he was Director of the Poetry Center). He has also been a technology entrepreneur, marketing executive, and consultant.

Tom has published in dozens of newspapers, literary journals and anthologies, including the influential *In the American Tree* and *The Norton Anthology of Post-Modern Verse*. He is the author of more than a dozen books, including *To the Cognoscenti*, published in 2007. Tom is co-author of *The Grand Piano*, an experiment in collective autobiography by ten poets associated with the rise of Language Poetry in San Francisco.

This interview with poet Tom Mandel was conducted in two phases — Spring 1998 and Winter 2007-8.

The first phase focuses on Absence Sensorium, *the book-length poem written collaboratively from 1993-1995 by Tom Mandel and Daniel Davidson, working via email and phone calls. Dan committed suicide in 1997 as the book was going to press.*

Absence Sensorium *comprises 526 seven-line stanzas; each line is either 7 or 11 syllables. The form is Spanish, called a* silva, *and was used by Luis Góngora, among others. Published by Potes & Poets,* Absence Sensorium *is available from Small Press Distribution.*

The second phase of the interview began in late 2007 after the publication of Tom's most recent book To the Cognoscenti.

Sheila E. Murphy: What aesthetic traditions most directly influenced the making of *AS*?

Tom Mandel: I wanted to write a long poem with a peripatetic feel, sort of "let me walk you through my experience," and had been reading Dante and some other long Renaissance poems as a way of thinking about the project. In one of Góngora's long poems I found a verse form called the silva and suggested it to Dan. We experimented with it and found that it was both extensible, as I'd thought it would be, and also ample enough to accomodate two minds.

Yet though *AS* is above all a poem of history, it was not influenced by Pound's idea of a "poem with history." Starting with the old verse form we chose, *AS* seems to *reach back* to root itself, rather than rooting itself in a method or theoretical position. But in the poem tradition plays a role of innovation; the gestures invoke or employ tradition, but are not traditional.

SEM: I'd be interested to learn your perception of *AS* in relation to other long, meditative or exploratory poems or poem sequences you value. With this in mind, what particular aspects of *AS* seem to you unique?

TM: *AS* is at once autobiographical and "investigative," to borrow a word I heard Steve McCaffery use when he was visiting a few weeks ago. I don't think that's unique but it seems somewhat unusual among recent long poems. To the degree that the poem poses questions of poetics they are asked about (and of) the object of the poem rather than its form or structure or its status as discourse. This too seems unusual, maybe it's a matter of degree.

What's unique of course is the collaboration. Rereading our work, Dan and I often could not remember which of us had written a particular section. Our contributions fused in the poem's crucible, yet as we wrote it seemed quite dialectical, often it felt as if we were as much contesting as considering. Contesting the object. This led us to treat the present as history — a traditional and even prophetic stance for the poet? — to return to your first question.

SEM: *AS* seems very immediate in its engagement with a myriad of details reflecting both your and Dan's read on the present tense. These details spiral into stories, political statements, lamentations, dialogues, chants, foretelling, even prayer. Did the "frame" of the selected form feel large enough or broad enough to include all that your minds sought to bring in to the work?

TM: The form was a stable element in what was an unstable act, as all collaboration is and ought to be unstable. We were able to challenge each other, to encourage, object, cajole, demand. Surprisingly, we kept on responding. The result was — probably inevitably — a poem that in a way is in cantos, though they are not foregrounded. What I mean is that we addressed each other in the writing, drawing a picture or telling a story to convey something one to the other, and these work like cantos, contained episodes along a path of the poem. Obviously, this is not the real meaning of the word, but I'm thinking of the narrative function of a canto in Dante, for example. Given that, the formal frame of stanza and line was a known, even a comfort, setting off into whatever came next.

SEM: Where/how does *AS* factor into your own development as a writer?

TM: That'll become clearer as time passes. I'm just starting another long poem and it most definitely takes off from *AS*.

SEM: How does *AS* seem to factor into prior or other work by Dan Davidson?

TM: To speak simply and frankly, as I must speak of my lost friend, Dan was immensely proud of *AS*. To speak of his work, on the other hand, I think that may be beyond me. His death still seems like the present moment, like Dan now, something very hot for which I've found an insulated carrier but cannot put down, hoping for a time to come when I can unwrap it, handle it, feel and think it through.

A few words, all the same. From my first read of *Product*, Dan's work seemed to me to define and occupy obsessively an analytic solitude, a subject whose sole object was the social. His work had force and scale in its abutment to the social, which it pushed and that way knew. An interest in interacting with the solitude I felt in Dan drew me to our collaboration. *AS* seemed to recoup other qualities in his person; I found myself thinking for example that he might be ready to play music again — he'd been a musician and song-writer for some years, but not during the time I knew him. I remember once sitting in his room, monastico-leftism-mess, and he picked up an acoustic guitar and began to improvise a fluent beautiful music. I hadn't known even that he played, and it was a shock.

SEM: What is most important about *AS* as to the genre to which the piece belongs, to your and Dan's work, and to you personally?

TM: "To be human is to be a variant" — where did I read that recently? What I like about *AS*, and want from poetry now, that I read and that I write, is variance and room for variance. *AS* is a phenotype that holds the genotype in judgment.

SEM: Let's talk about the format selected for *AS*. Is there significance in the length of stanzas and the syllabics of the lines, or were these choices made arbitrarily?

TM: Not arbitrary, although I'd thought of the silva as a seven-line stanza, wrongly as it turns out. The other day I looked it up in the Princeton Encyclopedia for the first time. It's a verse form wherein each line contains either seven or eleven syllables but strophic breaks can occur freely. So I'd misconstrued it. But the number seven is not arbitrary it is immensely significant, even perfect. And eleven is a variant on seven. Yet, when you repeat something you are applying it and you are changing it. That is, a world arises, particular not formal, which also changes the formal device, adaptively one hopes. As the rabbis used to say, "to the wise a hint is sufficient."

SEM: Was this poem created with any preconception relative to its length?

TM: Dan and I had written a couple of earlier collaborations, short poems just for fun — to see what would happen, that is. We wrote a sestina and a villanelle. So it seemed natural to stretch out. We quickly found that we had a large project on our hands. But we did not want to establish a set number of stanzas, the regularity of line and stanza length seemed enough. *AS* ends with the 526th stanza. That is, at a certain point we felt it was time to end it and we did something to bring it to an end.

SEM: Were *Prospect of Release* and *AS* written concurrently? How would you compare these works in terms of focus, aesthetic contribution, process and direction?

TM: I finished *Prospect of Release* in 1992, and Dan and I began *AS* about a year later. They are very difficult works to compare, quite different. In *AS* the stanza form is used to propel the work. In *Release* the variant-sonnet is used to contain the individual unit of the work. I use a sonnet form in *Release* which I've never seen elsewhere, the stanzas are of 4, 3, 3, and 4 lines in that order, a form that reads as balanced and internal   unbreakable even armored. But repeated lines, phrases, words throughout *Release* propel the thought, the single, variant, broken thought that is thinking into, through and out the work. I could never write another poem like *Prospect of Release*, because it is as unique as that single thought. But I could write another poem like *AS*, despite the fact that its conditions were unique and my collaborator dead.

SEM: What thematic currents in *AS* seem most important to you?

TM: I think I want to ask you that question. What themes stand out for you?

SEM: I'm very interested in learning your perceptions about collaboration as an aesthetic possibility for writing. There seems to be growing interest in the practice of collaboration. Can you speculate as to what is behind this? Clearly, you and Dan have brought collaboration to new heights with *AS*.

TM: Collaboration is deep in all human making and doing, of course. It's great for it to become more of a possibility in poetry. It's a cliché to point out that my generation of poets worked hard — more effectively in writing than in theoretical elaboration I believe — to de-establish the "I" or subject from its authoritative and even monarchical position in the poem. This is something that seems to need doing repeatedly, as the attempt so often merely remodels the ego's throne room in the name of a revolution that turns out to be one of taste(viz. Surrealism).

The theoretical discourse behind the language-poetry version of this effort is pretty much uninteresting to me, not because of a distaste for theory — not at all, I was raised on philosophy — but because it's mostly legacy theory, to coin a phrase, and incompetent to grasp let alone re-frame its object.

In fact, the "I" in any form — sovereign, exploded, evasive, missing, etc. — is a boring mystery, an excuse for a lot of tight-ass poetics that thinks the corner it has written itself into and must write out of is somehow more interesting than that "I" itself. Nope.

Perhaps the theoretical work of the last decade on complexity and emergence will open a bigger window on the processes by which poems are written and communicate, than what passes for critical theory, or Theory capitalized, or poetics as we have it, or whatever. But, I should write about this rather than just make these pronouncements, and I don't have the time to do that writing, so . . .

. . . I'll say some more about collaboration. In the case of AS, collaboration with Dan turned out to be dangerous, as we entered into a deep and entangled dialogue and then my interlocutor killed himself. I have found it difficult to disentangle my spirit from this loss.

SEM: A number of the following questions relate to thematic instances, stemming from your asking me about what themes stand out for me.

Throughout *AS,* there exists the sense that experience consists of a "pileup" of present tenses that eventually comprise a history, fluid in character and laden with differently shaped "rules." At some point, there is a reference made to glass breaking into slivers that soon after do not show. Over time, things change, gestures evolve, and the remainder is transformed, sometimes to the point of imperceptibility. Quoting another passage, "An accurate picture of the inner world/ finely sifted over seven hundred years/ of plasticity, invention and pleasure/ fell to nothing in a day." And from another, "The present is the perfect rebuttal/ and is the easiest to apply. The past/ is completed before the plaster has dried." Would you address the issue of present tense, history, and experience?

TM: Note that the first lines you quote were written by me. Reading the second passage, which was written by Dan, I notice for the first time the play on grammatical tenses: present perfect, past complete (as in the passe compose tense in French).)

The view of history I inherit, and I think it's "our" view of history now, derives from Walter Benjamin's famous image of the angel of history who moves forward, back to the future, focused ineluctably on the past which piles up as wreckage before his eyes. This image is an isomorph of Benjamin's statement that "every great act of civilization is also a great act of barbarism," which I know I'm not quoting quite accurately here.

It is important to think radically the meaning of these passages from Benjamin — to think with them rather than about them.

The antinomian endgame Benjamin's vision implies, thoroughly motivated by the twentieth century he witnessed, must be absorbed well beyond an identification of the evidence for its truth in Benjamin's time and in ours. It is not enough, in other words, to bracket what humans have done in history in an ethical category of revulsion, to make it into the other human 'We,' of which we are only formally a part — the Nazis, the church, the Chicago police. It has to be faced in the present tense, and the present tense is 'We' in a realer sense. It's Tom Mandel, it's Dan Davidson, it's Sheila Murphy; reader, it's you.

Not enough either to ignore or suppress the experience, the grammar, of intellectual and imaginative transformation which enters our lives from all that's happening with technology in our time. *AS* couldn't have been written without computers and email. This interview ditto.

In saying this I'm anticipating the end of the poem with its extended meditation on participation and resistance and its focus on what we make now, which though it seem the future is another past. In *AS*, the question of history immediately poses that of the individual, twinned in this telling but still the individual. How does the teller bear the tale he makes and tells? Experience in *AS* is a question posed. What I do rises up and asks me what it is I do. I'm not making the future but the past; what do I make?

We don't have available to us a level to which we can rise for resolution, as, at least formally let's say, Dante did. Or, we do, but we are aware of its evasiveness.

I like to think of the phrase "Grant unto Caesar that which is Caesar's," for example, on which so much of Christianity depends, that division of the world. I like to remember how easy especially Roman Christianity found it to cover in the dark the distance created in the daylight of this phrase. And I like to remember that these words are a moment in a centuries-long dialogue among the rabbis of the early centuries about how to view Rome. Without Rome, the rabble would destroy us Jews or the Egyptians would, one of them says. So instead the Romans destroy us? another replies. The issue cannot be resolved, but somewhere in the Talmud a prayer is repeated, somewhat humorously and altogether seriously, "that the eye of the policeman not fall on me." But, it did.

SEM: One of the primary issues I derive from this book concerns privacy and communion, which could be turned and seen as privacy IN communion. One line, "Approach is easy, access indecisive" seems at least distantly related to this aspect of *AS*. When communion is referenced in the book, the sense is of a difficult, demanding one, imbued with a sense of its own unlikelihood. Could you say more about communion as related to *AS*?

TM: I think it's community or communication but not communion. Whatever else *AS* is it is a dialogue between two very different individuals and in that dialogue we repeatedly model but also miss the difficult acts of communication and building (or accepting) community which seem so critical in a world where very very little is of that form. The great value of poetry now is in modeling ways in which an individual creating form engages, in however demanding a way, the community we build on communication. What you are seeing as "unlikelihood" — I think that difficulty is rather how critical such communication is.

The community we need and model in poetry is not like created, objectified culture — e.g. canon, value, meaning. It is like the communication among ants who by that communication span the distance between two branches (or roots) which otherwise would seem to be impossibly apart.

SEM: Memory seems to function as a device for survival, a gradually depreciating supply of itself. On one level, memory (an arbitrary construct?) seems self-validating, either artificially or with some value. How do you perceive memory in *AS*?

TM: The questions you've been asking in this session turn me into a philosopher, and I'm not a philosopher, or rather I'm very given to philosophy but I hope I'm a better poet than a philosopher. Still, they are good questions, but I experience a struggle between answers that have to do with our intention and those in which I'm a reader of the poem. I don't know which are which or which are more useful.

In a notebook last year, I doodled out part of a song that went:

> 'I remember, I remember.'
> Memory's the great pretender,
>
> Claims it happened and really was
> One way or th'other — all because

It seemed so in my head today
As present (presence) past my way.

If memory is an artifice or construct — tho I think actually it is a form of adaptation — it is nonetheless of inexhaustible supply and not self-validating but a kind of glue to bind something problematic to something else which is posed as a known. That's the way it works in *AS* I think — and here I am answering as a reader, not providing insight into an intention — but the collaborative process gave the poets the opportunity each to question what might be a fixed value in another's words, so there is a lot of fluidity in the position memory occupies.

SEM: As *AS* progresses toward the final (approximately) quarter of the book, there seems a buildup of intensity, wherein explorations from earlier in *AS* concerning present tense, history, communion, and survival confront contemporary life. The imperative of self protection intersects with politics and a larger, perhaps more threatening, picture. A fundamental solitude that permeates *AS* seems especially true here. Quoting again, "how to guard / our silence from an alien ear" and "No adjustment of your set is possible" seem also apt. I sense that we are looking at politics and life as spun from a great distance. Can you respond?

TM: The buildup of intensity in *AS* seems to me to be exactly the intensity of the poem experienced at a point where you have already read a lot of the poem, where you have a lot of the poem to bring to the later part you are reading. I'm interested in the phrase you use: "politics and life as spun from a great distance." I think that corresponds to an intention deep in the poem; the object of the poem seems to arrive as if from a great distance and with a lot of torque or spin on it. How to deal with its object, the poem itself what must it say and be? — it was very demanding. Let me tell you a story:

I had a curious experience once while attending a concert of the SF symphony. The pianist Charles Rosen, also a wonderful scholar and writer not only about music but literature and literary history, was playing Schoenberg's piano concerto, an angular, harmonically-demanding work in two movements. In Laura Davies Hall,as in many modern orchestral halls, a curving section of seats mounts behind the orchestra. During the second movement, a man seated a few rows up in this section in a place where the piano, no more than a hundred feet from him, might seem to be pointed directly at him, and where I could easily take in the pianist and him in a single glance — began to twitch violently, then to flail his limbs uncontrollably in a mounting crescendo which seemed to be not just attuned to the music but a part of it, a strange dance to Schoenberg's music.

The man was alone, the seats around him empty; was I the only witness to this transfixing scene? I was on the other side of the hall, and there was nothing I could do. Shortly before the end of the concerto, however, a couple of people entered his section of seats and helped him leave the hall. I later learned that the man was an epileptic, he was having a fit. I also learned, by the way, that he had recovered and was all right.

As it happened, I met Charles Rosen a few years later in Chicago. I asked him about this strange event; what had it been like to play Schoenberg accompanied, as it were, by someone in an epileptic fit. He remembered the concert, but he had been concentrating on the music and his musical collaborators. He was unaware of the audience when he played; what I described was news to him, strange and shocking.

SEM: The book posits an ongoing tension between "participation and resistance" in human existence. Would you address this?

TM: A tension and an identity, or at least the need and the attempt to keep both active, an attempt that can fail. Yes this theme is at the heart of *Absence Sensorium*, a theme that can never be resolved.

SEM: Your comments about variance and room for variance stimulate another question: Do you judge form in light of its capacity to generate variance?

TM: The variance and the variants a form spawns, yes that's what interests me — what I think is interesting for poetry — in form and the question of form. To me the whole debate about form, formalism, 'experimental' poetry vs. 'conventional' poetry is without interest. That is, it focuses attention on literary-critical issues rather than actual literary ones, issues of making I mean. Most of what presents itself as experimental poetry is minimally variant, is as conventional and indistinguishable from its sources and its neighbor-poems as most of the poetry of personal narrative.

Somewhere in *A Poetics*, for example, Charles Bernstein, rather glibly I think, dismisses poems of memory, personal apotheoses, as all like each other. In the context, his mention is of poetries of ethnicities and the way they so often turn out to be not new but identical to previous poetries — I probably better look up this reference and get it straight — essentially he's saying you can't tell one of these poems from another one, despite their stress on the uniqueness of the moment and the memory. I know what Charles is talking about, and I even agree with him. But, wrong or right, what Charles is saying here reproduces exactly what his opposite number traditionally says about 'experimental' or 'formally-demanding' poetry. "It claims all to be individual but you can't tell one from another!" Obviously, this indicates that the remark is itself a rhetorical topos, you can apply it invariantly wherever you want. It says and means nothing.

Osip Mandelstam writes somewhere that "an artist considers his world-view a tool and an instrument, like a hammer in the hands of a stonemason, and his only reality is the work of art itself." A stonemason doesn't waste time telling you what a good hammer he has, all new and different.

SEM: The words "Everything survives its end" seem particularly painful, given the circumstances following the completion of the book. Perhaps more hopeful, "What will replace thought" calls into question the centrality and eternal nature of that kernel of existence? Can you comment?

TM: Perhaps instead we should see "Everything survives its end" as hopeful. I don't know. I wish what we wrote had a message. It does. I wish people could get the message. Well they can. I wish poetry could make a difference. It must make a difference, and perhaps it will. Perhaps it has. It does.

SEM: I'm very interested in your comments about what I consider a syndrome of disguised mimicry, wherein certain practices are anointed "new," while their predecessors are branded as "old." Students especially may gravitate toward a passkey approach to writing, in an effort to sort "the good" from "the dross." This is probably de facto a process of secretly having a canon. In fact, *competence* (a writer's ability to work effectively in a form) seems a more pertinent issue in this case, certainly moreso than style. You've indicated that some distinctions are at least inappropriate and misfocused. Issues of *making* are more central. Could you talk about what you consider the most important aspects of *making*, as applied to AS?

TM: To orient yourself in any facet of life, you have to read signals in the environment. The most prominent ones are in essence indicators of what we might call "fashion." They tell you something about the subject at hand, but mostly they tell you whether it is in favor and in what ways. Until you are a fair way down the road and have gone through this orientation and reorientation many times, how can you know the significance — even the status — of this set of orientation signals? You can't, that's why you need them in the first place.

Most people now receive a really poor education and just haven't read a lot by the time they start to bear down on writing and living. This is a handicap and probably also a lucky break in some ways. It's a handicap because you don't have much to compare those orientation signals to. Things seem new which are not; things seem valuable which are maybe less so than you think. Other phenomena, especially those which are not assertively connected to the dialectic of fashion, escape notice altogether. And the social structure of the intellectual landscape may escape you altogether.

I guess I'm saying that part of the problem may be the lack of a canon, rather than a secret one. But that's just my preference for saying things that make me seem like the conservative I'm definitely not — pleasure in giving a little shock to someone for whom an avantgarde poet's announcement of the need for a canon may be disorienting. Not just in giving a shock, however, for in disorientation real ideas begin. So we need those little signals and we need to recognize them and drop them.

In conversation many years ago, Ron Silliman described us all as having constellations of figures (poets) in our minds and we orient ourselves via these schemata. When you are young, the constellations consist entirely of work by others, and almost always work by older others. Time passes, and the points on these schemata are occupied by facets of one's own work and work of significant colleagues. It seems like both the starting point and the later points can be enabling or disabling and require work. The past seems fixed, really like constellations, and one doesn't see sometimes the labors of thought — the making — which goes into that shape. If you can't escape the sense that there is a fixed issue of form wherein gradations of value inhere, you are in trouble as a writer. That is why we have nth generation NY poets and nth generation language poets and still people who think that surrealism is the possessing key.

This to me is the key to understanding what it means to stress innovation, to demand the new. It is a demand on a poet that she be free of such fixed attachments, that her work seem to come from some other place than that. I read work by new poets, Julianna Spahr comes to mind, that comes to me with this freshness. I read work by people on the other hand who are making a claim for "experimentalism" and "innovation" which seems totally unwarranted as a characterization of work that is essentially one or another predictable version of the now totally tired (to me, I should stress) American experimental tradition. Often, the sheer recognizability of such work — it fits in a well-defined box; it's what's comfortably "next" — draws it some acclaim. People like their expectations fulfilled. But new poetry should confound our expectations with an object that does not fit but rather creates expectations.

SEM: The awareness of active readership as a concept seems to be gaining momentum. At this meeting place of the writers, their work, and the reader, what are (at least) some of the important aspects that a reader must bring to the gathering?

TM: There are many kinds of reading of course. We don't read a new work of writing in the same way we read even a modern literary work with an established place of some kind in our culture. We don't read Tom Raworth the way we read Sam Beckett; nor read Miles Champion the way we read Tom Raworth for that matter. In fact, how useful is the word "read?" really. I read the sports section; I read Thomas Bernhard; I read a review of a new recording of Nielsen's 6th symphony; I read the distance to Lewes DE on a roadsign. Stopping for lunch, I read the name of the restaurant, the menu, then, while waiting for my salad, I read a new poem Doug Lang just gave me.

Active reading refers to what happens after I read, and that makes me re-read perhaps. When I read Jane Austen, it's like looking at someone across the table from me. All of the work is facing me and I it, and I'm trying to figure it out. But, when I read Jane Austen, it's like being shoulder to shoulder with someone very far away, and we are looking not at each other but at a shared scene, and she is opening shaping defining teasing that scene for me; or we are collaborating to figure that world out we're both facing. So what you bring to reading is what you bring to finding your way to Lewes DE, picking lunch from a menu, caring a lot what your friend has put on the page, sensing your place in the world from the writing acts in it undertaken by a close contemporary.

SEM: Your story of the Charles Rosen concert is rich and offers infinite possibilities. Sometimes when focusing on a particular historical situation, I find myself awakening to layer upon layer of realization of the significances from multiple viewpoints, in addition to sensing several adjustments resulting from the positioning of these viewpoints in time. There is no complete story.

TM: Or none that is not complete, or there for us to complete. Situating event in context to purpose about describes every waking moment.

SEM: Your remark, "A stonemason doesn't waste time telling you what a good hammer he has, all new and different," prompts me to ask what you believe would be a useful exercise for students hoping to write, either alone or collaboratively.

TM: On seeing the work of Spinoza, Thomas Hobbes is said to have remarked: "I durst not speak so freely." I don't know whether my sense of what a starting writer should do is of a kind to be welcomed.

I notice that you frame the question as about "students hoping to write." But, my first advice is to stop being a student. Stay away from schools (especially graduate schools) of creative writing or poetics, above all. Believe that the new is what doesn't yet exist rather than what was just announced. Cultivate a disregard for what others see as valuable but a regard for those others. Move to a large city where you can be anonymous. Fill your mind with exceptions. Take seriously what people think is trivial. See if you can reconstruct a baseball game from a box score. Hang around with the most interesting people you can find.

SEM: In consideration of the type of experience that *AS* is, I'm wondering about the way time factored into the making of *AS*. Was the project "slow and steady" or were there pauses between segments? Were there points at which you needed to halt the work and clear the slate, or did it progress at an intense pace?

TM: There were some slowdowns relating to life issues of availability for the work, and there were other periods of really intense communication. Overall, however, it always had momentum. It was never on the back burner but always the current project for both Dan and me.

SEM: Would you discuss the issue of access as related to *AS*? It seems that this work would be reachable (at least to some degree — impossible to project another person's ability to grasp) to individuals not already steeped in literary theory and contemporary poetics. Like other work of yours, this book offers the reader a way into the outer reaches, if the reader is willing to go. But there are ways in, in any case. Is this important to you, and is it conscious, or just the way the work evolved?

TM: I deeply hope you don't need to have studied literary theory or poetics to read my work! Poetry determines theory not the opposite. I use my own reading in — penchant for — philosophy (I really don't like the word theory and am glad to see that it is fading from use) and theology in just the way I use my experience of the quotidian world and other more formal interests. I need to know some math and physics to write, because I need them to understand the world, and I can't write without some understanding of the world. I need to know something of the history of writing to write, because this history is necessary to the development of vision and technique, necessary in other words — like physics and math — to have something to say.

All of writing is about having something to say. Otherwise there are more rewarding ways to spend your time than spilling words on a page. Unless by so doing you reach practical goals like being published, winning a grant, getting invited to the conference, or getting tenure. There is nothing whatever wrong with these goals, they're just normal issues of survival or professional advancement, the exact equivalents of being promoted at GM or made partner in the law firm. They have of course nothing to do with writing, with poetry.

Somewhere Max Weber refers to two ways to communicate. By explanation and by example. A poet has to do both.

There is an ineluctable value for articulation in writing; however it may be counterbalanced by other needs and interests it never departs wholly and usually leaves a way to get to it (a sign or map of itself) at the heart of a piece of writing, however complex in form, that comes to have value for readers, for people. Perhaps the path in a work that leads to articulation takes the reader to as you call them "the outer reaches." Certainly, I could not know that about my own work or make such a claim for it.

But articulation does lead to the person writing being a whole and offering an example. What we call poetics is a section of a discourse that may lead along this path. Often, the wholeness or articulation or "something to say" is not visible in the piece of discourse we examine as poetics or theory. This does not mean it is absent, though it does mean that we may find ourselves misled by such a piece of thought. We may find ourselves devoted to the facts of truncation rather than those of implication.

People want what concludes a sense of meaning and shores up a sense of self. Just as they want a template for what is "good" writing and "new writing" though this is by definition unavailable, so they want what I just lumped together in the phrase "some practical goal."

Our natures lead us to frame whatever is before us as the legitimate object of desire. A male pigeon courts a female pigeon, does his display. Absent a female pigeon, he will court another male. Absent both, he will court your shoes or a crack in the sidewalk. People are not significantly different in this regard.

SEM: Do you think of a "composite third person" as the author of *AS*, or would you prefer to think of the situation in a different way? I'm interested in hearing about the development of the writing presence that created *AS*.

TM: I think of myself as the author of *AS*, and I think of Dan as the author of *AS*. I don't have a third thought which seeks to resolve these two. The second of the thoughts I have in an incalculably and irrevocably and annoyingly other way than ever I would have imagined. Think how much fun it would have been if you'd been able to interview Dan and me, and we'd been able to collaborate on being interviewed. Think of what a great human experience that would have been. Dan can't have that experience, and he has denied it to me as well. Infuriatingly, he denied me the chance even to say, "Dan — wake up! Don't forego the great experience that will come." Hence, I must say it now and here, and it must mean something totally different from what it would have meant to shout it in his living ear.

SEM: To what extent were you thinking of a hypothetical reader as you wrote *AS*? Was the reader for you Dan, or Dan and others? Or no one in particular?

TM: Dan was the first reader for what I wrote — very much in the way one usually occupies the first reader position for oneself. And vice versa of course. His responses — in the form of what he did next on the book — took the place of let's say rewriting of which there is almost none in *AS* (save corrections). I at least had no hypothetical reader in mind. Dan was "in mind" but as the writer, not a reader: another version of myself in other words.

SEM: To what extent have you participated as a reader of *AS*? What are some of the things you've learned from reading it? As you read the work now, (how) has the work changed?

TM: That is a wonderful and difficult question. In a way, it asks "how have you changed?" as much as how has the work changed. I don't think I have a good answer right now. Perhaps I'll find my way back to the question as we go along here.

SEM: If you were to project ten years into the future, what difference do believe the Internet will have made in developing communication toward "the community we build on communication"? Would you be willing to share how it feels to you to use the Internet for communication? (How) is it different from other ways?

TM: To project even two years into the future of the current transformation is impossible, let alone a decade! It's obvious what the limitations of the net are as social space, community space. Range of activity and expression are very limited; emotional range is really shallow; spontaneity hardly exists at all. There is no real social development without that people give to it with all their faculties, and the net circa 1998 just doesn't have a way to accept most of what people are able to do.

That said, it's pretty extraordinary what happens between and among people even now. With a large number of people around the world my relations have changed immensely, deepened and become more significant, because of e-mail. And the Web offers people a pretty rich context for prepared communication and a context for spontaneous group communication which is...improving — that's the best I can say! As you know, I'm involved in this stuff, specifically in creating tools for open social space online. We have a long way to go.

Some tools and technologies are available; lots more are needed. One certain thing, at the point at which we really can experience social space online, we won't be thinking about the Internet, anymore than you now think about the telephone network when you call a friend. Dial tone, ring, busy signal — we don't experience these as technologies but as facts about the world.

(The following segment of the interview began in the autumn of 2007.)

SEM: Tom, your new book, *To the Cognoscenti*, appeared a few months ago. As you reflect upon your own work over the past 30 years, what emphases or changes seem most important to you now?

TM: That period — the seventies — is on my mind these days, because of writing *The Grand Piano*. I suppose I'm quite a different person from the one back then, although others would know better than I.

I imagine I began by thinking about poetry and then about people who wrote poetry; I don't think about these subjects very much any more. I think about poems, and I think about poets. Seems quite different to me.

A poet is the intention of a poem. Over time, as one becomes one's own biggest influence — or rather one's experience does — the work gives up particularity for a greater individuality, becoming more like a body of water, a meadow, a desert of sand than it is like a cityscape or even a dwelling.

In that sense, my work of thirty years ago has changed — perhaps more than I have. Recently, because of writing a piece for the GP, I reread a long poem written in 1978 called *Some Appearances*. It ends

> The stairs had been carpeted one by one
> We perceive the object riddled with its error
> Senseless parallels along which we padded
> Now tell me your theory one more time

SEM: I sense from your response a renewed vitality of the empirical, or at least a questioning of an orphaned sense of theory. Would you comment on the place of experience in your recent thinking?

TM: Sometimes I think of myself as the only member of a literary movement to be called "restlessism." Of course, there may be many members of the school who know nothing of one another because that ignorance is part of what defines it. Still, I lay claim to having founded it.

We do tend, as human beings, to value highly whatever we possess in abundance. When I was young, and my thinking was unimpeded by experience while being propelled by the quick, fresh hardware of youth, I valued theory more highly than I do now that I have an abundance of experience. Now I value experience above all else.

This is true despite the irony as to theory in the poem I just quoted — *Some Appearances*, written in the '70s. Or perhaps the irony conveys my interest in theory back then. After all, the first thing irony does is assert the phenomenon it ironizes. One could say the same thing about the title of my newest book, *To the Cognoscenti*. Are there any?

I note that your question associates the empirical and experience — and seems to oppose them to theory. I've just been reading a lovely essay by Deleuze with the title "Immanence: A Life." I think it was the last thing he wrote. It argues for a "transcendental empiricism" not of sensation nor of representation. It is "a qualitative duration of consciousness without a self."

Perhaps this conception allows us to recapture theory and experience in a single frame: the frame of poetry – *'frame' he says, and means a rim of flame.*[6] But, don't you want to ask me where I was born and what I learned from my mother?

SEM: What do you see as (some of) the most exciting aspects of current or recent poetry? Oh, and lest we forget your prompt, what role did your early life play in your writing?

TM: Uh oh, now I'm in trouble. I get sent a pretty good number of books, and I try to read as many of them as I can. But, that's not enough for me to make an intelligent comment without leaving out too much by too many.

Mostly, the names on my reading list would sound like the waiting list for the old folks home.

I suppose my biggest interest in new poetry is that there be new ways for it to reach people. My measure in this regard is a 13-year old in Lahore. How does new writing find her and vice versa? The advantage of mainstream media is that, for example, she may be found by e.g. Rae Armantrout's work because of the New York Times. The disadvantage of the burgeoning academic interest in new poetry (and this is not meant as a critique of "the academy": that's too easy) is that it expresses itself in contexts that won't find my 13 year old — in hiding places, endpoints, resting places of reputation.

I suppose she is my measure for two reasons: first off because I've met her; I know her. But also because my own relation to poetry was changed by what found me at that age: a Time Magazine article about Ginsberg and the Beats. It led me to the San Francisco Renaissance issue of the Evergreen Review, a volume I bought at a literary bookstore in downtown Chicago back then (I might have been 14) and which I still have on a shelf somewhere.

I'm waiting for more people to make innovative use of the Internet for poetry. There are lots of blogs, of course. Ron Silliman's is great. But other than Flarf (which I love) I haven't seen much new work that actively uses the compositional possibilities offered by new technologies, tho maybe that means I'm not looking hard enough. Many online magazines seem to mimic print — a terrible idea. Others make use of the greater extensibility of contexts online. Fascicle

---

[6] Mandel, T. *To the Cognoscenti*. (Atelos, 2007) p47

would be one good example. There's interesting design, especially in the use of Flash by for example *mark(s)*.

But so much more is possible — and needed. So I'm waiting for that and, probably, wondering why I don't make something myself.

As to my early life, my mother, more about that another day. Or read *The Grand Piano*.

SEM: Let's conclude with some of your early influences and experiences, combined with what advice you might offer to new writers and readers of what we may continue to call innovative writing.

TM: Back to my mother? She wanted me to be a Doctor not a poet. She had been kicked out of medical school in Vienna when the Nazis arrived and had in mind that I would make this right. A few months before she died in the mid-nineties, she got to see my daughter get her MD, so all's well that ends well.

The first poetry I read was Charles Greenleaf Whittier — is that how you spell his name? — in a book printed during the war on paper that had grown brittle and brown. I was a little kid, sitting behind an arm chair in the living room of my family's small apartment in the Uptown neighborhood of Chicago. I liked the way the words were splayed on the pages and that the brittle pages felt so frail.

My first influences were the beats — Kerouac, Ginsberg, Brother Antoninus. Then I read Eliot, of course, everyone did, and Pound. I was absorptive rather than selective since I didn't know (or care) what was what. I remember with pleasure the Oscar Williams anthologies of modern poets; I loved the work of Gene Derwood, for example — does anyone read her any more? Please do; hmmm, maybe I can drop in a link right there.

I was lucky enough to go to the famous Big Table Reading in Chicago in 1959 when I was still a teenager and hear Allen Ginsberg read from Kaddish. Gregory Corso read that afternoon as well, but Kerouac wasn't there (although I saw and heard him read from On the Road on television! on the Steve Allen show), nor was Burroughs. You can't have everything – still, why not try?

I Just Realized

I'm in a sierpinski
triangle. I have to
lean in close to read

the writing on the wall.
It says: *"it's been*
a long time since that
last off ramp

you must still be on
the I'll-do-it-my-way
highway."

It says:
"iterate"
I'll start tomorrow.

Count Cook Quarrel Sing

Black white blues jazz flamenco fado coimbra fado lisbon son rhumba (add something here)

are traditional arts that you can play
if you aren't raised in the tradition
and overcome what there is
to overcome, something more for you
to overcome. lennie tristano. So what's your point?

poetry is a traditional art
written in the tradition of poets
by poets and can be written as it is
most often by other people too
who write poetry

I didn't know how to listen
to his dark machine
until he died

john cage had something critical
to say about jazz
liking john cage is like liking something else
that's great
those poems can be good too, why not?

a peasant – not to confuse with
he who wears feathers of a pheasant

unlike his friend
jack spicer liked the shape of a balloon
before the hot air went in

o silhouette balloon, serve up my soliloquy

back when you heard
tapdance on a radio

this poem is by me
you need not believe

unless you are convinced
by something it expressed
that isn't so…

(add something here). & what's not tradition? how about the Olympics.

No Takers

A silent animal, a snake
a square of glass, puttied
        in a wood frame
in the form of a question mark
in the form of buildings
        like teeth colored by
            peeling paint
obscured wood
frame houses clustering
pink or shady gray
        with a
            touch of pink
a spray of bubbles
        on teeth.

A smile like smoke its smolder coils
into future darkness
        glum & beautiful & so
easily satisfied that we
desire only the fruit
we've already tasted, having
        no voice in the matter
    that made us wise.

From what state did they fall?
    Who will be restored
will we all?
Something moved. A guidewire
        a teacher reveals
    hidden,

then knew, nothing
and all between them,
unclothed
          the consequence
of an act its quantity
here and now, downtown

                              in the know or in the neighborhood
          on earth,
where
we require an instrument if we are to play,
                    an earthly paradigm
and ancient target
          stung at the root.
Serpent, emissary, servant
messenger, whose length
                    moving in shade of grass
filled with desire
to taste, latent with
desire, obeys
          this new will,
                    as the letters
fell into place. would it be this story
to restore their state.

It will happen here
but imply other events
          Shade climbs the object
one cannot see into the buildings
                    the geometric skyline
clarified on the backdrop
          of near done day.
          One has to eat first
to feel desire : *has to*

337

in the sense of an obligation.
House and inhabitant fading
            into hilltop trees
for a moment paused
                  then they fell (for a cause).

The wing of a fly is beyond reach
            of whatever set it going.
                  Expanding, hot,
            shifting to red
desiring a partner
                  from dust
watered by mist
before the division of territories,
            'lust' 'hissed'
plain sense is that organism.
No more, afterwords, can understanding reach
            among the trees,
to cut the shoots,
                  but gaining on
early evening with breeze
            feeling it get cold
they lower shades and turn
            lamps on in room corners
nothing much
outside on the schedule
                  the outside shut out
            turning bedcovers down
find skin smooth
            like eyes parting low
behind a scrim the big buildings
            dim beyond shades.
First they, then again

and wants to come
'do you want' 'oh yes'
     moaning and pushing
     eyes roll back
pulsing again, one
     of two hearts
become the only sound
within flesh each others arms enclose.
       O pleasure, never fade.

"Play" meaning free movement
and nothing forbidden, but the consequence
     of an act
breathes out of immortal shape
     into each other
our world where struggles, mor(t)ality,
     desperate, fill the lack
in one another's breath/breast
we hear something moving
     what is it?
do you hear it?
Virtually vanished then palpable
     dark, regular shapes
reappear. Lights brighten the houses
set off night, the darkened sky
     shaping out buildings
against its black
and shifts in the breeze.

Earlier, they heard a rustle among
     trees, the cool part
     of the day,
a moment of fear.

They could not maintain the mortality
                    of sublime effects.
          Where the thinker sees a storm blown up
from paradise, to replace
one utopia with another
          song overwhelms, erupting
among the communities.
          To cognize her
in their world
          in spiritualized body
has come naturally.
                    Embodied
in the history
          of creation, indelible
          it was altogether
                    a new development
an adventure
                    in mortal state.

Black square on the edge
          of white light
beneath overhead fixtures
          framed in middle distance,
an oblong billboard flanks
                    pinpoint patterns
of an illumined skyline where
dark houses fuse with trees
          black as clouds
their shadows swarming over the
          windowshades as, moving
in the room, they cross it
          to adjust the set
exhaling,

exiled.

Ascetic, forebearing, preoccupied,
a look of concern witnesses
from a window near my desk
the buildings seem to fall
into a gaze at their bases.
Desire wells up
between them. We understand
desire embodied
in creatures, but tar around
the vent pipe
seals a second creation.
Remember
that all believe
a promise whose fulfillment mutates
the believer's nature, an ecstatic
visit in which
everything but body
is spiritualized – body maintained
in tribute to need.

Perceive
exile as service.
As we are
other and accept no commands
the source must be authentic.
Even a letter
incises its name
on a miracle it covers,
hiding in an apparent norm.
Use caution, beware,
don't stumble – a Place guards

our species but may have
        left only you
in accident's hands, and if
you do look away, be
           one whose piety
        loses focus on the world;
then worry not, will guards
        you, knowledge and remembering are
with you – even when in
        ignorance you forget
the facts, wicked and silent
you are put to death,
           still you observe
the silence we lack. You
        awaken a desire in us
           to welcome the
sacrosanct in its communal pose.

Tom Beckett
interviewed by Nicholas Manning

Tom Beckett is the author of *Unprotected Texts: Selected Poems 1978-2006* (Meritage Press) and *This Poem/What Speaks?/A Day* (Otoliths, 2008).

Nicholas Manning: Tom, the situation of this interview is distinctive I think, as it's a case of the interviewer become interviewee. This provides me with an opening into an aspect of your poetics, as I've often thought that this type of reversal is one that also occurs in your poems. That is, not only do you, as poet, imagine the reader, but you become reader, while writing.

In one of your recent poems for instance, "What Speaks?", there appears the interesting figure of the Ventriloquist. The first thing that comes to mind is that the ventriloquist is a visioning of the poet who, perhaps ineluctably, speaks always via another self, in another voice. This dummy self is in some ways a "false" incarnation, as it is not truly embodied. But perhaps also, on another level, the ventriloquist is equally a model of the reader: that reader who desires, secretly or not, that the poet be an "unembodied form" of his or her own feelings and ideas.

Would you see poetic "ventriloquism" functioning on both these levels, of both speaker and receptor?

Tom Beckett: Nicholas, "What Speaks?" is a poem I've been attempting to write in public, for the last two years, at my blog, Chiaroscuro Metropoli. I've about 10 pages of relatively solid material for my efforts. That said, I'm a little lost, a little bemused by the state of the poem thus far. It begins with

A failed attempt
At voice recognition,
A phenomenology of reception
In the way one opens
At the thought of another
Within

I share Zukofsky's worry in "A" that one seldom recognizes the sound of one's own voice. One has a voice in one's head and has the voice that is out there in the world. They seldom coincide. Can we call that "alienation"? Is that a term that means something to anyone anymore?

There's something about a division of voices, a shift in the perception of voices, that evokes for me questions surrounding gender and sexuality, also of agency/power.

The Ventriloquist, not to mention its companion the Hypnotist, are pretty literally fucking with the subject of the poem. We are all "dummy selves" to one extent or another, more than we care to recognize (let alone say).

Writing for me, Nicholas, is—you're right—reading. But it is also self-interrogation. It's a way for me to locate and embody my provisional thought.

NM: It's been fascinating for me to watch your intricate and almost palimpsestic rewritings of "What Speaks?" over time. Could you talk about this process of very vigilant rewriting in your work? Since we've mentioned Zukofsky, can it be compared to the vision of art in "A" -1 as "Desire longing for perfection" ?

TB: Well Nicholas, I don't hold out much hope for perfection. But *desire* and that notion of palimpsestic writing, of writing over the original manuscript until it becomes obliterated by the new text, resonate together for me. As Lyn Hejinian has pointed out on several occasions, a first thought is often not one's best thought. Poetry writing is about both envisioning and re-envisioning. It's also about taking chances with one's materials.

Speaking of desire, one model for me has been David Bromige's *Desire: Selected Poems 1963-1987* (Black Sparrow Press, 1988). When it came time to assemble that volume David made it his project to rewrite, in some measure, each poem included in the volume. I thought that a brave and beautiful gesture.

Rewriting has become more and more important to me as I've gotten older. I'm 54 years old and my days are filled with interruptions. I'm often struggling to hear myself think. When I'm working on a longer piece like *Vanishing Points of Resemblance* or "What Speaks?" I need to have the whole text in my head and so I begin at the beginning over and over again.

Most of what I write I have few qualms about throwing away. Most of what I write is a rehearsal for what I haven't yet learned to do.

NM: Now that we've touched on the notion of desire Tom — such a central and recurring element of your poetics — I wonder if you feel that poetry provides us with a privileged, "safer space" for the deployment and exploration of desires — in themselves, but also in their consequences and corollaries — than does our lived experience? Or is a "poetics of desire" similarly fraught with burdens, risks and difficulties?

TB: It is all intertwined.

I am what I do and I am what has been done to me.

I speak and leave things unspoken.

I am myself written over and overridden.

I am said and unsaid.

Poetry is apart from me and a part of me. It is a shadow, a projection, a construct. It is a mode of perception made of language which is present and of language which is suggested.

Poetry *is* for me "lived experience." Desire runs all the way through it. "Burdens, risks and difficulties" are part of the terrain.

NM: If poetic and phenomenal perception are so very intertwined for you, would it be fair to say that you don't ever feel the risk of poetry becoming autotelic, isolated, "hermetic"? Do such terms have meaning for you? Or do you feel they represent a rather false fear?

TB: What's intertwined can become twisted and ravel, but I don't want to pursue images of selvage and of self's edge, or of knots and negation too far, tempting as it might be to plunge into a deep pungent vat of badly mixed metaphors.

Of course doubt, worry and fears are part of the process of trying to write poetry. I don't want to fail, yet I often do. Desire is, you know, often experienced as frustration.

Ultimately one writes the poetry one can write. The results aren't always pretty.

NM: Continuing with poetry twined by life, it seems that over the writing life of some poets there are sometimes major shifts in views, subjects, perspectives, praxis, (one could mention early and late Auden). But I have the impression Tom, not at all negative, that your preoccupations from the early poetry through till today show a great deal of coherence. Do you think this is true? More generally, what do you think of this idea of poetic "transformation" or "development"?

TB: While I won't pretend to objectivity about my own work, I'm pretty aware of my limits as a writer. Make no mistake, I've written plenty of crappy poetry. But I've learned to be a fairly ruthless editor of my work. I'm not a product of a University writing program. I don't have that sense of writing as *career*. I've learned what I know, written what I've written, on the fly and in fast company. And I've persisted, in spite of myself. That said, you're right, my preoccupations have stayed fairly consistent over the years.

NM: Having come to this "fast company", let me delve a little deeper with you into recent poetic histories. In your interview with Tom Fink and Crag Hill in your *Unprotected Texts: Selected Poems 1978-2006*, you recount a fascinating moment in which Lyn Hejinian, referring to the Language Poets, remarks: "I think we are Romantics, don't you?" Thomas Fink then calls this "an overdetermined signifier", and he is right! But let's wallow in overdetermination for an instant: what do you think Hejinian means by this? How might such nomenclature be applicable to your own work?

TB: Good question.

Our exchange occurred in Cleveland, Ohio, sometime in the 1990's. I've never been good with dates and am not much of an archivist. John Byrum, Jessica Grim and I were co-curating the Earwitness Public Poetry Reading Series at the time and had brought Lyn in as a reader. In addition to Lyn we were fortunate to be able to host a number of other terrific poets that year: Joan Retallack, Bruce Andrews, Ron Silliman, Leslie Scalapino, Bob Perelman come to mind.

My sense of Lyn's remark is pretty simple minded. Language Poetry is in its essence a utopian project. There was a desire to effect a paradigm shift in the body politic through a re-tooling of perception through language. What could be more romantic? Or more crucial to envisioning meaningful change? If reality's fabric isn't constituted out of language, where the hell does it come from?

As to how all of this has influenced me? Totally.

If I didn't believe poetry has the capacity to change lives I wouldn't have stayed involved.

NM: This writing under the lens of the utopian is interesting for me, as it's often struck me that your poetry is, as well as utopian, profoundly pragmatic. Can pragmatism and utopianism combine in a poetic? Should they?

TB: I'm more interested in the "can" part of your question than that "should" part.

Pragmatism (what can, what must be done) and utopianism (the desire for the realization of pure potentiality and the rationalized reign of unfettered Id) taken together express an integral of which the lower limit is the possible and the upper limit the improbable/dangerous.

For the last 30 years I've worked by day in the rather gritty field of Public Health doing the journeyman work of a Sanitarian. It is a profession which endears you to no one. Mostly people would rather not see you. Often they lie to you. Occasionally, real progress gets made. Mostly though one is operating between opposing forces, pleasing no one and fighting a war of attrition.

I think a poetic which is not risking failure has already failed. I think a poetic which is comfortable with what it can do will not accomplish very much.

As a Public Health person I react to situations in an attempt to prevent or ameliorate subsequent developments. As a poet, I try to find pathways out of where I am.

NM: Though there are not often instances of explicit "conversation" in your poems, I have the sense that they nevertheless exhibit — to borrow two terms from Mikhail Bakhtin — quite complex effects both of "polyphony" and "dialogism". I thus want to ask: is this creation of often very subtle dialogues in your poems influenced by your long and crucial attachment to the mode of the poetic interview? As an extension of this idea: is the dialogue created by an interview similar or different to the (im)possible dialogue articulated in the poem?

TB: I think it fair to say that my approaches to poetry, interviewing and editing have co-evolved. What the crossover effects might be from interview to poem I couldn't say. I've often thought though about Ezra Pound advising a would be little magazine editor to think in terms of constants and variants when assembling a roster of contributors. I've applied the idea of constants and variants to the process of interviewing poets—to the process of selecting questions to ask those poets.

I've developed a repertoire of "big" recurring questions like this favorite opener:"Where did/does poetry begin for you?" Questions such as this present an opportunity for the interviewee to go wherever she wants to go, and to establish the beginning of a stance toward the interviewer. That response then becomes something to work with, build on and interrogate. Fundamentally though, interviews are jazz, occasions to find out what one can learn through improvising in and around a number of themes. In the most successful interviews interviewer and interviewee are playing together, trying to push one another toward a place that will be surprising for each party. Of course it doesn't always work out so tidily.

When I started the E-X-C-H-A-N-G-E-V-A-L-U-E-S interview site I made it my project to promote interviews of "innovative" poets but not just poets who are preoccupied by the things which preoccupy me. One of my notable editorial biases: a lack of emphasis on "career" academic poets. I wanted to focus on poets for whom poetry assumes a centrality in their view of life and the world. It's not just a job or a business. It is a passion.

Another goal was to encourage interviewees to become interviewers for the site. In this I wasn't as successful as I had hoped to be. However, Eileen Tabios, Sheila Murphy, Geof Huth, Thomas Fink, Crag Hill and Mark Young answered the call with aplomb. Sheila and Mr. Fink did so on multiple occasions. An abler crew of associates would be hard to find. I feel truly honored by these artists' trust.

NM: Bakhtin also famously rejected the position of certain formal logics which suggests that if two people disagree, then one of them must be wrong. Your interview style in Exchange Values seems more curious than it is combative. Do you often disagree with the poets whom you've interviewed? If so, do you tell them?

TB: Truthfully, interviewing can be a gut wrenching process. And it is, make no mistake, work. Not everyone who consents to be interviewed is open to the work involved or to truly opening up to participation in a somewhat eccentric exchange. Then, too, sometimes interviewees bring agendas and are resistant to being taken off of their talking points. Sometimes I've made missteps and have pushed inappropriately Interviewing poets is challenging. Part of the process has been starting and then starting over again—working to find a register in which both parties can work together.

I am profoundly curious about how poets think about their processes and their worlds. I hope the work done at E-X-C-H-A-N-G-E-V-A-L-U-E-S by myself and an extraordinarily various and talented cast of characters will inspire similar curiosity in others.

Writing is a kind of wiring I want to be connected to in as many ways as possible. E-values has helped to facilitate that ambition for sure.

NM: You've spoken before about the relevance of politics and philosophy to your writing, but I'd like to touch on a perhaps even more tendentious issue. What about spirituality? Recalling Jerome Rothenberg's "Technicians of the Sacred", is poetry imbued with a sacrality for you Tom? Is this still a viable idea? Has such transcendence become undermined, or at least de-emphasized, in contemporary poetics, specifically American? Might this be a good or bad thing?

TB: I do not think of myself as a spiritual person. Nonetheless, I believe an analogy can be made between a poem and a prayer. And as I wrote in "What Speaks?" —

"A prayer is a means of programming one's mind."

Pascal suggested that if one professes a belief with sufficient frequency one will eventually really believe it.

Transcendence? I prefer to think in terms of unexpected moments of ecstasy, of jouissance.

It is hard to generalize about North American poetics. Of the writers I'm most interested in only Fanny Howe has made spirituality central to her work. I have the highest respect for Fanny's writing.

NM: This makes me think of that Gertrude Stein quote: "I rarely believe anything, because at the time of believing I am not really there to believe." Stein is an important figure for you, isn't she? Would you agree with her here? And could you talk about her influence on your work?

TB: It is impossible to overestimate the importance of Gertrude Stein. Her investigations constitute a practical phenomenology of consciousness. I have been reading and learning from her for over three decades.

Belief is a difficult thing for me to speak about out loud. I am a skeptical person by nature. My position is that questions are more important than assertions.

These days when I think about Stein I think less and less about techniques of repetition, near repetition and grammar, and more and more about fundamental questions about our so called realities.

Stein was, to my mind, William James' best student. She found a way to map a process of thinking through language toward a place which was—is—entirely of its moment. A place I aspire to also.

NM: "A practical phenomenology of consciousness" : what a superb summary of the scope of Stein's poetic. I suggest it could easily be applied to yours Tom. I hope you'll accept this.

At the beginning of this interview you spoke of poetry being "a way to locate and embody *provisional* thought" (my emphasis). This might be seen to foreshadow your valuing here of questions over assertions. My query though: is it necessary for poetry to be sometimes very explicitly, or even wholly, assertive? Perhaps you'll suggest that questions are a powerful mode of assertion, and of course that's true! But I wonder if this isn't an easy way out. Is there a distinction to be made here? Does poetry "assert"? If so, what?

TB: Poems if they're to be of use *must* assert their presences as they traffic in appearances and occur as embodied tunes. When I stated earlier that "questions are more important than assertions," I was speaking to my person— to the poet I think I am—and not the poem.

That said, I have written many times before of poetry's impulse as being fundamentally erotic—that is, in terms of *risk*, a poem is most akin to an unasked for kiss. A poem conceived in such terms is at once an assertion *and* a question, no?

NM: Yes, but is it in fact 'unasked for'? Kisses are often, even usually, preceded by a subtle mutual permission: perhaps poetry functions similarly, with tacit questions paving the way for our kissed assertions . . . I suppose that's why, when I have read before Tom your very rich positing of our relation to poetry in terms of this eroticized risk, I've always wondered: yes, but who is seducing whom? Is the poem really more seducer than seduced? If so, should the reader be playing hard to get?

TB: The reader is always already hard to get. Don't you think? Particularly readers of poetry.

Yes, I think that the kiss is unasked for and that it is usually met with indifference. It is rare for a poem to be truly engaged by a reader. Most readers are pretty cool cookies. While poets crave heat. At least this one does.

Who is seducing whom? It is a game of mirrors.

In a sense my poetry writing is the trace of an involved auto-eroticism that is desperately seeking linkages with the outside world. In the work, seduction attempts to become a feedback loop. "You show me mine./ I'll show you yours."

NM: "Masturbatory" is a term often used to describe certain art's supposed (self-) indulgence, but it seems to take on a very different tone in the context of your poetics. I'm thinking in particular of such moments in "Vanishing Points of Resemblance" as "I caress myself, pretending to touch someone else", or "I want to suck my own cock like a thumb". How might we read this? Ernesto Priego for instance interestingly remarked in a review of "Steps: A Notebook" that "'Unprotected Texts' has the melancholy tone of masturbation as an act of love." Is a poetics of auto-eroticism inherently melancholy? Celebratory? Both?

TB: I don't want to suggest ways in which to read my poems. I do want to say this: that "Vanishing Points of Resemblance" began as an attempt to write a novel about mistaken identity. I was mistaken about the form it would take. It became something else altogether—a sort of hybrid work. It is a text which is very important to me.

Listen: I'm not in love with myself. I am, however, fascinated with the other I am—and with projection in the psychological sense. Sex, in my writing, is an occasion for thought and explorations of limits. As I wrote in VPoR: "The relation of mind and body to possible worlds is what I pretty much inadvertently set out to explore. At some point I turned out to be my method."

Melancholy, celebratory? Both. But VPoR is dark, for sure. It was a last ditch effort to figure out if I had anything worthwhile to say as a writer.

NM: Given our spectral mistaken identities, talk to me about pronouns. Are they the most conjectural part of language for you?

TB Yes. Pronouns are often my actors of guesswork and surmise.

NM: I'm interested in what lies at the base of your reluctance to suggest possible readings for your own poems. Some poets do this without thinking it

implies a normative imposition. Aren't you as valid a reader of your poems —
albeit of a slightly different sort — as anybody else?

TB: Cowardice would be the short answer. I'm afraid of closing off heuristic
possibilities. I'm a ferocious critic of my own work but not always a good one.

NM: At one point in "What Speaks?" you talk of a process, perhaps that of
poetry, as being "a series of abandonments?" This immediately brings to mind
Paul Valéry's rather over-famous formulation: "A poem is never finished, only
abandoned." Yet in your poem Tom this phrase is, importantly, succeeded by a
question mark. So let me be direct: are your poems abandoned, or do they
reach for you at least a partial state of finition? Alternatively, does the
"question mark" regarding their completeness always recur?

TB: What an interesting question.

I'm in general agreement with Monsieur Valéry's pronouncement, particularly
in light of my experience with longer texts like "What Speaks?"

I've decided to call "What Speaks?" done because it feels like it has come to a
point that I find it pointless to try to move it beyond. Having spent over two
years working on the piece I know it will haunt me for awhile, that there will
be separation anxiety, that I will return to it from time to time like a spurned
lover. I'll stalk it a little to see what it is up to.

I'm still not sure I understand what was actually accomplished in "What
Speaks?" I hope one of these days I have an opportunity to read it in public.
That is often a rather telling way of coming to re-see a text.

Yes, Nicholas, my poetry almost always feels partially completed. My thought
out races my ability to grasp it. I am always questioning what I am doing and
what I have done.

NM: I haven't yet had the pleasure of seeing you read, but I'd like to ask: what
do you discover during these moments of civic airing which are the public
performances of your poems? As reader, do you adopt a mask, or do you
rather feel it is "yourself", or one of your selves, on display? Do the poems
change in your mind after such presentations?

TB: I discover terror. Which is partially, I suppose, a matter of being an
infrequent public performer of my work. (My appearance in Cambridge, MA

353

this past November was my first reading in seven years.) It is also a matter of feeling totally exposed, of masks falling away.

Reading a poem to an audience is different than reading it to oneself in the privacy of one's home. The text becomes exteriorized in ways it wouldn't otherwise. Self-consciousness ramps up. One's heart beats a little faster. One manages to pace oneself to the logic of the poem or speeds up out of nervousness and stomps on the line. It becomes a very physical process, especially reading a longer work like *Vanishing Points of Resemblance*. Performing that text for the first time, in Cambridge, was an emotional milestone for me. I was fortunate in having a warm and sympathetic audience. I'm pretty sure that in other venues VPoR wouldn't have been as well received.

Poems certainly can change after performances. I think one hears oneself differently when talking to an audience than when talking to oneself. That can be instructive. And sometimes an audience will usefully call one's bullshit to one's attention. That can be a wake up call. But sometimes audiences are just wrong. One can't please everyone. If you're taking any sort of stand as an artist, there are going to be people who will hate you on principle. That can take some getting used to.

NM: What are your feelings about the official 'histories' of Language Poetry as a movement, both as they have been written from the outside of this grouping and, increasingly, from the writers of the movement themselves, from within? To be frank, I'm specifically interested in the degree of inclusion or exclusion you may feel or have felt at different times with regard to the complex and various inscribings of this important poetic moment.

TB: This is the question I saw coming and have been dreading it.

I sought out the Language Poets, they didn't seek out me. I think the Bernstein, Silliman, Bromige and Howe Issues[7] of my magazine, *The Difficulties*, hold up pretty well all these years later and that they performed a crucial function when they were first published. They continue to be quoted from in articles and books, continue to be alluded to in footnotes. I think each issue accelerated the reputation of each subject-author, placing the work against broader contexts, interrogating and explicating methodologies, exploring Language Poetry as social project. My work as editor/publisher of *The Difficulties* was extremely important in terms of my own growth, too, but it will always be a

---

[7] There were 2 other, earlier, issues – TB

footnote to the greater project of Language Poetry. That said, *my* poetry writing has never been given serious consideration within that Language Poetry project. I was, I think, tolerated by Language Poetry principals while I was editing and publishing *The Difficulties*. Afterwards they haven't had too much to say to or about me. I'm probably too much of a loose cannon and probably too loose with their canon.

My involvement with the Language Poets was intoxicating. (I have some quarrels with these people. But I like most of them very much.) There were several years of figurative hangover after that involvement. I was quite discouraged for a number of years, but I've worked through my frustrations and moved on. To the best of my ability.

Consider that when I started *The Difficulties* in 1980 I was 27 years old, and that I wrapped that project up around 1990.

I didn't have an opportunity to publish my first full length poetry book (*Unprotected Texts* from Meritage Press) until 2006 when I was 53. My initial involvement with Language Poetry started half a lifetime ago. I have not forgotten those times. I've, in fact, taken some lessons from them. But I have moved on.

NM: Do you have a sense Tom of what the future of your writing may bring, or what you would like it to?

TB: I live in a continuous present haunted by the past. The future doesn't exist for me anymore.

I hope to continue writing as long as possible. I hope to be open and attentive. I hope that my writing and other literary efforts can be of some use. Beyond that, my dear Nicholas, I don't know what to say. Thank you for your time and patience. I've enjoyed this exchange with you.

NM: Thank you Tom. This has been more than a pleasure for me: it's been an honour.

What Speaks?

A failed attempt

At voice recognition,

A phenomenology of reception

In the way one opens

At the thought of another

Within.

Another front.

Inside

The Situation —

Room — me?

Meat. Muttering

Utterances, iterations.

Ejaculations. Shouting.

Interrogations.

Hollow

Cravings only

Bad plots
Fast food

Or sex

Can fill.

Letters splatter in a puddle.

Graphite nights

Going down

On erasers.

The Ventriloquist.

Weathers.

Ventriloquist professing to be both comedian and archaeologist.

(S)he wears a glass version of skin.

(S)he can't see its own body.

Covers.

Ladders.

Everything some other thing.
Before sleep (s)he prays for an erection or for a line of poetry to be
delivered upon waking—either or both would be OK.
(S)he sees them as the same thing.

A prayer is a means of programming one's mind.

Everyone is an element of a constellation.
(An element of multiple constellations.)
Everyone is an entire constellation, too.

"Knowledge = paralysis. Action = epilepsy—involuntary."
—Nietzsche

(S)he can't remember the convulsions.

Parent-thesis: maybe I should interview—no, interrogate my own
fucking selve (deliv-, deliber-atively—damn it—misspelled, but not
salvaged) at the edge of the plural, almost raveling.

You-bris. Check Derrida on circumfession/circumfiction.

Forethoughtskin.

Buzzing

Yet static moment

Of insight

And over-bright

Light just before

A gap.

The Ventriloquist, weathers: the other either mirrors.

Figures.

Erasers.

(S)he thought the Ventriloquist understood the word "overheard" to
mean something akin to "written over," as in "written on top of" — in
terms that is of a kind of layering of utterances.

According to the Ventriloquist, I found my structure in you. A world
of sounds composed only of weather.

I am a fiction

Called the Old Man

At the Scene

Of the Rhyme.

Venetian blinds

Ladder shadows.

Reality is never

Completely realized

But its drafts

Make oneShiver.

What about assumption?

The object cannot

Be taken in

All at once.

While the Ventriloquist masturbates (s)he shudders and shutters
the window.

Perception: a species of feeling.

Thought: an organ of the body, another skin.

Language: a pheromone.

A phenomenology of reception in the way.

Weather fronts. Structures churning. The Ventriloquist rehearsing.

I'm not speaking to the Ventriloquist. (S)he won't let me.

What is missing here?

One is being diagnosed?

Separation as a semblance

That can be decomposed?

A series of abandonments?

The Ventriloquist reads a horoscope to its date, the Hypnotist.

It

Speaks to one

From a place

Which is not

Visible.

What speaks?

Where is it spoken?

A process

Of disappearance

Slips

To the rear

Of overheard

Pleasure.

S(he) says

Our skin

Is templates.

(S)he says

Writing

Is stripping.

Suggestions

Constituting that

Second language

One didn't think

One knew

(let alone

penetrate, be

entered by).

Constituting another,

That Is,

Failed attempt

At a project

Of return—

Generative dream

Of Ventriloquist

& Hypnotist.

What can

Be done?

What should

We do?

Structure is a question

(S)he needs

To be

Magnetized now.

The Ventriloquist's

Lips are quivering.

Attraction holds

Out its

Sleight of hand.

(S)he's a

Distorting mirror.

One will come

To resembling.

Fragments

Of experience

Are assembled

In a face

One recognizes,

Wants to see

Out of

But never

Wants to be.

Words are mouthed

But the membrane

Between thought

And act

Is what's

Called experience.

In the gap

Where one lives

The others gather

Across the divide

That one is.

Blind spot,

Wet spot.

The whole

Idea of

Separation

Puts on

A shimmering

Sheathe.

Trying

To coincide

With one's selves.

Water

In a collander.

Impossible desires.

The Ventriloquist and the Hypnotist walk into a bar called
Chiaroscuro Metropoli.

Speak through

One.

Think one forward.

Build a shadow.

Project

An Avatar.

The law is

9/10 possession.

One's plea

For possession.

A funny thing

Happened on

The way

To the bar:

One noticed

Redundancies

In the Universe's

Punchlines.

I am

Not beautiful

The Ventriloquist

Whispers

Through me.

(S)he is

Getting sleepy,

Very sleepy.

The moment decays.

Voice-overs

Ever after

More or less

Nothing's ever

Exactly the same.

Interviewer Bionotes

Thomas Fink is the author of *"A Different Sense of Power": Problems of Community in Late Twentieth Century Poetry* (Fairleigh Dickinson University Press, 2001), as well as a prior book of criticism, and is co-editor of a 2007 collection of critical essays on David Shapiro. He has published five books of poetry, most recently *Clarity and Other Poems* (Marsh Hawk Press, 2008). His paintings hang in various collections.

Sheila E. Murphy's *Collected Chapbooks* is due imminently from Blue Lion Books. A new book of collaborative visio-textual art with K.S. Ernst, *Permutoria*, has just been released from Luna Bisonte Prods. Her home is in Phoenix, Arizona.

Bruce Holsapple works as a speech-language pathologist in central New Mexico. His poems have appeared in The Poker, House Organ, Blue Mesa, and First Intensity. A long essay on Philip Whalen is forthcoming in Paideuma. He is the editor of Vox Audio.

John Tritica is, as was Mary Rising Higgins, a founding member of L)Edge (in 1986), a poetry circle in Albuquerque, NM. He is the translator of Swedish poet Niklas Törnlund: *All Things Measure Time* (1992). *How Rain Records Its Alphabet* was published by La Alameda Press in 1998. The collection *Sound Remains* has just been issued by Chax Press.

Nicholas Manning teaches comparative poetics at the University of Strasbourg, France. His chapbook *Novaless I-XXVI* is available from Achiote Press, the complete *Novaless* is available from Otoliths, and a new volume, *Hi Higher Hyperbole*, is forthcoming from Ypolita. He is the editor of The Continental Review, (www.thecontinentalreview.com), a video forum for contemporary poetics, and maintains a weblog, The Newer Metaphysicals.

Acknowledgements

Many of the poems included in the individual selections are being published here for the first time, but a number have previously appeared in the following journals,

> Australian Book Review, Blackbird, Carnet de Route, Colorado Review, Gutcult, Heat, New American Writing, Octopus, Otoliths, P.F.S. Post, Salt, Talisman, Vanitas, and Word for /Word

website,

> Fieralingue: The Poets' Corner (curated by Anny Ballardini)

anthology,

> *The Hay(na)ku Anthology, Vol.II,* (eds Jean Vengua & Mark Young), Meritage Press, St. Helena & San Francisco, CA, 2008

artist's print portfolio,

> KK Kozik, *Gotham Haiku*, Four-color etching and aquatint prints, NewYork, VanDeb Editions, 2007

and in the following individual collections.

Ernesto Priego
> *The Body Aches,* Ex-Presso Doble, Claremont, CA , 2005
> *Not Even Dogs,* Meritage Press, St. Helena & San Francisco, CA, 2006
> *"...And Then The Wind Did Blow...",* Meritage Press Tiny Books, St. Helena & San Francisco, CA, 2007

Karri Kokko
> *list'n,* dbqp, Schenectady, NY, 2008
> *Vapaat kädet,* poEsia, Helsinki, Finland, 2007

Stephen Vincent
> *Sleeping With Sappho,* Faux Press, Newton, MA, 2004
> *Walking Theory,* Junction Press, New York, NY 2007

Tom Mandel

Letters of the Law, Sun & Moon Press, Los Angeles, CA, 1994

Mary Rising Higgins

)joule TIDES((, Singing Horse Press, San Diego, CA, 2008

Also from Otoliths

E-X-C-H-A-N-G-E-V-A-L-U-E-S

The First

XI

Interviews

Curated by
TOM BECKETT

Otoliths

The First XI Interviews has interviews with Crag Hill, Thomas Fink, Nick Piombino, Sheila E. Murphy, Eileen Tabios, Jukka-Pekka Kervinen, K. Silem Mohammad, Geof Huth, Barbara Jane Reyes, Paolo Javier, Stephen Paul Miller and Jean Vengua.

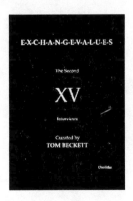

The Second XV Interviews has interviews with Mark Young, Michael Heller, Bob Grumman, Shanna Compton, Sandy McIntosh, Jim McCrary, Gary Sullivan, A.L. Nielsen, Michael Farrell, CAConrad, Anny Ballardini, Denise Duhamel, Nick Carbó, Jack Kimball, Geoffrey Young & Jordan Stempleman.